THE VIKING VOYAGE

THE VIKING VOYAGE

JUDY LOMAX

HUTCHINSON
London

© Judy Lomax 1992

The right of Judy Lomax to be identified as Author of this work has been asserted by Judy Lomax in accordance with the Copyright, Designs and Patents Act, 1988

This edition first published in 1992 by
Hutchinson

Random House UK Limited
20 Vauxhall Bridge Road, London SW1V 2SA

Random House Australia (Pty) Ltd
20 Alfred Street, Milsons Point, Sydney, NSW 2061, Australia

Random House New Zealand Ltd
18 Poland Road, Glenfield, Auckland, New Zealand

Random House South Africa (Pty) Ltd
PO Box 337, Bergvlei, 2012, South Africa

A CIP catalogue record of this book is available
from the British Library

ISBN 0 09 174754 6

Typeset by Raven Typesetters, Ellesmere Port, South Wirral
Printed and bound in Great Britain by
Butler and Tanner Ltd, Frome & London

For Knut Utstein Kloster,
(who dedicated the voyage to Gaia – Mother Earth)
and the crews of the Viking fleet

Contents

BAFFIN
BAY

GREENLAND

Davis Strait

Ammassalik
July 3
depart July 5

course
changes
in pack ice

LABRADOR
SEA

Narsarsuaq
Narsaq

Julianehåb
July 9

July 22   July 8

60°N

course change
to avoid ice

N

ATL

O

CANADA

July 24

Mary's   Cape Charles
Harbour
l'Anse aux Meadows
August 2

Fogo Island
August 7

NEWFOUNDLAND   Trinity Bay

St Pierre   St Johns
August 9

45°N   SCOTIA

NOVA   Halifax
August 17
depart Sept 2 out of
harbour and return
depart Sept 4

Gloucester

USA   Boston
Sept 11
depart Sept 17

Washington   Newport, Rhode Island
DC   Sept 20
Oct 9   depart Sept 23

New York
Sept 25
depart Oct 2

75°W   60°W   45°W

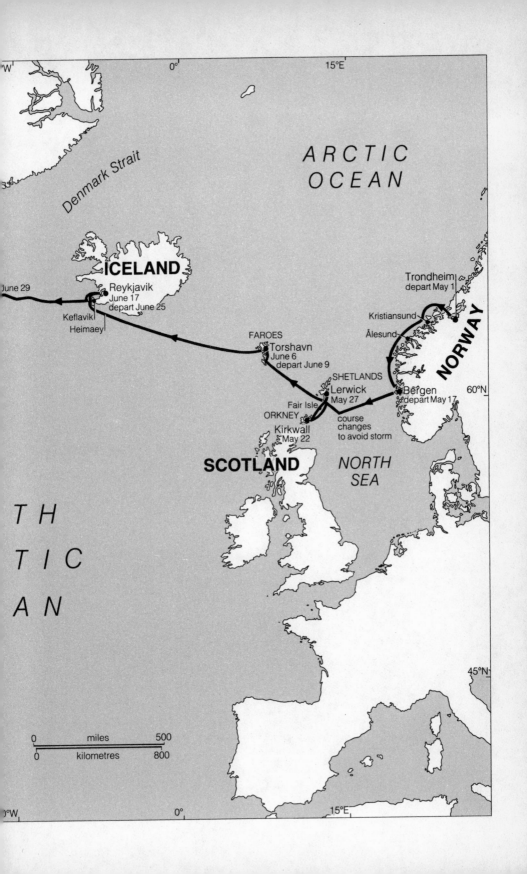

Illustrations

Preface

The novelist, Arthur C. Clarke was the first to comment: 'How strange to call our planet Earth when clearly it is Ocean.' If you are an astronaut and you happen to look down when over the middle of the Pacific, there is truly nothing to be seen but water, a whole hemisphere of it, in all of its forms, blue seas, white clouds and white ice at the poles. The land where we all live is a mere thirty per cent of the Earth's surface.

There is no better way to get to know the Earth than by voyaging across the oceans on a small ship. A good proportion of my working life as a scientist has been spent in voyages of discovery in the Atlantic Ocean on ships that travelled from the Arctic to the Antarctic. Such voyages are a delight and a way to grow familiar in a personal sense with the Earth itself, and a way to discover new things about ourselves and about the science of the Earth. I was therefore pleased and honoured to be asked by David and Judy Lomax to write this preface to their book, which is a personal account of the transatlantic voyage of the Viking ship *Gaia*.

I was moved to hear that the ship had been named *Gaia* by the President of Iceland, Vigdis Finnbogadottir. For me there is no more appropriate name for the Viking ship that was to set out on its historic voyage of influence and discovery. I am indebted to Vigdis Finn-bogadottir for her choice of the name of the Earth itself for the ship that was to voyage across the Atlantic in memory of Leif Eiriksson and then go on to Rio as the true representative of the Earth and of our children.

Many of the significant discoveries about our planet and ourselves have come from the voyages of small ships; from the voyages of the Vikings who brought back the news that there was a limit to the oceans and a new land across the sea. Consider also those great navigators like van Dieman and Drake who circumnavigated the globe and confirmed for us its true shape; or Darwin's voyage on the *Beagle* that gave us his vision of the evolution of the organisms; or the ocean voyages that discovered the mechanism of plate tectonics and how the sea floor divides and spreads.

Even now ocean voyages complement the view of satellites and reveal the physiological processes of Gaia, such as the way that algae living in the ocean act to move the chemical elements as gases to and from the air and sea. Other voyages showed how the ceaseless emission of dimethyl sulphide by marine plants regulates the clouds, winds and climate over the oceans.

The oceans are one property of our planet that make it the strange and beautiful anomaly of the Solar System. If it were like its siblings Mars or Venus it would indeed be dry Earth with no oceans and no life. We all know that the presence of water was essential for the appearance of life on Earth, but how many know that without life there would be no water?

Among the many reasons therefore that justify another name for the Earth is the fact that it is not dry. The name Gaia fits a planet that behaves as if it were a living organism, and can keep itself moist for life, in the same way that a cactus or a camel survives the desiccation of the desert. Space is drier than any desert, the presence of the system Gaia has saved the Earth from a fate, like that of Mars or Venus, of unremitting aridity. It was the theory of Gaia that made us first realise that just as life needs water so water depends on life.

Almost everything about the Earth seen from space reveals a living planet. If the glance is in the infrared instead of the visible, the gases that go to make up the air, oxygen, nitrogen, carbon dioxide, methane and the many trace gases, all can be seen. Their proportions are those of a living planet and just as different from those of Mars as is a woman from a stone statue.

Gaia is travelling to the earth summit in Rio as a tangible representative of the planet itself. She carries the message from UNICEF asking the leaders of the Nations gathered at Rio to curb human excess for the sake of our children. Her presence shows that the right way for us to live on the Earth is like the crew of a small ship that we have made for ourselves. Good sailors know their lives depend on keeping their environment the ship in good heart, and so it is with us. Gaia, the planetary system, is not fragile but we are: unless we recognize the nature of our planet and keep it fit for our children they will suffer even though the life of the Earth goes on.

Global processes start from the acts of individuals. The person or the organism that takes good care of the environment lives in a way that favours its progeny and will succeed. The good they do multiplies and becomes the way of life. Those that foul their environment make life difficult for themselves and they are diminished.

We have seen how the voyages of individual explorers and scientists have shown us how beautiful and intricate is the earth and helped us to understand its true nature. Their achievements stand out in sharp contrast to the confused chattering of those who stayed on dry land. I would like to think that *Gaia*'s presence at the Rio conference will in a like manner bring the clarity of the sea air to the land-locked debate about people and the earth environment.

James Lovelock

1 A Good Idea

'You don't sound Norwegian or Icelandic.'
'We're not – we're British.'
'I thought this was a Norwegian–Icelandic project.'
'It is.'
'So how did you get involved with it?'

It was a question David and I were asked over and over again during the five and a half months we spent sailing across the North Atlantic on a replica Viking ship.

The difficulty about answering it was deciding where to begin – whether to go back a few months to the day when we were invited to join 'Vinland Revisited'; or to try to explain how over thirty years David's rash comment that 'you can't frighten yourself sailing' had eventually led to plans for our own transatlantic neo-Viking 'Bugger Columbus!' expedition; or indeed whether to start a thousand years ago with the visit to Vinland by one Leif Eiriksson – whose precise dates and spelling are variable, but whose landing in North America was later recorded as a European first and certainly preceded the continent's much-vaunted so-called discovery by approximately five centuries.

Everyone knows about Columbus – but few people outside the Nordic countries have heard of Leif Eiriksson, although he is a national hero in both Norway and Iceland. His grandfather, Thorvald, was banished from Norway, in about the year AD 960, 'because of a killing' – a vague explanation, but the only one on record. Like many other Norwegian outlaws of the time, some criminals, others seeking political freedom or fertile farmland, Thorvald fled to Iceland with his family, including his son Eirik, who later became known as Eirik Rauðe – Eirik the Red: he had red hair and a violent temper. When Eirik was in turn banished from Iceland for three years – because of some more killings – he explored Greenland, where he set up a new Norse colony. It was from

1

Greenland that his son Leif set sail before landing somewhere in North America, which he called Vinland.

It was during a transatlantic voyage with our yacht *Cloud Walker* that a Nordic influence entered our lives. Our eldest daughter, Jane, introduced us in the Canaries to a Norwegian yacht skipper, who later became our son-in-law. Everyone called him Rikki, from his middle name Erik; his full name was Harald Erik Bjerke, to distinguish him from his father, Harald Christian Bjerke.

After sailing *Cloud Walker* via the Caribbean to the United States, and then up the coast from Florida to the Canadian border during the next summers, what to do next – or rather, by what route to sail her back to Europe – dominated mealtime conversation. The choices were via the Azores, my choice, or the more demanding northerly passage via Greenland favoured by David.

'I have an idea,' he announced one day. 'In 1992 there will be a great hoo-ha about it being five centuries since Columbus discovered America – but the Vikings got there first, five hundred years earlier . . .'

Of course. The Azores would have to wait, ousted by the idea of beating Columbus celebrations with a voyage across the Viking North Atlantic route. The next stage of the idea was our son's.

'If you are going to sail that route at all, you shouldn't be thinking of doing it with a modern yacht,' Alistair remarked impatiently. 'The only way to do it properly is with a Viking ship.'

'That's a good idea,' David and I said simultaneously. The idea was born. It would be an adventure with a dual mission – to find out how the Vikings sailed, and to publicize their pre-Columban nautical achievements. First we would bring *Cloud Walker* back to Europe via Greenland as a reconnaissance of the Viking route in reverse.

'Count us in with the Vikings,' Rikki and Jane said. Rikki would be skipper, leaving David free to concentrate on filming what we were convinced would make exciting television. I would write the book. The crew would include representatives of the places on the Viking route.

We read sagas in translation, and started to accumulate books about the Vikings and the Norse history of their North Atlantic settlements. The rape, pillage and plunder with which they had terrorized much of Europe had, we discovered, been less in evidence at their cold northern destinations, where from the ninth century they were looking for farmland rather than fights. They had encountered little opposition, since most of the land they took – like the Faroe Islands and Iceland – had been inhabited previously only by a scattering of hermit monks who preferred flight to fighting. There was no conflict with the nomadic Inuits in Greenland. It was only in Vinland that there was any opposition – which was why the New World era did not start five hundred years earlier. According to some historians, Columbus knew all about the Norse voyages to the continent which he is generally supposed to have 'discovered'.

There were of course one or two problems to be solved, like where to find a suitable Viking ship, and how to pay for it. It should, we decided, be an authentic copy of the sort of boat the Vikings probably used for long sea passages and for trading, a *knarr*, rather than a longship. Total authenticity was however impossible: we would not, for instance, be able to use plaited walrus hide for the halyards; and although we planned as far as possible to adopt Viking sailing techniques, we would allow ourselves modern safety and navigation equipment, and an engine.

We submitted our plans to Magnus Magnusson, as the best known Norse expert in Britain. His reaction gave us confidence: 'Your Vinland proposal . . . sounds tremendously exciting and full of potential,' he wrote. 'I am most impressed by the care you have taken in swotting up the background, and the robust realism of the proposal itself.'

2 Viking Ships and Sailors

One name kept cropping up in correspondence about our plans: Ragnar Thorseth, who had, we discovered, already sailed round the world in *Saga Siglar*, a replica of a *knarr* or Viking trading ship found at Roskilde in Denmark. We first heard about him in November, when Rikki's father, Harald Bjerke, sent us a Norwegian newspaper cutting: Thorseth, 'the last remaining Viking', was planning to honour both Christopher Columbus and Leif Eiriksson by crossing the Atlantic in 1992 with three Viking ships. The three ships which were to join in the Columbus celebrations were *Saga Siglar*, and replicas of the Oseberg and Gokstad ships. Both originals had been built, buried, rediscovered and reconstructed in Norway. The Gokstad replica had not yet been built.

Thorseth had started his round-the-world voyage with *Saga Siglar* by sailing in the wake of the Vikings across the North Atlantic. Other twentieth-century Vinland expeditions had been undertaken with more modern vessels – like that of John (J. R. L.) Anderson with the gaff-rigged ketch *Griffin*. Several earlier, memorable sailing expeditions to Greenland had been led by the American Newbold Smith with *Reindeer*, and as a way of reaching and climbing the country's icy mountains by Bill Tilman, an Englishman greatly admired among British yachtsmen in spite of his male chauvinism, his attacks in print on various long-suffering crew members and his habit of putting his yacht aground.

It was nearly a hundred years since the Atlantic had been crossed by Magnus Andersen's *Viking*, a full-sized version of the Gokstad with the additions of a deeper keel and extra top- and fore-sails. Andersen and his crew of twelve made no attempt to call at various islands colonized by their predecessors, but sailed non-stop from Bergen to Newfoundland in twenty-eight days, and then on to the 1893 Trade Fair in Chicago. The expedition was just as much a 'Bugger Columbus!' operation as the one we were planning: it was to celebrate the four-hundredth anniversary of the arrival in the New World of Columbus that Chicago was holding its fair.

'We have put the Spaniards who couldn't find men to sail Columbus ships [to the Chicago World Fair] but had to tow them, to shame,' wrote one of Andersen's crew, Severin Simonsen. 'Well what can they say now? Now we are in America, in spite of the fact that they thought we'd never see land again.'

According to Magnus Magnusson, 'the key man in all matters to do with Viking boats' was Ole Crumlin-Pedersen, of the Institute of Maritime Archaeology in Roskilde, in spite of Magnusson's irritation with what he called 'one of Ole's few mistakes'. 'He calls a *knörr* a *knarr*, which is simply wrong: it is based on a confusion caused by the fact that a *knörr* was also called (in one text) a *knarri*, and by the fact that it is familiar in its genitive form *knarrar*' – an example of which he quoted: 'A buxom lady in *Landnámabók* (Book of Settlements) earned herself the proud nickname of *knarrarbringja*, literally *knörr-bosomed.*'

Whatever the shape of the lady's bosom, or the general familiarity or otherwise of its genitive, since it was the *knörr* or *knarr* which interested us most, we had to decide what to call it. With apologies to Magnus Magnusson, we decided to settle for *knarr* as the version which appeared to be most common in English. This will not surprise him since he already felt that in this instance grammatical accuracy was a lost cause – 'as hopeless as my attempts to persuade people that *Valhalla* is a genitive plural, and should actually be *Valhöll*'.

We hoped that we would not need to refer too often to Odin's five-hundred-and-forty-doored 'hall of the slain', to which the Norse All-Father's fallen warriors were welcomed by the blood-lusting Valkyries. It seemed an exhausting reward for the sacrifice of their mortal lives in battle that Odin's freshly slain soldiers should then be expected to spend their afterlife stuffing themselves with boar's flesh washed down with mead brought by a goat living at the top of Yggdrasil, the tree of life, and fighting in preparation for the Last Battle, when the gods will meet their doom at Ragnarök – including Odin himself, a somewhat schizophrenic-sounding deity. As Lord of Death and Wisdom, he was equally responsible for war and the darkest of dark magic, and for poetry and wisdom – 'a tricky fellow', as a Swedish friend claiming direct descent put it: 'It would be more advisable to put one's trust in Thor, the Viking's friend.'

Ole Crumlin-Pedersen's reply to our letter asking if we could pick his brains about Viking ships avoided the nominative-genitive issue, and referred us to Thorseth, whose name we assumed to be linked with the more amicable and trustworthy deity. The name cropped up for the third time in as many weeks in a letter from Oslo's leading Viking ship expert, Arne Emil Christensen, who confirmed the newspaper article sent to us by Rikki's father, and offered us some advice: 'Whatever you do, stay away from scaled-down replicas of the Gokstad ship, they tend to be unstable.'

One small Gokstad look-alike, *Odin's Raven*, had demonstrated its instability by capsizing on the way from Norway to the Isle of Man for the Manx Millennium in 1979. Quite apart from any inherent design problems, I felt that calling a boat after such a 'tricky fellow' might well have courted disaster. Nevertheless, the first Viking shipping expert we were to visit on a research trip to northern Germany, Denmark and Norway was Alan Binns, technical adviser both to the 1979 *Odin's Raven* Manx Viking ship committee and to the Kirk Douglas film *The Vikings*. As we waited in the rain on a raw March afternoon for the ferry to draw out of Harwich, we hoped that the lettering on the life rafts – VIKING – was a good omen.

Mild misty drizzle obscured Alan's village, through which an earthwork wall had been erected in Viking times to separate the countries which have since become Germany and Denmark. Behind the fortifications straggling across Jutland's southern border between the North Sea and the Baltic, there was a flourishing Norse trading centre, which served equally as a launching point for marauding fleets. The old hamlet of Hamburg, a long day's row away, was allegedly attacked by six hundred assorted ships in AD 845.

Retirement from his lectureship at Hull University had not suppressed Alan's natural energy. Although he looked like a youthful archetypal eccentric professor, his mind was far from absent, especially on the subject of boating technicalities, whether Viking or non-Viking. He talked knowledgeably and at length, hardly pausing while he donned an efficient-looking apron, poured wine, laid the table and prepared and served stew. There was no nonsense about not allowing me to wash up. Emily was allowed to try on the helmet Kirk Douglas had worn in *The Vikings*. Her face was almost hidden under it.

After supper, Alan drew diagrams to demonstrate Viking sailing technicalities. 'You must take account of the "water keel" of bubbles surfacing just under the rudder,' he enthused. 'The turbulent water below the keel creates an extra keel, giving depth below the physical keel, which is almost non-existent – this makes a Viking ship comparable to a Dragon [a racing yacht].' His ideas and opinions bubbled along like the extra water keel he described. We were sometimes lifted along on it, sometimes left floundering in its wake, but appreciated his infectious enthusiasm and his ability to look at things from a viewpoint untainted by awe. 'Of course, you have to realize that Viking ships were basically just motor sailers, with oar power instead of engine power,' he told us, working out the equivalent oar-to-engine power at roughly thirty oars to ten horse power at a steady pull, fifteen for a spurt, depending on the ship's measurements and proportions.

After his experiences with *Odin's Raven*, Alan too advised us strongly against a scaled-down version of 'Gokstad', best known of all existing Viking ships. 'She wouldn't go to windward or even to any acceptable extent off the wind without taking in water over the low freeboard,' he explained. He was equally adamant that we should avoid a full-sized Gokstad replica: 'Gokstad ships never actually sailed to America, and I'm pretty sceptical about whether they even sailed to England. It's very noticeable that at the end of the ninth century, when ships like Gokstad are being used, Viking fleets stop making direct crossings from Denmark and start going down to the Rhine and then across to the Thames and back up again – and they always religiously do that even if they are in a hurry. So the clear implication there is that ships of the Gokstad type were not considered seaworthy enough for a direct crossing.'

The replica *knarr* we had set our sights on was in his opinion just as much out of the question: 'You can forget that. First of all, the settlers in Iceland – and even more the settlers in Greenland – would not necessarily have had such substantial ships at their disposal. You have to remember that they were farmers, settlers, often refugees, and they'd have had to settle for what they could get. They would often only have driftwood available for ship building, and they were not on the whole very wealthy.'

Our inability to raise the money for such a boat seemed to him equally obvious; and even if we could, we would not be able to have total authenticity: 'Now that the walrus is a protected species, it's not possible to cut its hide into strips and weave them into rigging ropes – not to mention the problems of baggy woollen sails which have to have buckets of water thrown over them to make them windproof. What you should consider instead is buying a second-hand femboring.'

This was a recognizable descendant of the Viking ships of the past, and was still built in northern Norway. Its chief differences from the

Viking style of ship from which it had developed were the additions of a cabin and a topsail. 'The Viking square sail was too small and presented too much windage,' Alan told us, almost triumphantly – it was one of his contentions that the Vikings used a more efficient trapezoid sail – before pointing out that statistically, according to the sagas, Viking ships were not impressively successful: 'After all, only fourteen of the original twenty-five which set out from Iceland to Greenland actually completed the trip.'

As extra persuasion towards the femboring, he launched into an analysis of the dangers and difficulties of sailing any kind of Viking ship safely: 'The deck's not watertight, and there are no scuppers. This is the crazy thing with any Viking ship. None of them have a continuous watertight deck, and none of them have any means of freeing any water. If you caulk a deck at the second strake down on a Viking ship, the bloody things are so inflexible that you'd just go on caulking and caulking – you can't get it tight. We certainly know that the deck planks were loose and liftable.'

He paused briefly, then: 'The most we got in *Odin's Raven* was five tons of water. There's no proper keelson – you get five tons in a boat that displaces ten . . .' He left the effect to our imagination.

From references in the sagas, it seems that a ship was considered seaworthy if a couple of men bailing almost constantly could keep the water at an acceptable level; we were not sure what was meant by 'acceptable', and we could not imagine having two spare crew members with no other duty than to stop the boat filling up and sinking.

Next morning, still in a misty drizzle, Alan took us to see the Nydam ship, built in the early fourth century and the same length as the Gokstad, but considerably narrower and shallower. It had never carried a mast or sail, but had been propelled by oar power alone, and although it may have been used for short North Sea voyages was not designed for long ocean passages. But its double-ended construction, overlapping planking and high bows and stern showed that the Viking style of shipbuilding had evolved over many centuries.

The mist cleared as we drove on to Hedeby, or Haithabu, a German compound name meaning 'the place on the moor'. Its position, on the shore of a lagoon with sheltered access to the Baltic, made it the commercial and social link between east and west, north and south. The salt-laden peace had all too often been disrupted by conflict. But the emphasis at the Wikinger Haithabu Museum was less on the stereotyped negative image of the Vikings – rape, pillage, plunder;

'from the fury of the Northmen good Lord deliver us' (not that this had ever been openly said in so many words in churches up and down the land, as I had been led to believe) – than on the everyday skills of people whose daily life depended on a mixture of farming, fishing, boat-building and trading.

At the Roskilde Viking ship museum, several hours into Denmark by road and ferry, we were shown a film about the excavation of the five Viking ships housed there. For generations – for as long as anyone's grandparents and their grandparents before that could remember – local fishermen knew about an underwater obstruction in the Roskilde Fjord. During a prolonged south-westerly gale, the wind sometimes whipped the water level so low that a long ridge was revealed across one of the fjord's natural deep channels. Occasionally sections of ship's timbers and stones from the ridge were taken home as souvenirs. Legend had it that these came from 'Queen Margrethe's Ship', which the Queen had ordered to be filled with stones and scuttled as a barricade against the waterborne enemies of her cathedral city of Roskilde.

Although bits and pieces were brought ashore from time to time, the first attempt at investigation was not made until 1953, the six-hundredth anniversary of Queen Margrethe's birth. It was however more a question of newspaper hype than of serious archaeology. A few years later, two private divers presented a section of ship's frame they had brought up from the wreck to the National Museum. For the first time, it became clear that the sunken ship dated not from the Middle Ages, but from the Viking era. There was great excitement when five Viking ships of very different styles and built for equally different purposes were eventually found – the Skuldelev ships, after the nearest harbour to the site of the slow and painstaking excavations. It is not known when or why the ships were sunk, the first three to block the fjord entrance to Roskilde, the other two to reinforce the blockage a few years later, although all five were built between AD 950 and AD 1050. The lifespan of a Viking vessel was no more than half a century, which puts the sinking into the eleventh century.

The discovery of the trading ship, proportionately broader and deeper, and therefore stubbier and sturdier, than any of the others, gave the first physical explanation of the much-quoted comparison of the bust of a mature and full-breasted woman with the broad swelling bows of a *knarr*. In an artist's impression of a longitudinal cross-section of a *knarr*, five crew members are sitting and standing on two separate sections of half decking, three strakes down, with various sacks and barrels stored aft of the mast and an assortment of livestock standing on planking only just above the bottom boards. We had already decided against carrying authenticity this far.

Outside the museum, several students were applying traditional Viking oil to the planking of a replica of one of the smaller ships. The planking had been cut and shaped with axes and adzes rather than electrically sawn, leaving rough irregular markings on the surface of the wood. The strong links between the museum and the university meant that the practical work of building, maintaining and sailing a Viking replica could be seen as a useful and enjoyable extension of study. Without student labour the technique of radial cleaving, splitting logs as much as nine metres long into thirty-two identical wedge-shaped planks – which enabled the Vikings to make their ships extremely light and flexible without sacrificing load-carrying strength – would have been prohibitively expensive. I was amused to notice that the students were using modern brushes and scrapers.

From Roskilde, we travelled by car and ferry to Oslo, where like all Viking ship enthusiasts we paid homage to the Gokstad and Oseberg ships at the Viking Ship Hall. We worshipped the elegance of their reconstructed hulls in their specially designed cathedral-like setting – and reaffirmed, for our purposes, our preference for the less elegant *knarr*.

'Oseberg', with her tall proudly curved bow and stern rearing up, drawing back and ending in a tightly sprung carved coil, the head and tail of a serpent, may have explored the intricate shore line and fjords leading deep inshore, either as a royal yacht or as a more mundane working vessel, before she met her noble end as a burial ship to a queen and her serving maid. No one knows which of the two women found with her, one young, one middle-aged, was the queen, nor whether, as is suspected, she was indeed Queen Ása, grandmother of the first king of all Norway, Harald Hárfagri – Fine-Hair.

Because the deceased were women rather than warriors, the contents of their ship-grave illustrate the domestic rather than the martial life of their time and station – a cooking cauldron, shoes of soft, stitched leather, fragments of tapestry which would not look out of place at Bayeux, a wooden ladle and broad shallow bread trough, a wooden-handled knife which would fit into any modern country kitchen, dough for bread, apples in a wooden brass-handled pail, combs and brooches. The most famous of the artefacts found with the ship under the protective blue clay of the burial mound was an ornately carved open cart. Whatever some Vikings may have done to deserve their rape and pillage reputation, others – or maybe some of the same – deserved to be remembered for their unrivalled skill in art, craft and design.

The intricate detail of the carving on Oseberg was impressive, but she had obvious nautical drawbacks, and looked suitable only for inshore fjords, with far too little freeboard for ocean waves. In comparison with her long slinky slithery elegance, the Gokstad looked stubby and solid, with an extra four strakes of planking above the waterline and fuller more rounded lines. The top of her high prow and stern posts had protruded above her grave, and so had not been preserved. The plain tapering finish of her reconstruction did not however look out of place, since she was altogether plainer, with none of Oseberg's carved decoration. Under way, with her single square sail set or propelled by sixteen pairs of well-synchronized oars, she must in her heyday have looked magnificent, worthy of her description by Magnus Magnusson, who called her 'a poem carved in wood', and 'the most beautiful ship ever built – such is its grace of line, the lean power of its hull'.

Rikki telephoned Bjørkedal in west Norway, where Ragnar Thorseth's *Saga Siglar* had been built by one of the few remaining traditional Norwegian shipbuilding families, also called Bjørkedal, meaning 'birch valley'. Maybe they could build another *knarr* for us; and it seemed better to make initial enquiries about this in Norwegian. Rikki explained that we were planning to sail a replica Viking ship to Vinland, and asked Jakob Bjørkedal whether it would be possible for the family boatbuilding firm to build one for us, and if so, how long this would take and how much it would cost.

'This is rather sudden,' Jakob replied. 'Ring us back tomorrow. We have another big ship on order, but maybe . . .'

Next morning, we received a telephone call from Ragnar Thorseth, suggesting that we should meet him. David was committed to flying home; but I just had time to fly for a few hours to Ålesund in west Norway, and still catch the night ferry on which Jane, Emily and I were booked with the car.

Jakob Bjørkedal was slightly less guarded next day over the phone: 'We are interested.' When Rikki told him that we had arranged a meeting with Ragnar Thorseth, he commented that in that case we were unlikely to want to commission a boat. 'Ragnar will want you to give him a lot of money for using his.'

At around midday, after various flights, bus rides and ferry trips had taken me north-west into increasingly rugged and spectacular scenery, with snow-covered mountains reaching down to the shores of deeply indented fjords spattered with rocky islands, I landed at Vigra, the airport for Ålesund, halfway between Bergen and Trondheim. From there, I had to take a bus and foot-passenger ferry to Ulsteinvik. As the ferry drew in, I recognized Ragnar Thorseth among the people waiting on the shore, although he was smaller, less ferocious-looking and older than I had expected, with a small paunch and white streaks in his dark crimpy beard.

Neither of us talked much as he drove across the island, surprisingly slowly for someone often referred to as an adventurer and latter-day Viking. His office was on the first floor of a two-storey building overlooking a small and unpretentious boat yard. Ashtrays overflowed among overflowing piles of paper. Ragnar found and washed two mugs, and filled them with strong bitter black coffee from a large Thermos flask. I outlined our plans, then came to the point: ideally we should like to use *Saga Siglar*, if he was prepared to charter her to us.

Saga Siglar was at a disadvantage in her shorebound winter state. All boats out of the water suffer a loss of dignity, and she looked in need of the sort of care and attention which wooden boats of every race and type demand constantly. Her watertight accommodation cabins were sitting forlornly on the ground looking scruffy both inside and out; but any cover was better than none, and at least all the essentials were there: a cooker, a table and benches, and enough tightly confined sleeping bunks. I felt that she was a boat I could trust my life to, and that she would not let me down.

We went back indoors, to more strong coffee. Ragnar looked down as he rolled a cigarette – his umpteenth; the nicotine stains on his fingers disappeared up his sleeves – and then raised his head. 'Would you mind if I was involved in your adventure?' he asked, almost it seemed apologetically.

He drove faster on the way back across the island. 'Yesterday I was fined for speeding,' he explained. I could not imagine a traffic cop on the quiet island road, but if there had been one about we should certainly have been stopped again – and then I would have missed the ferry.

There was time to waste in Ålesund between ferries and buses and the plane. Everything, including the early onset of darkness and the juxtaposition of snow, mountains, islands and liberally scattered skerries, felt very foreign. I wondered about cultural differences between us and the west Norwegians, and about what my meeting with Ragnar and his sturdy Viking ship might lead to.

On the plane, I made notes in the Viking diary I had already started. 'I have rarely liked someone so much, or felt so at ease, at a first meeting,' I wrote, 'although perhaps this was not reciprocal. It will be interesting to observe the meeting between Ragnar and David. Perhaps David won't like Ragnar, or vice versa. I hope that Ragnar will not feel threatened or bounced by David's size and enthusiasm, and that David will not feel upstaged by Ragnar's experience and ownership of the boat.'

Back at home, David was at first grudging. He wanted his own adventure, not Ragnar's; and as he had not met Ragnar, he did not know whether he was someone with whom he would enjoy sharing an adventure. After a couple of days, he started coming round to the idea. Rikki and Jane had just bought a 60-foot Norwegian ex-whaling boat, *Sversling*, which they planned to convert into a permanent nautically mobile home, and which we all agreed would be the ideal expedition support ship, with Rikki as skipper.

Two months later, a provisional financial proposal reached us, in a letter written in Ragnar's absence in Spitzbergen – 'in connection with his film project about the icebear' – by his partner, Sigbjørn Notøy. He quoted an all-in figure for six months charter and the wages of four crew members, subject to final agreement by the end of the year. We estimated that for the entire expedition we would need to find in the region of a quarter of a million pounds.

In June, just before we set out to sail *Cloud Walker* from Canada to Norway via Greenland, Iceland, the Faroes and Shetland, Ragnar wrote to us from Spitzbergen, where he was still filming polar bears from his motor-sailing yacht *Havella*: 'Hello to both of you . . . my interest in your plans has not changed and you can count on me and *Saga Siglar*.'

3   Recce at Sea

Before setting out with *Cloud Walker* for our Viking reconnaissance cruise from North America to Norway, we steeped ourselves in translations and interpretations of the medieval Icelandic Saga accounts of the Norse voyages to Vinland, which is believed by many of the experts to have been Newfoundland. It is, however, difficult to believe that such good and experienced sailors, and such enthusiastic searchers for fertile farmland, would have stopped there. From time to time a Viking ship must surely have sailed as we did, up the coast from Nova Scotia and up the Strait of Belle Isle between Newfoundland and the mainland where Quebec now meets Labrador.

Our approach to Newfoundland was dramatic. For hours, *Cloud Walker* – with David, me, a friend whose experiences of a mid-Atlantic rescue from an upturned trimaran we hoped would not come in too useful, and ten-year-old Emily on board – surfed down a series of huge breaking seas, with the speed sometimes off the clock of our trailing log. Then the cloud parted to reveal a rugged coastline half a mile ahead. Loran and radar gave us the courage to proceed – although we had vowed never to rely on electronic navigational aids – until at a quarter of a mile we saw a gap in the cliffs. A series of vicious squalls, downdraughted from the steep sides of the entrance to Bonne Bay, almost flattened us. The force of the wind whipped the surface off the water, so that it seemed as if there were two distinct levels. Even in July, there was still snow on the Gros Morne mountains lowering above the bay, halfway up the island's west coast. We tied up alongside a semi-derelict fishing wharf at Woody Point, one of half a dozen small settlements along the bay's southern arm. A profusion of wild flowers in abandoned paddocks provided a multicoloured backdrop to faded clapboard houses.

A retired fisherman, known to everyone as Uncle Bill, gave us fresh rhubarb and told us about the good old days when Woody Point was a

14

flourishing fishing community, before the introduction of modern fishing methods and container lorries, and the decline in fish stocks. He showed us an old exercise book in which he had written out his family tree back to the arrival of the brig *Hope* from Poole in the 1840s.

Along the coast at Port-aux-Choix, an overnight sail away, we talked to fishermen who were mending their boats while they were on strike over the price they got for their cod. A modern shanty-town development of half-finished bungalows sprawled uphill from the waterfront. Some years ago, one of the locals who was digging out foundations uncovered the bones of more than a hundred four-thousand-year-old skeletons – two of which were now on display in a new museum building behind the fish factory. Along with other coastal groups between Maine and northern Labrador, the Port-aux-Choix Indians, and Dorset Eskimos after them, had survived by hunting, fishing and collecting whatever was naturally available. Then they had vanished – exactly why, or when, no one knew.

Another overnight sail, during which the sunset all but merged into a technicolor dawn, took us across the Strait of Belle Isle to the Labrador fishing harbour of Red Bay. Gillian, the daughter of one of the many unemployed local fishermen, provided Emily with a day's companionship of her own age, and a lasting pen-friendship. Her father escorted us in a home-made dory driven by a powerful outboard to the excavations of a sixteenth-century Basque whaling station.

Red Bay, a straggling settlement of a hundred or so white-painted houses built on granite, seemed a tough enough place to visit even in a twentieth-century summer, let alone to stay in over a sixteenth century winter. For much of the year, the Bay and Strait are frozen – Emily's new friend went to school by boat in the summer and by skidoo in the winter.

As we sailed on round the top of Newfoundland, we turned our minds back a few centuries, from the Basque fishermen who had made the long voyage north in the sixteenth century, to the Vikings who had sailed west five hundred years earlier to a tiny place on the north coast called l'Anse-aux-Meadows. Even now, it is too isolated to seem a natural candidate for international fame. This was thrust upon it in 1960 when a Norwegian husband-and-wife team, explorer Helge Ingstad and archaeologist Anne Stine Ingstad, discovered that a row of grassy humps known locally as 'the Indian Camp' concealed the remains of a Viking settlement.

At last there was tangible evidence to back up the sagas. Finding this proof had become an obsession for Helge Ingstad, who had already examined thousands of miles of American and Canadian coastline by sea, land and air. The initial excavations were supervised by Anne Stine, and in 1978 l'Anse-aux-Meadows became UNESCO's first World Heritage site as 'part of the heritage of mankind'.

Since we did not have a detailed chart of the complexities of rocks and shallows in the approach to l'Anse-aux-Meadows, we sailed past it a few miles offshore. The sea was a deep rich green-blue beneath a clear sky although there was a distinct chill in the wind. A whale humped and blew half a mile to seaward, the place where it had surfaced marked after it re-submerged by a gathering of seabirds on the water's surface. Inshore, spray leaped warningly against the skerries. We carried on to St Anthony, just around the north-eastern corner of the island, and visited l'Anse-aux-Meadows from there with a hired car. The fog was so dense that day that the reconstructed Norse sod houses on a plateau above the water's edge were cocooned from the outside world. Apart from the handful of other visitors in jeans and anoraks, we could have arrived just after the original inhabitants had moved out. A small replica Viking boat stood outside the houses, inside a sheltering wattle fence.

The grass mounds which had first attracted the attention of the Ingstads had been reinstated after the end of the excavations. Beside them, Parks Canada had built a reconstruction of the settlement. Inside the main building, a long low turf house supported by a framework of wooden beams and posts, it was surprisingly warm for such a dank foggy day.

'Even in the coldest winter it doesn't get much colder than right now, because of the insulation provided by the sod walls,' our guide, a tall girl with a mass of curly red hair, told us. 'The walls are six feet thick – there's two feet of sod here, on the inside, then the posts go into two feet of gravel core, then there's another two feet of sod. The gravel core cuts down the use of more sod, gives the building more support, and provides a drainage system; the rain soaks into the gravel rather than into the sod itself.'

Emily and I sat on one of the long wooden benches running down either side of the main living-cooking-sleeping room while we were shown a Viking-style sheepskin sleeping bag, warm and cosy with the wool on the inside, and told how it was thought the Norse inhabitants had conducted their everyday life at the original settlement – cooking over a pit in the earthen floor in which they heated up stones, with a second fire for heating and lighting and roof vents to allow at least some of the smoke to escape. As there were no windows, it must have been dark and stuffy, but otherwise comfortable enough, even in winter.

Outside, the lushness of the grass alongside a stream running down into the shallow bay added to the natural attractions of the site. Wild flowers grew in profusion, as did great patches of something like giant cow parsley which I later discovered was angelica, and which can often be found at Viking sites. There was no sign of long-term habitation, or of conflict; no bodies were buried there, nothing abandoned in a hurry, no weapons have been found. It seems to have been a peaceful settlement, and to have been destroyed by fire after it was abandoned – why, or by whom, no one knows.

Whoever they were, and wherever they came from or went to, the Vikings who spent a few winters there organized their departure well, packing carefully and leaving only a few individual items behind: a spindle whorl, indicating that there were women as well as men, and that they had sheep for wool; a pin of the type used to fasten a Viking cloak; a concave stone used as an oil lamp; some wood chippings from boat repairs, and a few nails at a small smithy beside the stream from which bog iron was extracted.

Scholars disagree about whether this was Vinland, or the gateway to Vinland, or a staging post on the way to Vinland, or perhaps one of many places where a number of Norse men and women spent a few winters. The argument centres on the interpretation of the first syllable of the name Vinland, and particularly the length of the letter 'i', and whether or not one of Leif Eiriksson's crew found grapes growing wild. If they really were grapes – and according to the saga the finder was a German who knew a grape when he saw one – then northern Newfoundland is almost certainly far too far north, even allowing for a temperature difference between then and now. Those who insist that l'Anse-aux-Meadows fits the sailing times, directions and distances hinted at in the sagas suggest that the grapes were some other sort of berry from which wine was made.

The meadow or grassland claim gained support after the discovery of the Newfoundland site. Although the mixture of French and English in the name l'Anse-aux-Meadows sounds as if it adds weight to the grass argument, the word 'meadows' is a corruption of *méduses* – so the uncorrupted French means Jellyfish Bay and has nothing to do with meadows.

Scholars have argued equally inconclusively about the relative

historical validity of minor variations in the written versions of the story
– and, until the authentication of l'Anse-aux-Meadows as a Norse site,
about whether the two Vinland sagas, *Grænlendinga Saga* and *Eiriks Saga
Rauða*, were based on fact or fantasy. Like all the saga material, the
stories of the various visits to Vinland were for many generations
passed on by word of mouth, so inevitably variations and mistakes
crept in over the years.

'I know people in l'Anse-aux-Meadows who've never been in the sod
houses, just because they don't believe they were really Norse,' our
guide admitted. 'Their grandparents told them it was Indians that
lived here – then along came this Norwegian archaeologist who said,
"No, the Norse lived here." So who would you rather believe, some
stranger or your grandparents? That's the way they look at it.'

'This isn't Vinland – it's probably a halfway staging post on the way
to Vinland, used a few times,' David wrote in our log. But neither of us
doubted that the Vikings had landed in northern Newfoundland. In
one version of the saga the first sighting of North America was made by
a man called Bjarni Herjolfsson. Bjarni, who had spent the winter in
Norway, discovered when he sailed home to Iceland that his father had
in the meantime emigrated to Greenland and decided to follow. He was
lost in fog for several days, and then saw land to the west. As it was
clearly not Greenland, he refused his crew permission to land on three
separate occasions before eventually reaching his destination.

'People thought he had not been curious enough,' the saga writer
recorded. According to this version, Leif Eiriksson bought Bjarni's
boat, retraced his route in reverse, and landed at each of the places his
incurious predecessor had sighted. The first he called Helluland, the
land of stone slabs, tentatively identified as Baffin Island; the white
sandy beach of the second, Markland – Forest Land – is thought to be
in Labrador. It was only at the third, which he later named Vinland,
that Leif was tempted to linger: the dew on the grass was sweet, the
salmon were bigger and more plentiful, the grass richer and the winter
milder than in Greenland. If the place where a river flowed out of a lake
where Leif and his crew ran their boat ashore and built their houses was
indeed l'Anse-aux-Meadows – and apart from the grapes, the description in the saga can be taken to fit – then our route from northern
Newfoundland to Greenland would be roughly that taken when he
sailed back home again.

A grey heaving sea and the dull light of a sunless dusk were linked by
the strangely solid cloud of our first distant iceberg soon after we set sail

from St Anthony. Whales surrounded us throughout our first evening at sea, sometimes as many as two or three dozen at a time, so that whichever way we looked *Cloud Walker* was at the centre of a circle of humping spouting backs – a powerful diversion from the discomforts of a cold and lumpy sail. On a later, equally uncomfortable, squally evening the sea was alive with dolphins, which surfed in groups of half a dozen or more down steep waves. As they crossed behind and in front of us we could hear them squeaking and clicking with apparent pleasure. Icebergs crossed our path or swept majestically across the horizon at regular intervals. The cold intensified the nearer we came to Greenland, until even off-watch in seven layers of clothing and under two sleeping bags we still never warmed up.

Emily was so seasick for the first four days that she even stopped reading – usually her personal cure. On the fifth day, she recovered, no doubt partly because we all thought it would be the last at sea. Ice conditions, which that year were at their worst, decreed otherwise. It was dusk when we first attempted to approach the coast, off Julianehåb, the village-sized capital of south-west Greenland. We hove-to for the few hours of near darkness, and at dawn saw the first signs of serious pack ice in the distance. An hour later we were in VHF range for a radio call to the Ice Central office which I persisted in calling optimistically 'Ice Control' at Narsarsuaq, one of the world's bleakest and most isolated international airfields.

'Do you have a fortified hull?' a disembodied voice asked. 'Are you used to navigating through ice?'

The answer was negative on both counts. We were given coordinates for a possible approach to the west coast of Greenland via Bredafjord, a few miles north of our intended entry, which was seriously blocked by pack ice.

'This was passible last time we flew, a few days ago, but we can give no guarantees,' our invisible Danish guide told us. 'You will certainly meet ice, but perhaps not more than two tenths, which should be OK for you. We hope to fly today, and will talk to you.'

We edged carefully into scattered drift ice, which gradually thickened into the alarming beauty of pack as we wove in and out under motor between translucent wedding-cake chunks. What would happen if our engine failed became an increasingly serious concern as we tried to assess how many tenths of the water ahead was covered by ice. Visibility was too poor for the ice-reconnaissance aircraft, so we had to rely on our own judgement. The anticipated two-tenths ice cover thickened to an estimated four-tenths; it looked thicker ahead. We were only too aware of the flimsiness of our unreinforced fibre-glass hull as we attempted to retreat, with occasional alarming grating sounds as *Cloud Walker* squeezed through some of the narrower gaps.

Fortunately we were in clear water by the time the wind rose to gale force. The barometer seemed oblivious of the sudden and vicious weather change, a Greenland speciality. It was an unpleasant night. By morning, the wind had dropped to nothing, and visibility to two hundred yards. We made another cautious approach considerably farther north than our first, hoping to find a way round the pack ice which is swept from Greenland's east coast round the southernmost tip, Cape Farewell, and on up the west coast until it is eventually dispersed by a weak gulf stream eddy of warmer water. Our second attempt to squeeze safely through the freezing fog into the relatively clear channels of the inner leads was successful. Ice formed under way on our clothing and on deck, and all ropes and sails were literally frozen stiff.

At last, with what we felt to be a well-deserved sense of achievement and an eager anticipation of thawing out, we tied up alongside a fishing boat in our first Greenlandic harbour, Paamiut, or Frederikshåb, the old Danish name by which it was still known on our chart. Apart from the freezing fog for which Paamiut is notorious even in Greenland, we soon became aware of another problem. Men and women alike, Greenlandic Inuits, whose traditions have been eroded by a modern semi-industrialized way of life, seemed all too often to be drunk. Greenland is said to have the highest rate of alcoholism in the world.

A few miles up the fjord from Paamiut, we spent a couple of nights at anchor off a tiny island where until the 1960s there was a small community, with its own church, school and fish factory. Then, we were told, the Danish colonial administration stopped its supply ship, forcing the islanders to move to the town. They were rehoused in apartment blocks which must have seemed soulless and depressing even when they were new. In a quarter of a century they had become slums, outside which groups of men and women sat drinking beer, and adding the empty cans to the rubbish which was periodically cleared away by Danish Jehovah's Witnesses.

From Frederikshåb, we worked our way south inside the pack ice, anxiously negotiating the mouth of a fjord into which a glacier was constantly spawning new bergs. The inner leads of a maze of interwoven fjords took us through a bleakly beautiful wilderness of rock and ice beneath towering cliffs. The barren mountains beyond them led only to the waste of the ice cap. Occasionally the sun glistened on bergs reflected in shimmering still water, but for a fortnight these interludes allowed only brief respite from alternating freezing fog and gale force winds, often accompanied by stinging rain.

'Dodging ice in SE 7–8. How did the Vikings manage in conditions like this?' David wrote in the log on a day under motor and triple-reefed mainsail; between gale force squalls visibility had just lifted to a mile and a half, revealing an alarming line of jagged pack ice ahead. Seals popped up to look at us in surprise. 'Cosy anchorage,' David remarked that evening, in a pool surrounded by rock on which there were still pockets of snow only a few feet above the water line. It was August 1st.

On one of the magic Greenland days which make up for gales, fog and ice, we finally reached the softer more fertile fjords of the area first settled a thousand years ago by Vikings from Iceland. The broad expanse of Bredafjord treated us to towering bergs cut by brilliant blue and green stripes and with treacherous turquoise swimming pools at their feet.

'What on earth is Iceland like, if this place looked green and fertile in comparison?' we had asked ourselves several times. But there was rich grass on the gently shelving slopes of Brattahlið, Eirik the Red's farm, where the country began to seem less cynically named. Sheep grazed around the ruins of the original farmhouse, and of the church, which according to one of the saga writers was built for Eirik's wife when she became a Christian and banned him from her bed because of his pagan beliefs. At the modern sheep farming village of Atarnateq, drying hay was draped over the remaining stone ruins of the Viking bishopric and farm of Gardar – and there too the name Greenland seemed less an advertising gimmick than an accurate statement of fact.

One of the bonuses of sailing is that every now and then it creates an unexpected lasting friendship from a chance encounter. This happened at Narsarsuaq, where we were trapped for three days by the weather and made the acquaintance of Thorstein – or Tony – Jonsson. Tony, who had an English mother and an Icelandic father, was the only Icelandic Spitfire pilot with the RAF during the Battle of Britain. He had later flown supplies into Biafra during the Nigerian civil war, and had recently retired from his last employment as a commercial pilot. When we invited him aboard, he brought with him an Icelandic friend. Rikardur Peturssen, who lived in Narsarsuaq, was introduced as 'the tame Viking', and with his flowing red beard he certainly looked the part.

Leaving Greenland proved as difficult as entering it, and for the same reason: ice, combined with strong winds. Cape Desolation lived up to its name, coming and going in wreaths of mist and rain, while gale force gusts did their best to catch us off guard and flatten us even with three reefs in the mainsail and no jib. A line of pack ice stretched as far as we could see in either direction. Visibility was poor even while the glimmer of daylight allowed by the rain lasted. By the time it started to get dark, we had still not found a lead through the ice, although we could see across it to open water; but we dared not risk pushing our way through when the wind strength was never less than force six, and often more. Seals interrupted their fishing to stare at us, then dived effortlessly under the ice.

It was, as David wrote in the log, 'a horrid night'. *Cloud Walker* did three and a half knots under bare poles through the hours of darkness, in quite the wrong direction for Iceland but the only one we could take. We could hear the grinding and rumbling of ice behind us and to seaward and prayed that it would not be blown inshore before we had found a way round it.

At dawn, the wind dropped over a sloppy and at last iceless sea. 'All adventures are horrid some of the time,' Emily commented philosophically. We gave Cape Farewell a wide berth before at last setting course for Iceland on another wild night during which we were joined by whales and dolphins in a northerly gale. Throughout the rest of the crossing, fulmars played last across the bows all day, and aurora borealis and phosphorescence enlivened night watches. A solitary dolphin jumped under a full moon as we approached Reykjavik, where Tony Jonsson had been watching out for us and immediately whisked us off to his apartment to meet his wife, Katie, and have showers.

The trouble with cruising under sail is that it tends to give a jaundiced view of every port of call. If the weather is good, there is a compulsion to sail on in case it changes for the worse, and it is only in bad weather that we usually spend more than a day anywhere. So it was in Iceland, where it rained and blew for several days before clearing enough for us to set sail for our next port of call along the old Viking route – the Faroes. After three days of exhilarating sailing, with a wind varying from fresh to gale force behind us and big following seas, we arrived to find that the entire population of the capital, Torshavn, seemed to be outside basking in the sun.

'It's the first day of summer,' we were told, 'and probably the last.' Next day, the weather was indeed back to wind and rain. While we were waiting for a forecast which did not threaten a force ten storm, the departure before the end of August of the last ferry of the year to anywhere else underlined the isolation of the islands. First in New-foundland, then in Greenland and again in Iceland, we had marvelled at the nautical ability and agricultural determination of the Viking settlers who had sailed to, and had then established themselves as farmers in, such apparently bleak and inhospitable places. In the Faroes, and then in Shetland, we marvelled again.

There were times on our North Atlantic crossing when I wished I was someone else, somewhere else, and I even said at least once to David: 'Remind me never ever to sail here again.' But sailing is like childbirth: otherwise no one would ever have more than one child, nor go to sea more than once. So by the time we reached Norway, we were even more determined to make the crossing again the Viking way.

4 Negotiations

Ragnar and Kari Thorseth had moved to Håholmen, an island so small we could not find it on any map. Although it was not much more than eighty miles from the larger island on which I had met Ragnar before, only a bird could go directly from one to the other because of the maze of mountains, fjords and islands separating them. Ragnar met us from the same little coastal plane I had taken before, but at Kristiansund, two small airfields north of Ålesund, with his younger son Eirik, who looked exactly as he must have looked himself at the age of fourteen. There was only one way to reach Håholmen – by water.

The wake from a fast motor launch rose steeply behind us as we approached a tiny harbour under a compact cluster of old fishermen's cottages. We saw first the honey coloured copy of the Oseberg ship, with its carved serpent's head and tail; then Ragnar's own motor-sailing yacht *Havella*, a sturdy double-ended boat in need of a new coat of white paint after a year in the ice of Spitzbergen: and finally, as we turned to come alongside, *Saga Siglar*, looking considerably less forlorn than the last time I had seen her.

Once the centre of a small self-supporting fishing community, the island had belonged to the Thorseth family for generations – Ragnar's mother had grown up there – until an uncle had sold it. When its new owner in turn put it up for sale, Ragnar and Kari seized the opportunity to buy it back, and with various government grants and labour schemes embarked on the long task of turning it into a holiday and conference centre.

From the top of a small hill, a three-minute walk from our first floor self-contained flatlet, the entire island property could be seen at once: twenty or so cottages in various states of repair, some with their original sagging turf roofs, surrounded on three sides by scrubby grass and on the fourth side by the harbour. A fishing boat similar to but smaller than Jane and Rikki's *Sversling* lay at anchor. To seaward, spray marked the skerries between the island and open water. On the mainland, mountains rose steeply above the shoreline.

As Ragnar admitted, the person responsible for Håholmen's transformation from a collection of semi-derelict buildings huddling above an abandoned fishing harbour was his wife Kari. They had met not long after Ragnar's first, and probably toughest, nautical adventure: a ten-day solo crossing of the North Sea from Norway to the Shetlands in a fifteen-foot rowing boat. He had timed his arrival in Lerwick to coincide with celebrations attended by Queen Elizabeth II and the Duke of Edinburgh to mark the fifth centenary of the marriage between a Scottish King and a Norwegian princess whose dowry gave Scotland the Orkneys and Shetlands; these had been Norwegian since the ninth century.

Neither marriage, nor local journalism – Ragnar's employment when he and Kari married – nor the births of their two sons, Njål and Eirik, had kept him on land for long. Well before the involvement of the rest of his family in the circumnavigation of *Saga Siglar*, Ragnar had a reputation in Norway as 'one of the leading Arctic adventurers of the age'. He had taken an eighteen-foot speedboat through the Northwest Passage and a snowmobile to the North Pole. His obsession with Viking sailing had been triggered by a crossing in 1975 by fishing boat to Canada and North America, via Greenland, in the wake of Leif Eiriksson.

By the time we met him, he had set up his own company to cater for the adventurous instincts of those richer and less independent than himself. His new brochure invited anyone with 'a genuine inquisitiveness and an urge to explore the unknown, normal good health and the spirit of adventure, as well as a healthy bank account' to plan an expedition to 'the indescribable Arctic', also called 'the Kingdom of Contrasts', with one of the 'most famous explorers of our times, Ragnar Thorseth'. A comprehensive choice of boats was offered: 'the expeditionary vessel *Havella* (fitted to a high standard of comfort and equipped with state-of-the-art navigational and safety equipment); a larger polar vessel with helicopter platform, suitable for twelve to sixteen persons'; or one of the two Viking replicas, *Oseberg* and *Saga Siglar*.

'She's OK,' David said after his first inspection of *Saga Siglar*, although he did not like the idea of having to climb on to the top of the sleeping cabin forward of the mast to reach its top-opening hatch.

'What do you think?' he asked me as I climbed down to investigate the bunks.

'Narrow, minimal-sized, a bit claustrophobic, but perfectly adequate,' I decided. The day cabin was equally basic and serviceable.

As far as we could tell, the hull, rudder, mast and rigging were sound, although of course everything would have to be thoroughly checked and there would inevitably be a certain amount of work to be done before the start of any long and demanding voyage. We knew that there had been problems with the original mast and rudder, both of which had broken; their replacements had lasted round the world. *Saga Siglar* – 'Sailor of the Sagas' – looked what she was: a strong, well-tested working boat, and consequently a little shabby. But normal maintenance, including a few coats of Viking-style oil on the hull, would soon smarten her up.

That evening, in the warmth of a sitting-room-cum-bar above the restaurant, we talked about the timing and general requirements for our Viking expedition. On a sheet of lined file paper, Ragnar wrote out a new agreement, according to which he would provide *Saga Siglar* fully equipped, and we would provide a back-up ship for the entire voyage.

'You're getting a pretty good deal,' he assured us.

We asked to film him on board *Saga Siglar*. He took his glasses off, although he did not discard his cigarette.

'She is an extremely good vessel,' he started, 'but of course you have to know how to sail her –' His English was good, although he had a marked accent, but he clearly did not feel entirely at ease using it; and in spite of his flamboyant achievements and reputation he struck us as shy and modest.

'You can sail her comfortably up to eight, eight and a half knots,' he told us, in his soft deep voice, 'after that you're sailing too hard and had better reef.'

'Is this the type of ship the Vikings would have used when they crossed the Atlantic?' David asked.

'Yes, it's the type of ship they'd have used when they went to Greenland, Iceland, Labrador and Newfoundland. It's a cargo ship, not a longship, not a warship. They never went across the Atlantic in their longships, this is the sort of ship they'd have used.'

Although the possibility that he himself might be our skipper was mentioned, he did not think it likely as he had so many other irons in the fire. But he was having another Viking ship built, he told us, a copy of the Gokstad – the commission that Jakob Bjørkedal had mentioned. She was to be launched in April.

'Maybe I can come with her as far as Shetland,' Ragnar suggested.

But he would not, he said, want to take her any farther than that in open sea, and certainly did not think that she would be suitable for a North Atlantic voyage, although he was still planning a 1992 Columbus trade wind crossing with *Saga Siglar* and the Gokstad and Oseberg replicas.

We had admired the elegance of *Oseberg*, launched in 1986, but did not like the idea of sailing her across the Atlantic by any route, although two extra strakes had been added after she had sunk under full sail in gusty conditions in the Oslo fjord. She had also been given a shorter mast and a smaller sail, since one reason she had proved so unstable even in enclosed inland water was that she had been over-canvassed.

Although there was no opportunity for a trial sail with *Saga Siglar*, we felt we could trust her.

On our last evening on the island, Ragnar showed us some of his Svalbad – Spitzbergen – film of polar bears: spectacular snow scenes, a furry white cub coming up to *Havella* for food, an adult polar bear carefully testing the edge of the ice with its paw before climbing out. That there was a large mine on the Russian part of Svalbad, of which Spitzbergen is the main island, struck us as a bizarre juxtaposition; Ragnar had not filmed it, however, as it had no relevance to his project.

We had felt that the Thorseths were a little stiff and ill at ease with us earlier, and no doubt we were with them; but as the cognac level dropped that evening we all relaxed, Ragnar perching gnome-like, cross-legged on an armchair. From time to time, there was a half-warning, half-joking 'Ragnar!' from Kari as he rolled and lit another cigarette or recharged his glass – but she too smoked heavily, and her hearty spontaneous laugh became louder and more frequent.

Now that we had an agreement about chartering *Saga Siglar*, all we needed, as Ragnar pointed out, was to find the money. Harald Bjerke, who had recently taken early retirement, agreed to act as our Norwegian agent; he had plenty of energy, time and business contacts, had from the first shown considerable interest in our project, and was delighted to have a new challenge, even if it was only in an honorary capacity. He arranged a meeting at Norsk Hydro, his first choice of potential sponsor, timing it to fit in with the launch of the Gokstad replica, which we had already arranged to attend. The day before we left England, we spoke to Ragnar. 'You should give a copy of your brochure to Per Paust at the Norwegian Foreign Ministry,' he said. Although nothing had been confirmed, official discussions were being held about Viking ships and Columbus year: maybe our expedition in 1991 might be 'the start of something big'.

'Well, what do you think?' David asked Harald after our Norsk Hydro meeting.

'Ninety-five per cent yes,' Harald answered, beaming and looking as if he would like to dance a little jig then and there; but he was driving, and so he had to restrain this impulse.

Norwegians are not noted for excesses of enthusiasm, and if Harald felt so sure – or very nearly sure – that the sponsorship approach would prove successful, we were impressed, especially as that was the feeling we had come away with ourselves. We had been promised a definite answer in May. The company logo was already a Viking ship, so for it to sponsor the expedition of a Viking ship seemed a logical extension. The proliferation of Hydro Viking ships on petrol pumps, fertilizer bags and trucks as we drove north and west from Oslo towards Bjørkedal with Harald and his American wife, Dolly, seemed a good omen. It was a long drive, twelve hours spread over two days.

We had left England in an early heat wave – and reached Bjørkedal in a late blizzard. On any other day it would have been easy to have driven past the one shop and half a dozen or so houses visible from the road without realizing we had arrived. But on this particular day in late April there were girls with radios to tell us where to park, and even in the bitterly cold wind and snow flurries there was a big enough crowd to give a sense of occasion. The unmistakeable prow of the new Gokstad replica was sticking proudly out of a barn in which the boatbuilders were still adding finishing touches. Half a dozen children, well-wrapped-up against the cold, were brandishing wooden shields and swords. Assorted adults were standing around waiting, watching, talking, photographing even before there was anything to film – except lowering snow-covered mountains behind the lake into which the ship was about to be launched.

At last, a tractor and an excavator were manoeuvred into position. Chains were attached through holes at the forefoot of the ship, and slowly, very slowly, she was pulled out of her shed a few feet at a time. Then there was a pause while log rollers were moved out from behind and carried round to be repositioned in front ready for the next few slow feet forwards. If it had not been for the machines and power cables, it would have been easy to imagine that we had slipped back a thousand years to the launch of one of the original Viking ships.

It took two hours to cover the three hundred metres to the road. Then, for the third time in a decade, the traffic – not that there was much of it – was held up for the slow majestic crossing of a full-sized

Viking ship built by Sigurd Bjørkedal and his sons for Ragnar Thorseth. The real festivities started once she was on the lake side of the road. A junior band, some of its members smartly dressed but shivering in red uniform, others too cold to take off their parkas and woolly hats, played a medley of brass favourites. It seemed unlikely that any ninth- or tenth-century ships had been launched to the strains of 'When the saints come marching in' – but why not?

A long line of volunteers hauled on ropes attached at either side of the bows, while others leant their backs and shoulders against the hull, steering a little to this side, a little to that, forwards a few feet, HALT! while the rollers were moved, and then on again – a skilled team operation.

There was a pause just above the water. Two small Viking boats, one under engine- and one under oar-power, emerged from behind some bushes. Ragnar, looking more like an Arctic spaceman than a neo-Viking in a silver fur-lined all-in-one outfit, undid the top few inches of its zip to reveal some hairy chest before posing, alone and with Sigurd Bjørkedal, for photographers. 'Today I am keeping a low profile,' he had told us earlier, 'this is the builder's day, not mine.'

Instructions were shouted for the final crucial moments of the launch by a master of ceremonies standing high above us in the bows wearing a baseball hat, and using a megaphone.

Then, with a sudden rush which almost brought disaster, *Gokstad* – as she was being called, for want of another name – plunged into the water. The wind caught her broadside on, sweeping her bows round and threatening to smash her against the shore. There was a hasty scramble for oars to push her off, then for a few minutes a confusion of blades; as she was taken into deep water, the rowers gained control of their long narrow oars and gave a passably coordinated demonstration.

On shore, a large painted wooden bowl, decorated with a traditional blue and red rose design and filled with strong local home-made beer, was passed from mouth to mouth. 'Nearer heaven you never come,' we were told when it was our turn to taste it.

'Do you realize that this is only a few days earlier in the year than we intend to set sail from Norway in a Viking ship next year?' I asked David as I tried to stamp some life back into my feet.

The launch was marked in Bjørkedal by a weekend festival, which would no doubt have attracted more outside visitors had the weather been kinder. There was a gathering of Viking craft in the small harbour at the head of the lake, to which the new ship was rowed and the smaller older ones motored. An exhibition of local crafts, including boat-building, had been mounted in the village school. Rides were being given in a cart drawn by two stocky west Norwegian horses, a picturesque breed, with a distinctive dark stripe through flaxen mane and tail, and similar to the horses taken westwards a thousand years ago by the Vikings.

We returned home trying not to be elated, but feeling that at last our plans were about to fall into place. Requests for information, and enquiries about TV, press and radio coverage, started to gain momentum. The *Guardian* quoted me as saying cheerfully that our expedition was a 'Bugger Columbus!' exercise. The Norwegian press made our motives sound more serious: 'We will strike a blow for the Vikings. It was Norwegian Vikings who were the first Europeans to go to America. We think that it's time that both the Americans and others were told the historical facts,' I was supposed to have said.

It was disappointing to be told in May that we would have to wait for an answer from Norsk Hydro until September or October. Harald had drawn up a list of potential Norwegian sponsors, from all of whom we had polite and encouraging but negative replies. At the same time, I continued to look for sponsors in Britain, but with no success. A major obstacle was that it was understandably less appealing to a Norwegian company to consider sponsoring a British-based expedition than an entirely Norwegian operation – but equally difficult to persuade a British company to sponsor an expedition with a Norwegian-built boat.

I telephoned Peter Davies, one of the directors of Southampton Yacht Services, which had done work on our old wooden boat *Eridani*. The company, founded in 1980 by Piers Wilson, former production director of the Southampton Camper and Nicholson yard, was small, but had gained such a widespread reputation for specialist wooden boatbuilding and maintenance that a number of large American yachts had been sailed across for major refits.

'What would it cost us if we asked you to build us a fifty-four-foot Viking ship? And would you be able to do it anyway?' I asked.

'Off the top of my head, I would say around £150,000,' Peter replied. And, yes, it would of course be possible, although it would need some research as it was not a type of boat they had ever built before.

The idea of commissioning our own *knarr* was appealing. It would give us control of the operation, from the laying of the keel through the building to the launching and sea trials, all of which would arouse considerable media interest, and would leave us – or our sponsors – with a Viking ship as an asset at the end of the expedition. We put it to Rikki and Jane that since Rikki had an American passport, as well as professional sailing qualifications, they might like to operate a Viking ship in America after our voyage. As our support ship was to be *Sversling*, their home would already be there.

'Very keen in principle on the idea of operating a Viking ship somewhere in America – sounds an ideal thing for us,' Jane wrote from Norway.

Another advantage of owning our own *knarr* would be that we could then if necessary postpone our expedition to the following year; if we were chartering *Saga Siglar* from Ragnar this would be impossible, since by then he would need her for his Columbus–Leif Eiriksson link. We explained our thinking to him in a letter at the end of June, since we felt that it was important to keep him informed about what we were up to, and also still wanted to keep our options open.

Tony Jonsson had agreed to be our Icelandic agent, and at the beginning of July he came to stay with us. He was despondent, however, because of an article which had just appeared in Reykjavik under the headline: '150 million [Icelandic kroner] public relations project related to land discoveries: Leif Eiriksson versus Columbus'.

'Jōn Baldvin Hannibalsson, the foreign minister, proposed during a cabinet meeting yesterday that Iceland should join Norway in an international public relations project regarding LEIF THE LUCKY in 1992,' the article stated. 'The reason for this being that the Spanish-speaking people will, that year, be celebrating the 500th anniversary of Columbus setting foot in the West Indies. By this public relations project the Norwegians and Icelanders intend to inform the world that it was the Icelandic Leif Eiriksson who discovered America 500 years before Columbus. The most prominent part of the PR project will be the sailing of knarrs from Norway to Iceland and on to the Western Hemisphere. This will take place at the same time as Spanish speaking people will be sailing caravelles by the more southerly route over the ocean.'

Iceland had already committed ten million Icelandic kroner (approximately £100,000) while the Norwegians were expected to contribute enough to bring the total to the equivalent of £1,500,000. It made our estimated cost of a fifth of that seem small. Since the article went on to state that the idea had been initiated during discussions in Norway, we assumed that this was the project hinted at by Ragnar, and a variation on his original idea of sailing his Viking ships with the

Columbus fleet. Although we wrote to ask him for further clarification, he did not reply; and there were no official announcements in the Norwegian press.

'You'll have to abandon your idea,' Tony said gloomily. He had been looking forward to being part of it, as a crew member of *Sversling*, subject to approval by Rikki whom he had not yet met. Although he was not young, we considered him eminently well qualified: he had amazing stamina, had for a while operated his own trawler, and had recently taken a number of fishing trips to Greenland, so he knew the coasts of both Iceland and Greenland, as well as having a wide network of acquaintances in both countries.

'The possibility of an official expedition needn't change our plans,' we said, 'we shall be doing it first anyway.'

With only a couple of weeks to go before we were due to leave to sail in the Baltic with *Cloud Walker* for a summer family holiday, I telephoned Peter Davies at Southampton Yacht Services again.

'You remember I asked you about building a Viking *knarr*? –'

'– and I gave you a figure off the top of my head –'

'Well, now I'm asking you seriously to give us an estimate.'

Before committing themselves, he and Piers borrowed all our books about Viking ships and called a meeting of their shipwrights to sound out their feelings about such an unusual project. They were unanimously enthusiastic. So were Piers and Peter, one or both of whom hoped to go to Denmark and Norway 'to study a *knarr* and meet experts' before starting the project. We already had a basic set of scale drawings of the Roskilde *knarr*, which we were given permission to use in a letter offering further advice and cooperation. Although the original Viking shipbuilders worked without plans, we did not feel that authenticity need necessarily rule out such assistance to modern shipwrights used to a different way of working.

Piers sent us a quotation which cannot have allowed Southampton Yacht Services any profit margin. If we pared everything else down to the minimum, we should still be able to carry out our expedition within the £300,000 we had budgeted. The prospect was exciting. A couple of Scottish yards gave provisional estimates which indicated roughly the same sort of figure, but the advantage of Southampton being only an hour's drive away outweighed the authenticity of having a Viking ship built in, say, Orkney. We had until the end of September to make the decision if we wanted Southampton Yacht Services to guarantee having a *knarr* ready to launch and test in the Solent by Easter.

Although it was still difficult to start making plans in Canada and the United States, I had written letters, had had some encouraging replies, and had worked out a provisional itinerary in the States which would allow our Viking ship to feature at all the major boat shows during the year following our estimated time of arrival in 'Vinland'.

Harald had come round to the idea of commissioning a new boat, although initially he had regarded it as impractical. 'You may after all be right in your belief that there may be sufficient advantages in being independent,' he wrote, and commented that 'summer time in Norway is a particularly frustrating period when it comes to finding people home and at work!' One of the people he put us in contact with, and with whom I had a long telephone conversation, was Alf Bjercke (no relation), Oslo chairman of the Norway–America Association and, as Harald put it, 'a man full of enthusiasm and ideas'.

A few days later, Harald wrote again: 'When I talked to Alf Bjercke yesterday, he suggested that I contact my old friend Knut Utstein Kloster since he currently "is interested in Viking ships".' Harald and Knut had both been students at MIT in America.

'I have just talked to Knut this afternoon,' Harald went on, 'and it turns out that he had the material you had sent to Per Paust at the Foreign Ministry on his desk, and that he is having a meeting with Ragnar Thorseth tomorrow. . . . Knut is heavily involved in Thorseth's Viking fleet expedition in 1992. They have government support from both Norway and Iceland.' As background, Harald explained that Knut Kloster had been involved in building up one of the major cruise lines operating out of Miami. 'He bought the old *France* which was renamed *Norway*, but has now left the day to day management of the company to others. His pet project at the moment is the planning of the world's largest cruise ship which will be like a floating city.'

At least we now had confirmation from Norway of the joint Norwegian–Icelandic venture of which we had heard through Tony Jonsson.

After sailing for a month in the Baltic, we entered the Gøta Canal on the Swedish east coast. From the middle of Sweden, I made two telephone calls to Oslo. The first was to Norsk Hydro.

'The decision has been made to put all the company's sponsorship money into the Winter Olympics to be held in Norway in 1994,' I was told.

The second call was to Harald.

'You have a meeting with Knut Kloster at 9.00 am on Friday morning,' he told me, 'but don't get any hopes up. He says he has enough ships already, but he is interested in swopping ideas.'

5   A Kloster Cruise?

Harald drove us to the offices of Kloster's company, World City Discovery, at the top of a modern building looking across trees to the Oslo fjord.

'Why is it called World City Discovery?' we asked.

'Knut has this ideal of the world being like a city, with no national barriers,' Harald said. 'His chief project for the last ten years has been planning the world's biggest cruise liner, *Phoenix*, which he sees as a floating world city, with international leaders having environmental conferences on board. Maybe he will succeed. He's that sort of person. When he turned the *France* into the *Norway*, no one thought having such a big cruise ship would work – but it did.'

A model of *Phoenix*, with three sloping conference towers on her deck, stood below a portrait of Knut Kloster's grandfather in the spacious room we were ushered into. A huge round conference table filled two-thirds of the space. Floor-to-ceiling windows along one wall gave a panoramic view across autumn-tinged trees and the Oslo fjord.

The four of us sat down in armchairs round an informal low square table. Knut offered us coffee from a Thermos flask. Although we knew he must be in his sixties, like Harald he seemed younger, as if he took regular exercise and ate and drank sparingly. He had more hair than Harald, and the lines on his forehead looked as if they came from concentration rather than age. Since we knew less about his Viking plans than he did about ours, we countered his opening question with a request for information.

'It started with a conversation between myself and my old friend Erik Bye,' Knut began. 'We thought we should do something about Leif Eiriksson.' Erik Bye was one of Norway's best known television personalities. The timing of their thought was not unconnected with the approach of the Columbus quincentenary.

'But we did not want it to be something which was just Norwegian, it

35

should involve Iceland too.' Since they were both acquainted with, and indeed friends of, Iceland's President, Vigdis Finnbogadottir, and since Leif Eiriksson was even more of an Icelandic than a Norwegian hero, their next move had been to talk things over with her. Her reaction could be roughly summed up as: 'Great idea.'

The whole project was still in a state of limbo – neither announced in Norway, nor worked out in any detail. The 'Bugger Columbus!' element was not to be emphasized in case it upset his supporters. Since Viking voyages in modern Norway were inextricably linked with the ships and name of Ragnar Thorseth, he was as we had assumed a key figure in the project.

One possibility under consideration was a race between a Viking ship and an unmanned model, controlled by satellite, of an ultra-modern ship, possibly *Phoenix*, to demonstrate the beginning and end of the millennium launched by Leif Eiriksson's crossing to Vinland.

Afterwards, David summed up his initial impressions of Knut: 'I found him stimulating, honest, intelligent. He seemed extremely shrewd and questioning, and was full of ideas and enthusiasm, but he was modest, not at all pushy, although at the same time I had the feeling he was used to getting his own way.'

Knut spoke quietly and quickly, even in English, and had a way of pushing his lips together and pulling his chin back while he was thinking which drew his mouth down at the corners. His eyes were always alert, but slightly hooded, as if he might bring the shutters down over their expression to retain his privacy. Whether he was speaking or listening, I had the feeling that he was also observing, looking below the surface for some deeper meaning. He had a disarming ability to admit the inconsistencies in his own arguments with an almost childlike openness. I could imagine him as a small boy with scraped knees and torn trousers smiling his way out of trouble.

The impression that we were being observed, and tested, was reinforced when we were joined by Knut's colleague Henrich Nissen-Lie, nautically informal in a navy blazer and with a sailor's blue eyes. He and Kloster made an excellent interviewing team, almost as if they had rehearsed a double act of sounding deceptively casual.

'Is there really a boat yard in England which can build a Viking ship?' we were asked. We passed over a copy of the letter and estimate from Southampton Yacht Services, and a brochure showing some of their previous work.

'Why do you want to make your voyage next year, rather than the year after?'

'Because we want to get in before the Columbus lot,' we explained. 'Everyone will be sick of re-enacted voyages later on. And unless ours is made first, it won't attract enough attention to make the point that the Vikings got to America before Columbus.'

There were two final questions from our interrogators which afterwards I felt sure were particularly loaded. The first was about how we, David and I, would get on together on a small boat on a long voyage: wouldn't we fight?

'Of course we'd fight – but we always do anyway – '

'No, we don't – '

'Yes, we do – so it isn't really much different on a boat.'

'And in fact we probably get on better at sea than on land – and we are used to sailing together.'

We were then asked what we thought of Ragnar Thorseth. 'We don't know him well, but we like what we know – and we'd be happy to sail with him.'

Knut Kloster and Henrich Nissen-Lie exchanged a glance, then politely dismissed us. 'We need to talk a few things over, and make some phone calls. We'll telephone you in two hours.'

Two hours later we were summoned to Henrich Nissen-Lie's office, where he told us that he had been charged by Mr Kloster – the only time we ever heard Knut referred to so formally – to invite us to join the official Viking expedition.

This was so unexpected that it took us some minutes to understand that we were being offered crew places on a voyage to be financed by Knut Kloster and backed by the Icelandic and Norwegian governments, and that this would be brought forward from 1992 to 1991.

'In other words, our timing and your money for your expedition, with Ragnar as skipper and us in the crew on his ship?'

That summed it up.

'Which ship?'

'Gokstad, which will probably be called *Leif Eiriksson*, with a back-up ship, possibly *Havella* although this has not yet been decided definitely.'

'Is that with Ragnar's agreement? And does he agree to having us on board?'

'Yes' to both questions. If Ragnar thought Gokstad could make the crossing, who were we to disagree? It seemed a sudden change of attitude, since it was not long since he had told us firmly that only a *knarr* would ever have been used on a long ocean voyage; but of course Gokstad was newer, bigger and more photogenic than *Saga Siglar*.

Knut Kloster's reputation for acting impulsively was clearly well earned. The confirmation of his invitation came a couple of days later, by fax: 'I hereby confirm our proposal in writing, after having discussed it with Mr Per Paust at the Ministry of Foreign Affairs in Oslo, but not yet with our Norse friends in Reykjavik. . . . You are invited to take part in the official Norse (Icelandic/Norwegian) Leif Eiriksson's 1000 years celebration voyage from Bergen to New York, via Orkneys, Shetland, Faroes, Iceland, Greenland, Newfoundland, Boston and Chicago. Departure from Bergen on May 17, 1991, with arrival in New York on October 9 (Leif Eiriksson's Day in the USA).'

Our response, faxed by return, was – of course – 'Yes, please,' followed by a fax to Ragnar: 'We are drinking to the success of the official Norse Leif Eiriksson's 1000 years celebration voyage.'

'It is our intention to have all agreements and contracts signed before October 1st,' Henrich Nissen-Lie faxed us optimistically.

A week later, Harald telephoned us from Oslo: 'Guess what! I've been asked to be project manager for the whole damn thing!'

We were summoned to Oslo for two days of meetings at World City Discovery a fortnight after we had first met Knut Kloster and Henrich Nissen-Lie, who greeted us warmly. The vibes were cooler from Erik Bye, whom we had not met before and who made a point of speaking in Norwegian. This was perfectly reasonable, except for our non-Norwegian speaking presence, and for the fact that a decision had been made to use English as the project language – not at our request, nor for our benefit, but because of the difficulty of communication between Norwegians and Icelandics. Although Scandinavians can usually communicate easily in a mixture of Norwegian, Swedish and Danish, Icelandic is a far more complex language; it is only in Iceland that the original Norse of the sagas has survived for a thousand years.

In view of the official joint nature of the project, we were surprised that there was no Icelandic representation at the meetings at World City Discovery, although for the first session there were two Norwegian government representatives. Ideas flowed from Knut Kloster. He spoke of a Leif Eiriksson voyage as 'a catalyst' which was to set a course towards a better world as part of a vision of the future: it must be something meaningful, an idea people would talk about afterwards; he wanted 'to mobilize the young people of the world to meet the challenges of the future'. His wish to save the world sounded sincere, but when he was asked how, he turned the question back to the questioner: 'You tell me how; I don't know how; I just want to start the discussion.'

The man most concerned with the how of Knut's ideas, and particularly with the 'how much', was Jørgen Randers, a slim humorous man with receding dark hair who told us, 'I try to keep Knut's feet on the ground.' Rather than curbing Knut's ideas, he seemed to enjoy entering into their spirit and finding ways of paying for them, or even of making them pay – Knut Kloster had the reputation of not being able to avoid making money.

It would have been too much to expect that once we had been invited to join the official expedition, and had accepted the invitation, it would all be plain sailing. The first hurdle was put up by the Norwegian government representatives. It was, they insisted, quite impossible for anyone in an official capacity to organize receptions with less than a year's notice, and so the voyage could not take place until 1992.

The arguments in favour of 1991 had by then been accepted by everyone else: if we waited until 1992, everyone would be sated with Columbus; if 'Bugger Columbus!' was even an unspoken aim, the Vikings had once again to get there first; and if the Viking voyage was actually during the Columbus year, this really would seem like a spoiling exercise. The final push towards 1991 rather than 1992 had been the discovery that the Columbus hoo-ha was starting in 1991.

It was Knut who broke the stalemate. 'We will start the voyage in 1991, and we'll go as far as Newfoundland. Then in 1992 we can start again from there and carry on down the Canadian and American coasts.'

'An excellent compromise,' it was agreed; the publicity for the first stage could be the advance fanfare for the second.

By the end of the second day, the project had been renamed 'the Vinland Voyage 1991–1992'. A tripartite draft Declaration of Purpose had been drawn up, with spaces at the bottom for signatures on behalf of the governments of Iceland and Norway, and World City Discovery. Leif Eiriksson's landing in America one thousand years ago was to be commemorated 'in a manner that is meaningful in our own time – both for the Norse community and for North Americans and other peoples of the world'. At the same time, the project was to establish a basis for international media attention and sponsorship, and focus on youth, environment, culture and communication, 'in a positive way which

looks towards the future'. As 'the people already in Vinland a thousand
years ago experienced their encounter with the Norse explorers in their
own cultural context', this important aspect was to be part of the
programme – 'in light of what happened 500 years later'. Columbus
was not named.

Two days of non-stop brainstorming continued during the intervening evening over dinner at one of Oslo's best restaurants, where
eight of us – David and me, Ragnar Thorseth and his partner Sigbjørn
Notøy, Jørgen Randers, Henrich Nissen-Lie, Per Paust and Harald
Bjerke – were Knut's guests at a large secluded table. I was
disappointed that Erik Bye had cried off, as I had hoped that a
convivial evening together might have dispelled some of the hostility I
sensed from him towards our presence.

Halfway through the evening, Ragnar confided quietly to me, 'I
don't know what I am doing here. While I was walking along this
evening with Siggen, I said to him, "I don't know what is happening."'
I knew what he meant. He was still not ready to celebrate, he said. 'I've
been this far with agreements before and then they haven't happened. I
shall not be confident until there is a signature on a contract.'

Over the next few weeks this pessimistic attitude proved so well
founded that we soon felt as if we were on a psychological roller coaster.

There was a sharp downward lurch when Knut faxed us several days
after the date originally set for the tripartite signing of the Declaration
of Purpose. He, Erik Bye and Norwegian government representatives
were about to go to Reykjavik for a meeting. 'The signals I now get
make it difficult to believe that the Declaration of Purpose will be
signed as it was developed here during the meeting we had on
September 26. In fact, it is quite clear that we stand rather alone here
now with the proposal for a voyage in 1991. Therefore, I regret to
inform you that we must keep the whole question of how to proceed
open until we return from Reykjavik. This is a joint Norwegian/
Icelandic project, and everything we do must be based on consensus.'
Icelandic feathers clearly needed smoothing.

'What's going on?' we asked Harald, who confirmed our suspicion
that Erik Bye wanted us out. 'He actually said so at a meeting the other
day. Maybe he feels that you are trying to take over his television
plans.'

These were for a TV series to be called *The Hunters and the Home-
Seekers:* 'a meeting, in the Arts, between Native North Americans
[Hunters] and descendants of the Viking Voyagers [Home-seekers]

who landed on North American shores 1000 years ago'. From what little we knew about Erik's complex and ambitious proposal, it seemed unlikely that our intention of making a straightforward documentary about a neo-Viking voyage would conflict with it, an impression confirmed when we read his preliminary four page outline.

Erik Bye had spent some time in America and had a genuine interest in and understanding of the Native North American culture which he was keen to link with his own equally strong roots in and commitment to his Norse background. We felt kindly disposed towards him, and after talking and thinking about his apparent antagonism we decided – to use one of the best worn of all clichés – to take the bull by the horns.

'Dear Erik,' David wrote, 'Judy and I get the feeling that you would prefer it if we were not involved with Leif Eiriksson 1000. Is this the case? If so, why? If not, let's talk about how we can cooperate.'

Erik faxed a long response: 'I am *not*, I repeat *not*, against you in any way whatsoever, personally, professionally or as possible participants in the Leif Eiriksson 1000 venture. . . . Understand my position: I have been involved in this from the start in a purely "advisory" capacity . . . My primary job, to begin with, was to help bring about an *official* joint Icelandic–Norwegian cooperative effort, so as to avoid what could have become a Norwegian Leif Eiriksson celebration, leaving the Icelandic nation out of the picture. That was an approach which I considered totally unacceptable. . . . So far, a lot of thinking about the project has been mainly moving about in the clouds – that is to say, we have had no clear-cut, specific outline of thought that anybody has been able to discuss . . . The meeting in Reykjavik is an *official* meeting . . . Clear-cut decisions *must* be made at this meeting . . . Since the Icelanders have not until *now* received any clear information from Norway and have not had one single opportunity of voicing *their* interest or of putting any of *their* ideas on the table, the Reykjavik meeting is crucial to the entire venture. . . . Provided that we reach a joint agreement at Reykjavik – including *your* position in the Norse venture – the time has come to start doing practical work. . . . If we pool interest and do this right – OK: – If not, leave the entire year to good old Christopher. . . . Perhaps the "proper way" is the Atlantic crossing? It just may be as simple as that! It will be decided in Reykjavik.'

President Vigdis Finnbogadottir, Knut faxed from Reykjavik after an informal luncheon with her and Erik, supported the project and the wish to make the voyage 'meaningful'. 'It is in a global perspective we must set the course: we see how important it is that the spirit of discovery in our modern times be aimed at shaping mankind's common future – to save the world that we spent a thousand years discovering.' He intended to make two proposals at a meeting in Oslo at the end of October: that the ship should not after all be named *Leif Eiriksson*, 'but something else (which will be disclosed at the meeting)', and that the whole voyage and all associated events should after all take place in 1991.

'It would be helpful to have a few more facts,' I faxed back. 'Concern for mankind's future, and idealistic aims about meetings of cultures, are excellent – but what does this mean in practical terms? Exactly what is proposed?'

'The task now is to establish a basis for moving ahead,' Knut replied, adding that what must be avoided was the impression 'that we are just beating our "Viking" chests': 'I see the voyage as a discovery expedition, where the course so to speak is created while we move ahead.'

Later the same day, a Saturday, he faxed again, 'for the sake of good order and to avoid any misunderstanding', to state that both he and Erik saw NRK's proposed television series and the voyage, including the documentary film, as two separate but interdependent projects. 'We are,' he finished with a verbal flourish, 'on the same wavelength in a global perspective.'

Knut was obviously spending his weekend thinking about his personal version of the Viking vision which by then had so many of us in one way or another in its thrall. So it seemed was Erik Bye, who phoned me at length. As well as wanting to pin at least one of Knut's visionary feet to a practical floor, Erik still felt that the Icelandics were not involved enough, did not have much money or many people, but were very proud. He saw his role as diplomatic, to ensure as far as possible that whatever he and Knut were doing was a joint nordic project.

Knut's two Saturday faxes were followed by a longer Sunday one: 'Dear Judy,

'It's a beautiful Sunday morning, and I am sitting here with my coffee – contemplating . . .

'I think it truly behoves us now – as a matter of mutual interest – to agree on a basic strategy which is aimed at developing the project . . .

'In a nutshell: we should nail down the kind of platform you propose to have firm ground under our feet – and then we should set our discovery course by distant stars – not by the light of passing ships!

There is no basic inconsistency between idealism and realistic opportunities. I firmly believe that.

'Erik and I had a wonderful brainstorming session in Reykjavik before we went to have lunch with Vigdis Finnbogadottir. That's when the idea of not naming the ship "Leif Eiriksson" came up. We played around with it for a while, and then Erik began quietly to sing the shanty "Shenandoah". And before we knew it, we were sailing up the Shenandoah river in Virginia, to our final destination – where it all began.

'This reminds me of the Tower of Babel that was supposed to reach to heaven: that's when the peoples of the ancient world dispersed across the planet, because of their inability to work together – confounded as they were in their overreaching pride by the "gift" of languages. Our expedition should symbolize the need for the world's peoples – all different "tribes" – to draw together again, to bridge their differences of language, culture, creed, and colour, and to explore the future attainment of common goals: "Come, then, with our differences and aspirations – not to reach to heaven but to reach one another!" It all began with the early voyages.'

Although 'Shenandoah' was an improvement on 'Leif Eiriksson' for length, impact and memorability, David pointed out that it was already the name of a famous American East Coast schooner.

Two days before the October meeting to which a revised Declaration of Purpose was to be presented, another new name was put forward, at the suggestion of Vigdis Finnbogadottir: *Gaia*. By then *Vigdis* had been rejected as too personal, *Phoenix* as too close to Knut's commercial interests, *Leif Eiriksson* as too cumbersome, masculine, and overtly patriotic, and only Knut and Erik had liked *Shenandoah*. It seemed no more illogical to take a name from Greek mythology, than from American Indian history; it was far easier to spell and to pronounce than any equivalent Norse name. Gaia, or Ge, an ancient personification of the Earth, the Greek 'Mother Earth' goddess, certainly avoided Vikingry – and added an extra dimension to Knut's 'world city' ideas by symbolizing environmental concerns. 'The Gaia hypothesis' formulated by the British scientist James Lovelock in the 1960s postulated that the planet itself was a living entity, a superorganism in which living things interacted with geophysical and chemical processes to maintain conditions suitable for life. The theory had subsequently been adopted, not necessarily accurately, by various 'green' movements.

Just when it seemed as if everything was about to come together – the day before the signing session – there was another downward lurch on the roller coaster. I was in Oslo for discussions about our own agreement with World City Discovery, and had been invited by Erik Bye to his office at the Norwegian Broadcasting Corporation, where we were talking amicably when his telephone rang. The new head of NRK, he was told, had refused funding for *The Hunters and the Home-Seekers*. Erik, a large man with a powerful voice, flew into a rage, resigned on the spot, and was still ranting when Harald, Knut and I left the building. Since the original three-party agreement had been extended to include a fourth party, NRK represented by Erik, his resignation and the collapse of his plans was a serious threat to the project.

'What do we do if Erik stays out and the governments then also withdraw tomorrow?' Knut asked.

'Carry on without them?' I suggested. 'It would make everything much simpler anyway.'

By morning, Erik had been reinstated at NRK. All four parties signed their joint Declaration of Purpose. The project, now officially called 'Vinland Revisited', could at last move ahead. Ragnar had signatures on his contract. Ours was signed, initially by fax, a week later.

Harald Bjerke and Henrich Nissen-Lie visited all the places on our neo-Viking route except Greenland. Local planning groups were set up in each official port of call.

From time to time, Knut faxed us some Gaian thoughts: 'As I see it unfolding, in each port of call the main theme so to speak will be:

HOW IS GAIA DOING?

'The Gaia hypothesis – simply put – says that in order to understand the various aspects of the planetary environment, the planet as a whole has to be regarded as a single living organism – to quote Fritjof Capra, who, in his 1982 book *The Turning Point*, went on to say: "Awareness of the earth as alive, which played an important role in our cultural past, was dramatically revived when astronauts were able, for the first time in human history, to look at our planet from outer space. Their perception of the planet in all its shining beauty – a blue and white globe floating in the deep darkness of space – moved them deeply and, as many of them have since declared, was a profound spiritual experience that forever changed their relationship to the earth. . . .

'"What the astronauts, and countless men and women on earth

before them, realized intuitively is now being confirmed by scientific investigations . . . The planet is not only teeming with life but seems to be a living being in its own right. All the living matter on earth, together with the atmosphere, oceans, and soil, forms a complex system that has all the characteristic patterns of self-organization. It persists in a remarkable state of chemical and thermodynamic nonequilibrium and is able, through a huge variety of processes, to regulate the planetary environment so that optimal conditions for the evolution of life are maintained."

'To what extent this hypothesis really holds water is I am sure quite a controversial question. But it seems to me that it is steadily gaining momentum and – frankly – I like to believe it is true!

'If the earth is alive, then what could be more appropriate for our expedition than to focus on the state of its "health" in the places we visit. . . ?'

Since Lovelock's ideas, and the name he had chosen to symbolize them, had become such an important aspect of the entire project, Knut asked us to see if we could arrange a meeting with him. But Lovelock was too busy writing his third book about the Gaia hypothesis to do anything more than wish us a polite 'Good Luck', although I met him briefly after hearing him lecture most stimulatingly in Oxford. I hoped that we would be able to avoid 'the mildew of insincerity' of what he impatiently dismissed as 'fragile earth' environmentalism.

There was no opportunity to ask whether he recognized his theory in the section of Erik Bye's proposal which Knut felt set the tone for our venture. 'A central theme in Indian culture, tradition and religion is respect for "Mother Earth". It is the age-old concept – known also to other human tribes – of Man as *part* of, not the conqueror and misuser of, our natural environment,' was how Erik put it. 'All over the world people are being forced to face the necessity of a *re-discovery of values* – if not for religious or other reasons, then clearly for the reasons of sheer survival.'

A compromise about where the ship was to be christened and registered was reached only weeks before the scheduled start of the voyage. Since the name had been suggested by the President of Iceland, it seemed logical that she should conduct the christening ceremony – and since the ship had been built in Norway, and was to leave from Norway, it seemed equally logical that it should be christened there. This all seemed simple enough, but there was the matter of protocol to consider. If the ceremony was to be conducted by the president of a foreign country, then there must be equally high ranking home representation – but there was no mutually convenient date. It was eventually agreed that the ship would initially be registered in Norway as *Gaia*, but would not be officially christened until we reached Reykjavik in June, when the registration would be changed to Icelandic. The ensigns of both nations would be flown, one from each side of the masthead, with the Norwegian ensign in pride of position until the registration, and the Icelandic thereafter: an unusual, indeed unique, arrangement.

Among the more relaxed aspects of the advance planning was the problem of clothing. Heavy weather sailing gear would obviously be essential, but then we would all have to emerge looking smart for the many official functions which were being laid on en route. 'Why don't you write to the "Clothes Show" for advice?' David suggested. This popular British Sunday TV magazine programme dealt with a different fashion problem each week. My particular problem was so unusual that it did indeed appeal to them and not long before we were due to join the crew of *Gaia* I spent a day being filmed in a nautical setting.

Knut responded in April to enquiries about the project in general, and his motivation and World City Discovery's involvement in particular, with an official statement which started by re-posing the questions: 'Who am I, what is World City Discovery, and why am I spending several million dollars on celebrating the fact that a man from Greenland . . . came to America a thousand years ago?'

He described himself as 'a third generation Norwegian shipowner, sometimes talked about as the one who pioneered the modern cruise industry in the late Sixties'.

Leif Eiriksson did not, he stated emphatically, discover America, which was already inhabited, but merely started a peaceful invasion which turned violent when the two groups clashed, as regrettably was so often the case between different cultures.

'What's so great about that? Nothing, really – and yet it touches the basic sense of having to stake something in the pursuit of important goals. The willingness to take risks. Simple as that. And that's a spirit we need more than ever, in the world today, with the tremendous environmental challenge we are faced with, and the deepening gap between the rich and poor in our common present.'

The primary aim of Vinland Revisited was 'to gain respect for the environment of which we are only a part' and to 'discover our common future'. World City Discovery – 'a strange little company' – was, he explained, dedicated to the proposition that free enterprise had an important role to play, over and above the clearly defined commercial objectives.

A personal patriotic motivation was admitted in the statement's closing paragraph: 'Finally, but not the least important, I am supporting this project because I am fond of my country, and proud of our history as seafaring people. From the early Viking voyages to our modern fishing and shipping industries, the ocean has always been our best friend, and – sometimes – worst enemy. That's how it is in Iceland too. We truly have common roots going far back in our history – and deep into the ocean.'

On a lighter note, a 1991 holiday brochure described a Kloster cruise as 'a trip across the globe on an unforgettable voyage of discovery . . . to exotic destinations . . . with faultless service, elegant accommodation and a cuisine which is a gourmet's dream'.

'What a relief!' David commented as we attempted to pack everything we would need for five and a half months into one kit bag each.

6 Shakedown:
Trondheim to Håholmen

Trondheim's claim to have been Leif Eiriksson's point of departure on his famous Vinland voyage was a good excuse for making it the start for Vinland Revisited, since it would be almost as difficult to disprove that he set sail from the Christian court of King Olaf Tryggvason at Niðaros, the original name of the city, as to prove that he did.

As a preliminary to our Atlantic crossing, the full Viking fleet – *Gaia, Oseberg, Saga Siglar,* accompanied by *Havella* – was to sail in convoy down the Norwegian coast, leaving Trondheim on one national holiday, May 1st, and setting out across the Atlantic from Bergen on another, Norway's Independence Day on May 17th. David and I, with our ten-year-old daughter Emily – who was coming with us down the Norwegian coast – met cameraman Andrew Dearden and soundman Nigel Chatters at Heathrow, and landed outside Trondheim late on Sunday evening. David had worked before with Andrew, a freelance who had spent a year filming with an air-sea rescue team, but had done very little sailing; Nigel, also a freelance, had a fair amount of sailing experience. They were to be our film crew throughout the voyage.

Our initial efforts next morning to find out exactly what was happening, where and when, revealed the unflappability of the Norwegian temperament. 'They are great in emergencies,' a friend with wide experience of working in Scandinavia had told us. 'What you have to remember is that they have a wonderfully relaxed it'll-be-all-right-on-the-night attitude – and it usually is.' The 'night' was still a couple of days off, and there was no emergency, but by mid-morning Dag Nordtomme, ex-singer, impresario and hotel consultant, was outlining Trondheim's plans for the Viking fleet's send-off.

'Ragnar Thorseth has opened public Norwegian eyes,' Dag told us. 'We're so proud of this man. He has opened a door. We want to honour

48

him because we feel as a nation that he is a very important person' . . .
so important that representatives of sixteen embassies had been invited
to see him off from Trondheim; Dag was not sure how many had
accepted.

Although he was about to enter Trondheim as a modern Norwegian
commoner, Ragnar was, as befitted his status, to leave as a neo-Viking
Earl – an honour which was to be bestowed at the inaugural gathering
of a Viking Club. The first Viking 'King' of the Trondheim district for
several centuries had already been chosen and crowned, and was to
officiate that evening at a ceremony devised by Einar Belboe, founder of
the Viking Club. Emily was invited to be a Junior Viking.

Einar, a local sportsman and leader of the Trondheim Gymnastic
Club in his spare time, by profession a marketing consultant, had been
working for five years on the resurrection of traditional Viking games.
Plans for Trondheim's 'Viking Land' were, as he put it, 'on ice': it was
to have been in the woods near the town, but money ran out and the
community changed its mind about the site. Einar said that he would
give it another five years before pulling out.

'There will be more sport here, and less fighting, than in the Viking
City of Jorvik in York,' he explained. 'The Vikings were great
sportsmen.' It was apparently not uncommon for a fully armed man,
heavily clothed as if for war, to jump a tall fellow warrior, turn round
and leap back over him – one of ten old Nordic sports on offer to a
would-be Viking, although no one was expected to achieve excellence
in or even to attempt all ten. 'Of course, the Vikings used steroids,'
Einar pointed out, 'their steroids were red mushrooms.'

Although on the surface Trondheim looked a wealthy city, it was, we
were told, suffering a financial crisis which had affected the local
Vinland Revisited organizing committee. When the Convention
Bureau, originally in charge, was disbanded because of lack of funds,
planning was taken over on behalf of the Trondheim Commune by
Torbjørn Fjesme. Looking like a gentle Viking giant with his massive
ginger-blond beard and head of hair and equally massive frame, he
patted his paunch when he said that no, he was not entering any Viking
sports contests.

Trondheim was in a sort of fight with Bergen, he explained. Bergen,
which later became the capital of Norway, was still a mere hamlet when
Niðaros – Trondheim – was the capital of the Viking world. By starting
our voyage in a sense from both capitals, we were fuelling rivalry. In
addition to the foundation of the new Trondheim-based Viking Club,

our departure was to be the occasion of the announcement of a Leif Eiriksson 1000 Committee, which was to plan Leif Eiriksson's official local millennium in the year 2000. Although there was nothing to fix this categorically in any particular year, give or take the odd decade or two, it seemed a little contradictory that Vinland Revisited was commemorating it nine years before Trondheim. But then there was the city's own millennium to look forward to, in 1997, which definitely made our Leif Eiriksson commemorative voyage premature, since he could hardly have left from there before the place existed.

'Trondheim is a very historical area, with very deep roots,' Torbjørn reminded us. 'You meet the history every day, for instance at the cathedral or the many churches.' Its two most illustrious historical figures were both kings, both called Olaf, and both the subject of sagas included by the thirteenth-century Icelandic writer Snorri Sturluson in his vivid and historically imaginative *Heimskringla*, or *Saga of the Kings*. Snorri gave particularly colourful accounts of the deaths of some of the earlier Ynglinge kings, descendants of the Norse god Yngvi, better know as Frey. One Yngling, Fjolnir, drowned in a vat of mead when he got up in the night; another, Sveigdir, disappeared into a boulder during a drunken chase after a dwarf; and King Vanlandi was trampled to death by a nightmare.

The life stories of the more recent Olafs had only had a couple of centuries or so of being handed down by word of mouth when they were recorded, but still need considerable pinches of salt. Olaf Tryggvason was according to Snorri converted to Christianity by a hermit on the Isles of Scilly. As a pagan, he had by then harried – a major royal occupation – in Friesland, Saxland, Flanders, and far and wide in England and Scotland. As a Christian, he split his time relatively peacefully – give or take the occasional 'great raid' – between England and Ireland, until he was overwhelmed by homesickness. By a combination of cunning, killing and converting he became King of Norway in the year 995. Christianity spread apace, in preference to the alternatives offered by the new king: death, maiming or exile.

The assembled chiefs of the Tronds wanted Olaf to sacrifice with them as other kings had done. After he had threatened them and had knocked the great god Thor off his pedestal in their temple, the people of the Trondlaw also agreed to be converted. That was, by tradition, when Trondheim was founded, although recent archaeological excavation has uncovered signs of earlier occupation. Once he had a city and a palace, King Olaf acquired some impressive longships (*Crane*,

Short Serpent, Long Serpent) with which he sailed on baptizing missions, harrying for Christ.

If *Eirik the Red's Saga* is to be believed (which given the greater historical credibility of other versions of the story seems unwise) Leif Eiriksson was charged by King Olaf with the conversion of Greenland; and that first Vinland landfall was less a nautical achievement than the result of a pair of navigational accidents, proving Leif's ability to make the most of a mistake rather than demonstrating any superiority as a seaman. It started when he was driven off course en route from his home in Greenland to Niðaros. The summer he had planned to spend in Norway passed pleasantly enough in the Hebrides, where he abandoned a pregnant aristocratic mistress in time to reach King Olaf's court in the autumn.

The King 'paid him many honours', not least of which was entrusting him the next summer with the task of persuading his fellow Greenlanders to abandon their innumerable Nordic deities. According to the saga, 'Leif put out to sea as soon as he was ready, was storm-tossed a long time, and lighted on those lands whose existence he had not so much as dreamt of before': lands of wild wheat, vines, maple trees; Vinland. From there he backtracked to Greenland to spread the words of Christ and King Olaf.

Trondheim's second Olaf, even more famous and Christian, was known prosaically as Olaf the Stout until a number of minor miracles accompanied his death and he became Saint Olaf. An unlikely candidate for canonization, he started professional Viking harrying in the Baltic when he was twelve, and was the chief engineer of the destruction of London Bridge, commemorated in the round 'London Bridge is falling down', while he was fighting with the English against the Danes. After taking the crown of Norway in 1015, he carried out the process of Christianization in much the same forceful manner as his predecessor, and founded some churches to keep it going.

His earthly downfall was hastened by a marriage alliance with Sweden which led to a Norwegian–Swedish raid to Denmark. This so annoyed the Danish King Knut, or Canute, by then already also King of England, that he set out with a large fleet and became King of Norway as well. Olaf's death, in a battle north of Trondheim during a bid to regain the crown, was accompanied by an eclipse of the sun. 'The summer after, there was much talk about King Olaf's holiness,' Snorri reported in the *Saga of St Olaf*. 'Of those who had before gone against him in full enmity and no wish to own the truth about him there were many now who believed it true that the king was probably holy.' His sanctity was confirmed when his body was exhumed from its original secret grave for reburial in Niðaros: instead of rotting, it was as good as new. Every year, a battle between Olaf the Holy and an opponent known as Tore the Dog is re-enacted in Trondheim at an outdoor theatre with seating for seven thousand.

There was an all-too-solid reminder of a much later episode in the city's history only a few hundred yards from the hotel – the Pir Centre, a German wartime U-boat hideout. Huge and hideous, with solid windowless walls twenty metres thick, it was built to last, standing over the end of a harbour created by the Germans with Russian and Polish slave labour. Several submarines could hide simultaneously in pens underneath the building. The RAF's wartime efforts to destroy it left a few pockmarks, and did more damage to its surroundings. Attempts to blow it up since the war proved only the impossibility of removing it without also demolishing most of Trondheim's city centre.

The estimated time of arrival of the Viking fleet was postponed so many times, because it was encountering headwind on its way north from Håholmen, that we began to wonder if it would arrive in time to leave. At last there was a rumour that it had been sighted not many miles off Skipakrok, Trondheim's historic river harbour.

We were waiting on the quay with a man in a wheelchair, half a dozen others with cameras, one with a silver box labelled 'Radio', the local drunk, and a few women with preschool-age children, when the ships came into sight. The bridge opened, the road across it rising slowly and stopping halfway between horizontal and vertical. *Havella*, pulling *Gaia* behind her, motored through the gap, followed by *Oseberg* and *Saga Siglar* under their own engine power.

It was the first time I had seen *Gaia* since her launch. Her mast looked alarmingly flimsy. She was flying three flags: Norwegian and Icelandic ensigns, one on either side of the shrouds from crosstrees angled aft, and higher, just below the pointed mast head, a huge striped Norwegian pennant, already a little frayed at the ends.

The ships manoeuvred slowly into position alongside the quay. 'Ragnar is being interviewed for radio,' Emily reported, 'and loving every minute of it.' Torbjørn Fjesme loomed over me: 'Hi Judy.' The man in the wheelchair – 'Maybe an old sailor,' Torbjørn suggested – spent some time gazing at *Oseberg's* curved carved sternpost, then wheeled himself along to look her over as thoroughly amidships. A dozen seagulls gathered to squawk a greeting, but as the strange new vessels were fishless they soon flew off.

Like a politician, Ragnar had temporarily acquired a small child, whom he held aloft for the photographers. 'Nice T-shirt,' he greeted me when he had been released from his public duties – it had a picture of *Gaia* on it. I described a sweatshirt I had had made for Jane – with Ragnar and the full Viking fleet above the caption 'Bugger Columbus!' – to the crew of *Havella*. One of them was Rikardur Petursson, whom we had last seen in Greenland. We introduced ourselves to Audun Gården and Steinar Kulen. Øyvard Karlsbakk, the expedition's radio operator, was to join us in Bergen. I hoped that the atmosphere of warm relaxed humour in *Havella's* wheelhouse would be reflected on board *Gaia*.

I had expected to meet the rest of the Vinland Revisited crew at the hotel's Viking Club dinner that night, but the project was represented only by Ragnar and Kari Thorseth, and Harald and Dolly Bjerke. Physically, the two couples could not have presented a greater contrast. Ragnar, with his grizzled beard and hair and crumpled-looking skin, had an almost piratical appearance even in a tie and jacket; and Kari, vividly made up, with so much thick black curly hair that her head made her body seem almost unnaturally slim, and wearing a tight-fitting short skirt and high-heeled shoes, could well have been a pirate's wife. The Bjerkes made a more conventional pair; Harald was tall, slim and clean shaven, and Dolly as usual smartly dressed and immaculate.

At a high table surrounded by lights and microphones, a score of founder members of the club demonstrated Norse quaffing and ribaldry, wearing full Viking costume, although they had decided against a demonstration of traditional rock hurling in the glass surrounds of the hotel. A beaming wench threw a laughing lover to the floor. There was no shortage of general horseplay, even before the entry of the Viking 'king' on a small and reluctant pony. It was dissuaded from bolting only by the lack of space between the potted plants, and by the weight of its bulky rider.

Ragnar was duly dubbed a Jarl and presented with two axes, one to keep, the other to present to President Bush. Their maker gave a detailed description of Viking axe-making. More feminine presentations were made to Kari, and to Anne Stine Ingstad, whose elderly husband had not felt able to take time off. During the ensuing eulogistic speeches Emily lost count of the number of times Ragnar's name was mentioned.

'They should say something about Knut,' she whispered to me, an omission remedied by Ragnar. In a brief speech of thanks for honours and axes he paid tribute to Knut's inspirational and financial role.

Until our departure, Ragnar had the use of the hotel's Leif Eiriksson suite, a two-storey penthouse complete with jacuzzi, ante-room, dressing room, sitting room, plush decor and lush plants. We felt as if we were being granted a royal interview when we were ushered into it by Steinar Kulen, whom we had met briefly on *Havella*.

'I've had it with Viking boats,' Ragnar told us, 'I'm sick of them. In my next incarnation I want to be a Viking boat designer, then I can include things like a self-bailing deck.'

'The Swiss have self-bailing Viking decks,' I reminded him, 'or so they say.' This was one of the claims made for a scaled-down Gokstad replica in an article in French which he had faxed me a few weeks earlier from Håholmen. 'Please can you translate this?' he had asked. 'English will do.' The ship, which had been built on Lake Geneva, was about to set out in the wake of the Vikings.

Joking apart, Ragnar felt it necessary to give us a pre-sailing pep talk. 'You have to understand my priorities. My number one priority is getting the boats across safely. That is my number two and number three priority. The next three priorities are keeping the crew happy.'

For the departure festivities all crew members had to wear neo-Viking tunics and leg lacings. 'You can't be serious!' I had exclaimed to Harald when he told us that a Norwegian dress designer was working on costumes. The simple woollen tunics, worn with plain leather belts – Harald had bought the entire stock of a bemused Oslo stall holder – were however comfortable, and served the purpose of identifying the crew. I withdrew my reservations, although a neo-Viking uniform did seem a little backward-looking for a project which was supposed to be setting a course for the future.

There was neither work nor school to keep Trondheimers indoors on the annual May 1st holiday, and it seemed as if they must all have turned out in the cool bright sun to cheer as a Viking fleet left their city. Ancient and modern mixed indiscriminately in the farewell pageantry. Norwegian, Canadian, American and British flags had been hoisted for the occasion, although unfortunately no one had thought of flying one to show that Vinland Revisited was supposed to be as much an Icelandic as a Norwegian project. American-style majorettes marched and twirled, a band played, neo-Vikings declaimed, city officials spoke. Ragnar was presented with two large polythene tubes of water in which some small salmon were swimming; I was not sure whether this was meant to symbolize the environmental aims of our mission, or the commercial interests of one or both of the governments backing it, or merely to publicize a local fish farm.

'The biggest salmon is Leif, the smallest one is Columbus. They will follow the ship to Vinland,' I was told. But the moment they were tipped unceremoniously into the water between *Gaia* and *Oseberg* they swam swiftly out of sight.

Among the embassies which had accepted their invitations were the British and the American.

'Will you be in Washington?' Ragnar asked the American Ambassador, Loret Miller Ruppe.

'You bet. You get there, and I'll be there to welcome you back!' she promised enthusiastically. 'Thank you for discovering us.' She turned to Anne Stine Ingstad: 'I feel so proud,' she declared.

Ten thousand people saw us off from the land at Trondheim, and dozens of boats accompanied us for the first few miles down river. Knut, Henrich, Harald and Per Paust all looked pleased as they waved from the shore. With so many other boats around, it was not a good time to learn new sailing techniques in a foreign language, so I concentrated on keeping out of the way, along with two journalists who were to be on board as far as Håholmen: Jennifer Merin, a dumpy and talkative New York freelancer with a crimpy frizz of fair hair into which she had plaited some leaves; and Tom Hennigan, a slimmer, quieter Canadian poet and lecturer in English.

The seven journalists distributed round the fleet had all been flown to Norway by a New York PR company appointed to ensure maximum media coverage for Vinland Revisited on the American side of the Atlantic. There had been considerable resistance to, even acrimony about, the company's appointment. The only person I knew who seemed to appreciate their assistance was Knut Kloster. We were told that one of the company's executives had admitted in Iceland, 'Gee, do you know that before I came here I didn't even know where Iceland *was* – I didn't know if there were *ten* people living here, or *ten million*.' Perhaps on the assumption that everyone else must be equally ignorant, their publicity material for Vinland Revisited included six-page descriptions of modern Norway and modern Iceland.

My only contact with the firm had been by fax and phone with Nicole Gorden, who was in charge of the Trondheim to Håholmen group of journalists.

'We're going to be shipmates,' she had told me.

'Really? I didn't know there were going to be any other women on *Gaia*.'

'Just a short passage. But no one has told me anything about the domestic arrangements – er, the bathroom facilities – on board.'

'Hardly surprising – as far as I know, there's not much to tell.'

'Gee, I guess that means we won't be waxing our legs much!'

Nicole was not after all on board, and it was hardly leg waxing weather as we were towed overnight into wind and rain.

Even so, the enthusiasm of Jennifer and Tom about being on a real live Viking ship knew no bounds. Outside, it was raining, cold, unenticing. Our breath was as white as the cigarette exhalation of the smokers, who were in the majority.

A noisy heater warmed the cabin, which was much less cramped than I had expected. The forward two-thirds were filled by a large plain wooden table, approximately four feet by seven, with storage lockers under fitted benches along each side and enough room for the crew to sit comfortably for meals. The spaces under the table had been divided into lockers for charts and film gear. The galley was separated from the rest of the cabin by open lockers for stores, crockery and cutlery, and there was a small fold-away seat beside an impressive array of electronic instruments: radar, global positioning, satellite navigation, electronic maps and log.

The sleeping cabin had a small entry-well into which boots, bags and oilskins had been hurled. Until Tom and Jennifer left, there seemed little point in trying to sort it out properly. The bunks, as we discovered during the few hours sleep we each had in turns on our first night on board, were cramped but surprisingly comfortable.

Our only brief stop during the day was at Kristiansund. Under way, people came and went between the boats by inflatable dinghy, for which Andrew and Nigel immediately adopted and anglicized the Norwegian word; from then on we all referred to the Zodiac as the 'gummiboat'. Ragnar disappeared on to *Havella*. Tom, who had stayed up all night because he suffered from claustrophobia, abandoned *Gaia* for *Oseberg*. Jennifer was transferred damply from one to the other so that she could find the best live radio link to Minneapolis.

There was still a sprinkling, sometimes a capping, of snow on the mountains on either side of the fjords, and very little sign of spring or greenery. As Emily remarked, the rocks of the landscape looked very like Greenland, with the addition of a few leafless leaning trees.

There were clearly a number of jobs to be finished on *Gaia* before our next departure. The life raft had not yet been bolted down, for instance, and there were no points of attachment for safety lines at night or in rough weather. Although Ragnar insisted that no one could fall out of the boat – and this would indeed have been difficult, since the walkway between the cabins and the hull was deep and confidence-inspiring – it looked all too easy to fall off the curved coachroof during sail-handling operations.

'It's quite warm out there,' Emily reported after a quick visit to the open air of the aft space – neither deck nor cockpit seemed the right word, and 'warm' was a relative description. 'Thingy' – she had not yet sorted out everyone's names – 'says we should be there in less than an hour.'

For everyone except the Brits and the journalists, reaching Håholmen was like coming home, since the others had already been working and living together there for a couple of months, some for much longer.

'Emily! Catch! Here are the keys to your room.' Ragnar showed her the outside stairs leading to the first floor flatlet we were to share with her.

We had wondered whether having her with us would cause any problems – not that she herself would be a problem, since she was used to being on boats, but it would not have surprised us if her presence had been resented. If it was, we were never made aware of it. Although all of us – David, Emily and me, and Andrew and Nigel – were obviously under scrutiny, I was relieved at how readily the others appeared to accept us. Communal meals in the Håholmen dining room, and relaxed evenings in the bar, certainly helped.

Effusively shepherded by Nicole Gorden, whose outfits outdid everyone else's for elegance if not necessarily for island practicality, the gang of journalists spent a day on the island, where they were joined by Knut and Erik Bye for discussions about the Project and the Planet. Ragnar, David and I listened, but did not join in. Knut turned a dining-room chair round and sat astride it, allowing Erik to dominate the conversation with his rich gravelly voice, the voice of an ageing singer and smoker. Although his bulky good looks had started to sag, he had not lost the combination of charm, warmth and sincerity which for many years had made him welcome on television sets in living rooms throughout Norway.

'These ships are like a Grecian column, perfect!' he enthused. 'The major contribution of the Nordic people to world culture is the design of the Viking ship. It's perfect.'

'What's the connection between this challenge to preconceived notions about history – the Norwegian challenge to Columbus – and our world view today?' Jennifer wanted to know. She found her own answer: 'We're on the verge of another kind of social disorder, so maybe there's another kind of parallel, another reason for setting off on a course of discovery – '

'Out there is the sea.' Erik pointed dramatically towards the open window. 'That is the Norwegian prairie. We ploughed it – so we hit Greenland and the coast of North America, Vinland – not conquering people, but trying to eat. If we look upon this as some sort of a jubilee for a European venture across the sea, then we're making a gimmick. What we need now is a rediscovery of ourselves. It sounds philosophical, but I'm not a philosopher. Symbolically, this journey – the Leif Eiriksson thing – has a great meaning. It shows that man is moving all the time. But how are we treating each other today? Who are we today? These are the important questions.'

'You have said all the time that we should really turn the whole thing round and try to look at this so-called discovery with the eyes of the people living in America at the time, not always with the eyes of the European and Norse people,' Knut put in.

'We didn't discover anything – they were already there,' Erik said. 'We were uninvited guests.'

Tom Hennigan joined the discussion. 'Your sensitivity is laudable, but the brutal political fact is that the successors to the people that were there, the Indians and the Inuits, have an impossible situation. What can you do, what will they see, that is valuable to them?'

Erik's answer was vaguely optimistic: 'We can help bring about what is in their culture, show what they have to say.'

Tom was not prepared to let him get away with a generalization. 'A few months ago in Canada there was an army surrounding them – they were there, but they were beleaguered – and the function of television was largely usurped by the government to discredit these people because they were constantly shown wearing masks and waving guns. The government effectively did nothing, and all that happened was that public opinion was turned against the Indians because they were seen constantly as thugs.'

From the Norwegian prairie only yards from the window came the soothing sounds of squawking seabirds and lapping wavelets.

The time in Håholmen passed quickly. There was much expert Norwegian and Icelandic carpentry on the quay, and gradually one technical task after another was completed. A row of pigeon holes was constructed, one for each crew member.

'That's *it*, Judy,' Ragnar said warningly. 'Each person has one space, nothing else is allowed in the cabin.' Perhaps as the only woman I was suspected of having more bits and pieces than the men. David and I fitted netting alongside and above our bunks, a simple enough addition to storage space but one which was greatly envied; so it became our task to rig up netting for everyone else. Helped by Emily, we were entrusted with the menial but essential task of oiling the hull, inside and out, and then the deck, with a mixture of a Swedish proprietary boat oil and turpentine.

'Tomorrow Jon Godal will give you a sailing lesson on *Gaia*,' Ragnar told us, after we had attended a lecture in Norwegian about tacking techniques. 'No filming – this is a sail-training session in English, specially for you.'

Though the bespectacled expert and the Norse crew members discussed the finer points of Viking sailing, there was a distinct lack of English except when we asked a specific question, which we did frequently, determined to learn as fast as possible. Any good intentions the British contingent had had about being fluent before joining the crew had been foiled by lack of time; and the others all spoke such good English that being with them did not force us to learn their language. But by the end of the day we were beginning to understand the basic nautical terms in Norwegian.

Sailing *Gaia* as the wind rose from force four through five to six was exhilarating, especially for the helmsman standing on a raised section of deck in the upward curving stern with both hands on the steering oar tiller, which had been carved in the shape of a sea monster that was trying to swallow the oak rudder.

'Push for port,' we were told, 'pull for starboard' – the 'steerboard' being the Viking-style starboard-hung rudder. I had wondered whether my comparative lack of strength would be a problem – *Gaia* was a big boat for tiller steering – but although she was often slow to respond, she was not heavy on the helm.

David's weight came in useful when the instruction came to hoist sail, which needed four people hauling and one tailing, or taking the strain. Tailing became my job, since I had less pulling power than the men. Once the yard had been raised halfway up the mast, one end had to be manhandled forward with much grunting and pushing and heaving until it was clear of the shrouds. Then the end of a cord lashing was pulled and, unless there was some snarl-up, the sail fell with a great crash of ropework, billowing forward in the wind while the yard was being hauled up the rest of the way.

Although *Gaia* was remarkably well balanced, going about was slow and frustrating. First she stopped, then she moved sedately astern, before at last swinging gradually, almost reluctantly, on to the new course. The manoeuvre required plenty of sea room, time and patience. She could sail much closer to the wind than we had expected, easily maintaining 60°; although she could point up another ten degrees or more, this was only with the loss of so much speed that it would rarely be worth it.

We found our first experience of reefing alarming, even in a gentle sea: it involved unsecured foot work on the cabin roof and balancing on the gunwale, as well as a certain amount of hanging on and leaning out. But at least by the time this manoeuvre had been carried out successfully – as a training exercise rather than from necessity – we were beginning to make sense of the cat's cradle of ropes. Three sets of reefing lines each reduced the sail area considerably. Controlling lines led aft from the corners of the sail – 'schøte' at the bottom, 'bráss' from the top ends of the yard. 'Buline', lines leading forward from the leading edge of the sail, could further control aerofoil shape; so could 'priare', three lines attached to the central vertical of the sail, the bottom one on the lower edge.

Afterwards, I patched a hole which had developed in the sail during the training session. Ragnar summoned all crews to the sitting-room-cum-bar in the loft above the dining room in the evening. He had told us firmly that we were not to expect sailing instructions to be given in English, and underlined his point by giving a long pep talk in Norwegian, with a strong west coast dialect. 'Just the occasional concession, a few words now and then in English, would have been nice,' Andrew commented afterwards.

Before we set out from Håholmen, the expedition's doctor, Odd Kvamme, took blood samples so that he could keep a check on cholesterol levels, and weighed us all. Odd was a qualified acupuncturist as well as being in general medical practice on one of west Norway's many islands, a considerably larger one than Håholmen. David and I were to be on Ragnar's watch with him, along with Ottar Bjørkedal.

7 *Gaia*, And Gaia: Håholmen To Bergen

By the time we left Håholmen, for a passage of sixty nautical miles down the coast to Ålesund, we felt part of the crew rather than mere passengers. The first few hours were in almost open sea, apart from an alarming jumble of skerries. *Gaia* showed her calm water paces admirably. 'We are beginning to know what is what,' I noted, 'but familiarity will never breed contempt aboard this wild horse ship.'

The shore was lined with bleak mountains, coming right down to the water's edge. There was some snow even on the tops of those immediately above the waterline, and the more distant peaks were white.

Odd, who was planning to work on a medical book about pain during the voyage, drew up a domestic rota according to which a different person was responsible each day for cooking *middag*, the Norwegian name for the evening meal which was to be served at the 18.00 watch change, and for setting out a midday repetition of Norse breakfast – bread, cheese, cold meat, smoked salmon, maybe some tomatoes or sliced cucumber. A huge Thermos jug was to be kept full of coffee, brewed in the only kettle on board and decanted through a tea strainer. Not being the type to shirk a duty, Odd had put himself in charge of the first *middag* – burgers and spuds.

Although I did not intend to slide into a traditional woman's role of galley slave, I would have offered to scrub the potatoes for him if I had not had an infected thumb which felt as if it was working up to a test case for his research. It was one of those mysterious minor injuries which occur unnoticed at the time on boats.

After supper, while Emily whistled and played patience, David and Odd examined the new electronic navigation system – not very Viking, but they certainly would have used it and all our other mod-cons.

A nocturnal arrival left us tied up, with the other two Viking ships outside us, beside a hotel which was one of the few modern buildings in Ålesund. With Emily, there were eleven of us on board *Gaia*, and only nine berths. Ragnar slept as usual on *Havella*, and Gunnar volunteered to move into a spare bunk on *Oseberg* so that three Lomaxes would not have to squeeze into two bunks. There were only four crew members each on *Oseberg* and *Saga Siglar*. The other ships had lighter yards, and as they were not crossing the Atlantic did not need two full watches. With ten of us on *Gaia*, Ragnar had enough crew members of his own choice without having to rely on the four of us from Britain.

In Ålesund, where art nouveau architecture replaced much of the old centre of the town after a fire early this century, we were presented with a heavy brown and white traditional Norwegian sweater each. They became our working uniform in harbour, where everything and everyone on board were the subject of constant scrutiny from people who seemed to have nothing else to do.

'Do you sleep with all the men?' one man asked me.

Various boxes of stores and equipment arrived from time to time and had to be stowed: washing-up bowls and liquid, work suits, kitchen roll, fastenings and heavy duty wire for lifelines along the sides of the coachroof, food supplies, two life buoys, cases of beer, tins of tobacco and packets of cigarette papers. Many of the stores we rewrapped in dustbin liners and put under the loose deckboards, all of which were numbered; a list of where to find what was pinned up in the galley.

The cabin heater was so efficient that we had to turn it down. Emily taught Jon to play her favourite card game, pounce or racing demon, while David and Odd did battle over a miniature chess set.

'This man isn't afraid of taking risks,' David remarked at one of Odd's rasher moves. Chess, which the Vikings used to play, became a favourite cabin pastime, both under way and in port. Odd played as intensely as he did everything else. Frode, the youngest, blondest, most macho of the crew, had not played before but learnt fast because he hated losing. Jon, who we soon discovered had an extraordinary capacity for sleep, minded less, but won more often. Gunnar, our handsome mate and the only professionally qualified seaman as well as the only Icelandic on *Gaia*, rarely had time to play; when he did, he revealed an imaginative, aggressive approach. Ottar shared my dislike of a game which was so time-consuming, and Ragnar refused every challenge because he said that chess revealed too much of the player's personality. David's position as ship's champion was frequently challenged but never seriously threatened.

Another short relaxed day's sailing took us seventeen miles from Ålesund to Ulsteinvik, where we were told that accommodation had been booked for the Brits at Steinar Kulen's hotel, but not for the rest of the crew. We had neither expected nor wanted to be treated differently from the rest, but moved obediently.

Steinar was fleet supply officer, for which nine years as a hotel owner, and sailing experience with Ragnar on *Saga Siglar*, were excellent qualifications. After years of twelve- to sixteen-hour days, seven days a week, a serious car accident had forced him to rearrange his affairs so that he could leave someone else in charge. The invitation to join Vinland Revisited gave him an opportunity to put this into practice, and to think about what long-term changes he wanted to make to his life. He and his wife, Solveig, who was also his business partner, were a remarkably handsome couple, one fair-haired, one dark, both slim, with an elegant Edwardian air even in their most casual clothes. Somehow Steinar managed never to look scruffy, and his beard and moustache always seemed well groomed.

Although I had liked Steinar's sense of humour when I met him in Trondheim, we had not had much chance of getting to know him. This was partly because he was on *Havella* and we had had an awkward 'them and us' feeling about *Havella* ever since David had been stopped by Ragnar as he was about to step on board her in Håholmen.

'Where do you think you're going?' Ragnar had asked, in the tone of voice of a teacher who has caught a child sneaking a look at an exam paper. David explained that he was taking a video camera to Audun, whom he had asked to film dramatic rough weather sequences of *Gaia*. 'OK,' Ragnar said. That had been one of two minor confrontations between them. The other, also at Håholmen, had arisen when David had asked what a second camera team was doing there, and had been insistent that he must in future be told about other film crews.

'This whole thing isn't being organized just for your benefit,' Ragnar had snapped back at him. I was not surprised that each seemed suspicious of the other, and hoped that the tension would lessen once we were all at sea together.

The weather, unpredictable in that part of Norway at the best of times, was at its worst while we were in Ulsteinvik. For two days, a strong south-westerly gale blew driving rain straight from the direction in which we were hoping to sail. As *Gaia* was moored at Fosnavåg, twenty miles away by road, we were grateful for Steinar's loan of the hotel minibus.

The scenery was wild and spectacular. Mountains rose almost sheer to their snow-covered tops above a maze of inlets, fjords and sounds. It looked as if an angry Norse giant had hurled handfuls of land into the sea, where they had become a jumble of rocks and islands. A Viking mast gliding silently behind an outcrop did not look out of place. A series of bridges linked five islands beneath craggy snowcaps. Before the road was built, with its tunnels and bridges, many of the small communities living in scattered clusters of houses on the islands were accessible only by sea, others only by climbing steeply up and then equally steeply down.

Ragnar and Kari gave a crew party at their luxurious split-level pine-clad house overlooking a stormy vista of rocks and islands. Antique family furniture sat easily alongside carved boats from the Philippines and other tastefully selected mementoes in the main living room.

We were joined by Knut Kloster and Henrich Nissen-Lie, who were both staying at Steinar's hotel. Speeches were made by Ragnar, Knut and Odd – in English, which drew the Brits into the magic circle of Norse camaraderie. One of many toasts was drunk to the announcement that *Gaia* would continue her environmental journey from Washington west round the globe to arrive in Seville at Expo 92 before returning to Norway. It was Rikardur's birthday, an excuse for another toast – 'Skol Rikard!' – and for the presentation of small carefully selected silly presents and cards.

In anticipation of a clearance which would make an early morning departure possible, we moved next day from the hotel back on to *Gaia*, where Emily was deeply concerned about a pair of homing pigeons presented by an Ålesund newspaper. We were to release them, with appropriate messages, somewhere in the North Sea. Meanwhile, they were nameless and confined to a small pink plastic cage.

'What shall we call them?' Emily asked.

'Pinky and Perky,' Nigel and I offered simultaneously. This was rejected in favour of David's suggestion of Knut and Vigdis – although we were not sure which was which.

Emily's concern was shared by Herdis and Rosa, the two Icelandic girls on *Oseberg* and *Saga Siglar*. David had met them during a preliminary filming trip before Easter. 'There are two amazing girls on Håholmen who've been working on trawlers in Iceland,' he had told me. As the surname of both was Gunnarsdottir, I had imagined big burly sisters. Nothing could have been further from the truth. They were not related, and had not known each other before. Herdis was small and blonde, with big wide-spaced eyes, a dainty tilted nose and the widest possible smile. Rosa, who was taller, was equally slim and attractive, with brown curly hair restrained at sea in a pony tail. On social occasions on shore, both looked stunning, although no concessions were made by their fellow crew members to their femininity. Emily got on particularly well with them.

Elin, Ragnar's secretary, whom we had seen first at the launch at Bjørkedal, came on board with her small son in the afternoon, and promised to bring some hay or straw as pigeon bedding. 'This is the best crew Ragnar has ever had,' she told us. We hoped this included us.

After supper, we were visited on *Gaia* by Pierre de Billot, the South African skipper of *Oseberg*. After living for several years in Norway, where he was taking a degree in business studies, he spoke fluent Norwegian but with an accent. When we had been planning to charter *Saga Siglar*, Pierre, who had sailed on her from Tahiti to Norway, had been suggested by Ragnar as possible skipper. We had been unenthusiastic; a South African seemed to have no relevance on a Viking voyage, but having met him, we agreed that we could not have wished for anyone more agreeable or competent.

David, Odd and I discussed Gaia and James Lovelock during the next day's tow from Fosnavåg to a mid-morning stop in a bight called Vingen, where we took it in turns to zoom to the head of the bight in the gummiboats for a foray ashore. There were no houses in sight, but dozens of six-thousand-year-old rock paintings, mainly of deer but with a few fish and goats, had been highlighted in red. The earliest inhabitants of the area used to hunt deer by rounding them up and chasing them over the cliffs – an early example of human cooperation.

As we approached the harbour of Florø, we were instructed to don our Viking tunics. One at a time, and then several together, local Sunday-outing boats fell into place until *Gaia* looked like a shark with an escort of pilot fish. Ragnar was brought across from *Havella*. While *Saga Siglar* and *Oseberg* sailed around to entertain the crowds, a large tripper boat came alongside *Gaia*.

Christopher Columbus was standing on its top deck in full fifteenth-century finery. According to a book recently brought out by Henrich Nissen-Lie's publishing company, with a foreword by Knut Kloster, the Columbus – or Colon – family originated from the very fjord we were in. A posse of local journalists, plus a German TV crew, climbed aboard *Gaia*, followed by Columbus himself, to the strains of a single horn.

'Welcome aboard,' said Ragnar, or perhaps it was Leif Eiriksson. They squatted together on the cabin roof to look at a map of their respective routes.

While photographers jostled for position, the rest of us on *Gaia* concentrated on holding off the tripper boat, which towered over us, threatening our hull with every lurch in spite of its huge fenders.

Once enough photos of the two bewhiskered seafarers had been taken, David accosted Columbus, alias Torbjørn Halvorsen.

'You're supposed to be Christopher Columbus and Norwegian?'

'Yes – didn't you recognize me? I've read the book. It isn't proved that he came from Norway, but it could be. He didn't speak Italian.'

'Did he speak Norwegian?'

'We don't know. He had no Norwegians around him, so he had no one to speak it with. He spoke Latin.'

The boat lurched. Columbus swayed.

'Excuse me – I've forgotten my sea legs in these five hundred years.'

'What was your last job?'

'I was the Lion in *The Wizard of Oz*.'

The German film crew, Ragnar discovered afterwards, was making a documentary about Norwegian attitudes to the EEC. He was afraid that they were looking for eccentrics to prove that Norway was 'just a funny little country'. 'It will be a farce,' he complained.

As we approached Florø, we had some exciting sailing – the best so far. 'Are you ready for some rape and pillage?' Ragnar asked Nigel.

'Actually, I'm feeling a bit tired at the moment,' Nigel replied.

Florø, Norway's most westerly mainland community and a traditional departure point for boats sailing to Shetland, was founded on fishing in the early nineteenth century. Its population of twenty thousand in the heyday of herring fishing had since been halved. Fish farms had been started in the surrounding area to satisfy European and Japanese salmon markets, and a helicopter site served North Sea oil platforms.

'There are two hotel rooms booked for you,' Ragnar told us. 'We are leaving for Eivindvik at eight o'clock tomorrow morning.'

'If it's an early start, wouldn't it make more sense for us to stay on board?'

'Not really. I want you to have some family life, and the crew should be able to invite girls on board and have some fun.'

Nevertheless we spent an amicable evening in the cabin. No one felt like venturing into the rain. A haze of cigarette smoke drifted across the chess board. I read about the original Gaia, the Greek Mother Earth goddess, a lady of doubtful morality whose son, born of a union with an older son, cut off his father's genitals on her behalf.

'Don't read any more,' Odd advised. We decided to concentrate on Lovelock's living earth Gaia theory. By the time we reached Bergen, Knut wanted us to have formulated a Gaia message and to have worked out ways of putting it across both during Vinland Revisited, and during the continuation from Washington round the rest of the world.

First we needed to clarify in our own minds what Knut believed – no easy task, as he had admitted that even he was not sure what this was. David tried to sum it up: 'Knut wants to draw attention to *Gaia*'s international message of a new optimism. He thinks that too many people have a defeatist attitude; they realize that the environment is in danger, but they don't do anything about it because they let themselves believe it's too late to avert disaster. He is convinced that individuals have the power to influence events and change the course of world development.'

'So what he wants to do is discover and publicize ways in which individuals can improve the quality of their environment for the benefit of future generations,' someone added.

'It's difficult to see how spending all this money on sending a Viking ship across the Atlantic is going to stimulate debate about what individuals can do to reverse the gap between the rich and the poor, which is another of the things he says he wants to do,' David commented.

'Does it have to be individuals? Isn't that the responsibility of governments?'

'The lead must be taken by individuals because politicians act entirely out of self-interest.' Nigel had a low opinion of politicians. 'They'll use environmental movements for their own ends. The nature of modern politics is so short-term and self-interested that promises are just talk. We have to keep politics out of it.'

'But everything is political,' David objected. 'To decide to take action in the cause of safeguarding the environment is in itself a political act. To do something, choices have to be made and laws changed. This is a political action – you can't escape from it.'

'Politicians react to pressure, so perhaps if individuals take the lead, even if politicians do use general concern about the environment for their own ends, these ends can be for the general wellbeing and future of Gaia,' I suggested.

'We have to stand outside and apart from any political parties,' Nigel insisted.

'And equally outside any religious groups,' I added. Lovelock's dismissal of the significance of the human race, which according to his hypothesis could easily be eliminated by Gaia if that seemed the best way to ensure the survival of the planet, had made him a controversial figure in some religious circles. It also seemed to have been conveniently ignored by many members of the environmental groups which had latched on to his use of the Mother Earth goddess as a symbol for his theories.

'That's the most difficult bit of the Gaia theory for me,' I told Odd when the discussion continued under tow in heavy rain next day. 'If Lovelock is right, and Gaia has a self-regulating ability to survive by getting rid of anything and any species which threatens her survival, then maybe in environmental terms that's the answer: mankind is the problem, so Gaia has to get rid of us. But what we are all trying to do is work out how to make sure that there is a future for us. That's the basic conflict between Gaia and religion, or at least Christian religion.'

'What does Lovelock say about that?' Odd asked.

'After the lecture I went to, someone asked him whether there was room for religion in his theory, and what his own religious beliefs were. His answer was that he wasn't an atheist, but he didn't know how agnostic he was.'

'We can't expect to find the solution when we start,' Odd admitted. 'If that was possible, these ideas would have been known already. What we can try to do is to start with clear minds, and hope to "make the road" while we are walking.'

The trouble with every Gaia discussion on board was that it was so much easier to make admirable generalizations than to suggest any practical course of action. Someone suggested that an analogy could be drawn between *Gaia*, the ship, and Gaia, the world. The prime objective on board must be the ship's safety and wellbeing, and personal motives must be set aside to ensure this. 'So *Gaia* the ship is herself a symbol of Gaia the world or the planet. All personal interests must take second place to the needs of the ship, and in the same way rivalries and national loyalties must be set aside for the wellbeing of the world.'

'Judy, can you write out a summary of what we have all been saying and what we think about this Gaia question?' Odd asked. We worked it out together, and started with a paragraph restating the general aims of the project:

'The Vikings were skilled and energetic adventurers. They were close to nature and relied on instincts and techniques their modern counterparts have long forgotten. Their spirit of adventure is the sort of quality which is needed now. It is the spirit modern man needs in the search for a peaceful common future and a course to save the world from environmental catastrophe and the consequences of famine, war, global recession.'

'So that's the summary of the ideals behind this whole thing, but what about the practical aspects?' I asked. Our one positive suggestion was that the cooperation between Norwegian, Icelandic and British during the transatlantic crossing should be extended by having as international a crew as possible during the continuing voyage round the world, to symbolize and demonstrate international understanding and cooperation.

After I had printed our joint crew contribution to Knut's vision of using the Viking spirit to establish international cooperation and care of the environment, Odd added a handwritten sentence: '*Gaia* is sailing to "rediscover the future", for the best of mankind.'

'What about whaling?' I asked him. 'Many people see the whale as the symbol of caring for the environment.'

'We have a different attitude to it in Norway,' he said. He refused to be drawn into a discussion on the subject even when David suggested that there might be an apparent contradiction between the ostensibly environmental aims of our voyage and its backing by two governments which had made it clear that they did not rule out a resumption of commercial whaling.

The rain scarcely stopped all day, so there were frequent migrations into the warmth of the cabin, although the scenery of the Sognefjord was too spectacular to miss. When the fleet was at last able to set sail, a competitive element set in. Hoisting the yard on *Gaia* was as usual not without snags. Sometimes the tangles could be easily sorted out, although this often involved what we considered hair-raising acrobatics over the water. It was perhaps partly because we were clumsier than the Norse that we were alarmed by the lack of safety precautions; but if a merchant seaman with thirty dry years at sea behind him could fall overboard – which had happened during a sail-training session with *Saga Siglar* on Håholmen, fortunately with no serious ill effect – so could any one of us.

Eivindvik's schoolchildren were given the day off in our honour, and were brought by bus to look at the Viking fleet. Afterwards we agreed that if *Gaia's* deck and coachroof could withstand the jumping and tramping of so many feet, it should stand up to just about anything. Frode, the established king of the gummiboat, filled it time after time with an alarming number of children. There was not a life jacket in sight; but people along the Norwegian coast were as used to boats and the water as inland children to stairs.

At midday, the *Kommandøren*, a monster blue, white and Perspex catamaran from Bergen, roared into Eivindvik and manoeuvred into a position a few yards ahead of us. Its propellers threw up swirling white water under the bows of the three Viking ships, and damage was averted only by some hasty use of fenders and ropes. Then a gangplank was lowered; since it was several feet short of the ground, several wooden pallets were found so that dignitaries and a second importation of foreign journalists could step ashore.

The single street leading directly up from our mooring was filled with umbrellas. Two ladies with tightly permed blue-rinsed hair put polythene bags over their curls. By the time the junior band had mustered behind its majorettes, it was raining heavily. See-through plastic macs were provided for the band, but the uniforms of the unfortunate baton-twirling girls were soon soaked through.

Undeterred, they completed their programme. Equally undeterred, but with the protection of a raincoat, a white-haired local poet read his new Viking poem to the assembled umbrellas, and the mayor gave a mercifully brief speech in a strong local dialect. We had to stand on the coachroof appreciatively while water dripped down the necks of our tunics.

Our last stop before Bergen was at the tiny harbour of Idalstø, where we were visited by the entire local primary school, muffled against a showery gale in a multicoloured assortment of woolly hats. We had a Canadian, Kaye Fulton, on board. 'I'd rather stay here on *Gaia*,' she said when the rest of the journalists who were to sail into Bergen with the fleet were summoned for an audience with Ragnar on *Havella*. 'I should have taken the opportunity when it was offered,' she admitted later. 'Now Ragnar has no other time free for interviews.'

Almost all the journalists we met asked us the same questions: 'What's in it for Knut Kloster? Why is he spending all this money? His motives sound highly idealistic, but are they genuine? Surely there must be some hidden profit motive, especially in view of his reputation that everything he touches turns to gold.'

'We think he is genuinely idealistic,' we answered time and time again. 'You have to meet him to be able to believe that, and in any case it's difficult to see how this particular project can be a moneymaker for him.'

We had however to admit that the reasons we, and the rest of the crew, were on board was primarily for sailing and adventure. Our film brief was to make a good travel and adventure documentary, with the environmental mission as the icing on the cake.

The passage from Idalstø to Bergen was fast, exhilarating and fiercely competitive. Although in light winds *Oseberg* could sometimes keep up with or even overhaul her, *Gaia* as usual proved her ability to outsail the rest of the fleet. *Saga Siglar* followed at a more sedate pace. We entered the harbour, running in front of a force eight gale and doing nearly nine knots with two reefs in the sail. There was no way out ahead and no room to turn. I felt a moment of near-panic, tempered by relief that docking safely was not my responsibility. Only some quick action with fenders over the bows, and some hefty pushing off by watchers on the shore, had averted the nautical equivalent of a crash landing at an earlier stop – and that had been without wind.

Of course I should have had confidence in Norse boat handling abilities, which had so far, with that one exception, proved superb. The timing of dropping the sail was precise. A Viking ship does not respond lightly to the helm during manoeuvres in confined waters, in which in the old days the oars would have been used. Frode, who had perfected a modern Norse technique of using the gummiboat instead of oar power as we came into and left harbours, bullied and nudged *Gaia* into position.

My feelings as we roared into Bergen and tied up beneath the picturesque old terraced houses of Bryggen were a mixture of pride, exhilaration and apprehension. There was so much to cram into such a short time – less than forty-eight hours – and then there would be no turning back. There were still any number of odds and ends to be done on the boats. Brief reunions would be followed almost immediately by partings. To make sure that I remembered to give Emily's air ticket and passport to Jane, who was to be *in loco parentis* for her at our home in Berkshire, I put them carefully into my handbag before we moved from *Gaia* into the hotel in which we were to spend our last two nights in Norway.

Then we were caught up in the rush of combining last minute preparations with the festivities arranged to ensure that Bergen gave us an even better send off than we had been given by Trondheim.

Helge and Anne Stine Ingstad opened an exhibition which showed
their role in proving that the early Viking voyages had eventually
reached North America. We were all guests of honour at a dinner given
by the city.

David and I attended a press conference at which some of the Gaian
threads which were to be woven into our voyage were revealed. Ethnic
flag waving was at a minimum: Leif Eiriksson, Vinland, Vikings and
Viking ships were hardly mentioned. Columbus was named only in
connection with a book hastily translated from Norwegian, *Westward
before Columbus*. We were to carry this book with us, along with *State of
the World*, sub-titled 'A Worldwatch Institute Report on Progress
Toward a Sustainable Society'. A letter from the Worldwatch project
director was enclosed in each copy of its 1991 compilation of reports. It
was no coincidence that its first and last paragraphs read very like parts
of the Vinland Revisited brochure, since this was the message Knut
wanted us to carry in the wake of the Vikings:

'During the last thousand years, humans have explored virtually
every corner of the earth. We have probed the depths of the ocean and
soared through outer space. But, having spent the last millennium
discovering the features of our habitat, the challenge now is to discover
how to keep it habitable. . . .

'What will the world look like a thousand years from now? The
answer depends in large part on what we do during this decade.
Winning the battle to save the planet depends on discovering how to
change our own behaviour.'

As part of our Gaian mission, we were to record whale sightings for
the World Wildlife Fund; carry a cask of frozen cow's embryos for
implantation in the Faroes; and distribute Norwegian Forestry
Commission saplings in islands with a shortage of trees. This latter
mission was a belated apology for the destruction caused by the
Vikings; the Icelandic forests which had been cut down so that the early
settlers could build ships and houses had never recovered.

A youth essay competition on the theme 'What on earth is going on?
How is Gaia doing? Are we in healthy shape?' was being run by AFS
Intercultural Programs, a student exchange scheme founded in the
United States but operating internationally. The winners of its first
round, held in Norway for foreign and Norwegian students currently on
the scheme, were introduced by its vibrant Australian Development
Director, Ailsa Eckel.

The fears of younger children had been gathered together in a booklet, printed by the Bergen-based organization Research for Children, 'Now – or Too Late'.

At breakfast next day, David raised the controversial subject of whaling with Knut. Iceland and Norway had just declared their intention of resuming commercial whaling. Knut seemed a little nervous. He introduced us to the Icelandic ambassador, to whom we did not mention whales.

May 17th, the date of our departure and of the annual Norwegian national holiday in celebration of independence, was a perfect spring day – rare in Bergen, a city noted for its rainfall. Dressed in our Viking tunics, we paraded with the Bergenese, sandwiched between one of a dozen competing bands and a contingent of strict time-keeping elderly uniformed marchers. Every possible local organization seemed to be represented: church groups handing out leaflets; KFUM and KFUK, the Norwegian equivalent of the YMCA and YWCA; people of all ages in national costume; civil servants and unions; children and senior citizens; young boys, in uniform and armed with crosspieces, from a Bergen non-military all-boys club; even a contingent in plastic Danish Viking helmets. Each group had its own colours, carried proudly at its head. Some marched, others straggled.

'We're just a rabble,' Emily commented, accurately enough. As soon as we established a rhythm, either the whole three-a-breast column came to a halt, or it speeded up, or we found another band marching towards us or parallel with us playing something entirely different. Of a population of a quarter of a million, two hundred thousand people were marching or watching the parade. Flags were waved and there were cheers and clapping from every window, balcony and doorway along the route. The approach of our flagbearers was greeted with applause, many people calling out to Ragnar by name.

The sky was blue, the temperature warm enough to be a promise of summer, the atmosphere convivial and relaxed. We snaked several times round the town in lines of three for an hour and a half before coming to a halt on a large open square beside an inner-city lake. There was a lengthy intermission while we waited for the rest of the procession. The Danish plastic Viking helmets were informally presented to us while we waited, and we passed the time posing for and taking silly photos of each other wearing them.

'There's Knut,' David said.

'Knut!' I exclaimed, running forwards and forgetting that I was wearing a plastic horned Viking helmet.

'Take that thing off – never let me see you wearing it again,' Knut said; he sounded genuinely angry. 'Some TV or press person will see you and make it look as if you are taking these helmets seriously.' We all hid our helmets from sight while various dignitaries, Ragnar included, spoke from a podium in the shape of half a Viking ship. What we could understand of the official speeches confirmed our impression that the Bergenese were fiercely proud of their city and their country.

For the first time in her life, Emily was wearing sunglasses.

'Of course I'm not crying,' she insisted, 'I've just got hay fever.' She had managed to cure it by the time we were sitting in a waterfront hotel dining room for a formal farewell luncheon. The mayor of Bergen gave another speech, attributing the decline in Norwegian fortunes from the fifteenth century onwards to the Danish decision to move the capital from Bergen to Oslo – 'because the Danes got seasick on their way to Bergen, but could reach Oslo in sheltered waters'.

After lunch, Emily bade us a tearful private farewell in the privacy of a hotel room.

She had never tried to dissuade us from leaving her for so long – five months – but she was nevertheless as upset as any other ten-year-old would have been. Since she would be in her own home, with an elder sister who had always been almost like a second mother, we were not worried about her wellbeing, although we felt twinges of guilt. But the scale of the day's celebrations had already been so overwhelming that our feelings were numbed.

The harbour was seething with small boats jilling around waiting to escort *Gaia* out of Bergen. First, though, there were more speeches and pageantry ashore, including a children's song, 'Kids Have Rights', and a playlet in joint honour of Ragnar and Leif Eiriksson.

Exactly at 4.00 pm as planned, we slipped our lines and moved away from the harbour wall, under motor assisted by gummiboat. Ottar and I dived for the bows with fenders as a large British-registered traditional wooden yacht cut across our bows. Miraculously, there were no collisions, although there was scarcely any clear water. Everyone from Bergen without a boat seemed to have lined the shore to cheer us off, and everyone with access to a boat seemed to have taken to the water. Fire boats squirted twin jets of water, creating a mini rainbow. There was enthusiastic hooting, shouting, and waving from ships and boats dressed overall.

A nautical procession of a thousand craft accompanied us out of the inner harbour. Three hundred boats continued with us for the first hour. White choppy wavelets sparkled and slapped against the hulls under a cloudless sky. Gradually, one at a time, our escorts shouted 'Good luck!' or 'Bon voyage!' and turned back towards Bergen.

The water gently lapped *Gaia's* hull as a light breeze carried her towards the open sea. To port, snow-sprinkled mountains merged with low white puffy clouds behind the darker hills lining the coastline. To starboard, scattered houses seemed to grow out of the rock.

Pierre came across by gummiboat from *Oseberg* to say goodbye before she too turned back. 'If this is saving the world, it could catch on,' he said.

It was just beginning to get dark, after the luxury of supper on deck, when there was a VHF radio call from *Havella*. We were five miles offshore, and many more from Bergen.

'Someone wants to know where Emily Lomax's passport and ticket are,' Odd told us.

8 Shelter In Shetland

It was almost dark when a fast motor launch came alongside. We handed over Emily's passport and ticket – which in the emotion and excitement of the departure I had after all forgotten – and in a flurry of spray the *Sea Express* roared back towards the land, which was disappearing fast astern.

'Thank goodness for Norwegian improvisation,' David commented. We could only imagine the confusion we must have caused, wonder who was the more distraught, Jane or Emily, and feel grateful to whoever organized the launch. It would have been good to be able to talk to someone in Bergen to say 'thank you'.

The only communication possible from *Gaia* was however to *Havella*. The mobile radio telephone used in Norwegian waters had been taken off; and the VHF worked only on the emergency channel. *Havella* had a fully operational VHF radio, as well as an SSB amateur shortwave radio. Øyvard Karlsbakk, who had taken time off from his job with IBM and was the only crew member on either boat older than us, was an enthusiastic radio ham and had set up a daily schedule. Among the people he planned to talk to regularly was a monk from a Benedictine monastery half a mile from our house in Berkshire. It was comforting to know that once Jane and Emily were back home we would therefore be able to keep in touch with them, indirectly at least, through Father Wilfrid, or Paul Sollom, as he was known to fellow ham radio enthusiasts.

I suppose that we all to some extent shared the same feelings as we lost sight of the land and started our first night in open sea – a mixture of excitement that at last the real adventure was starting, and apprehension about what lay ahead, and about how we could cope with it. Andrew was perhaps the most apprehensive: he had the least sailing experience, but would be under considerable pressure to produce results whatever the conditions. The overall responsibility for everyone's safety, and for the success of the venture, lay of course with Ragnar, who was relieved to be at sea at last. So was I, although my private fear was of succumbing to seasickness and giving the men an excuse for thinking me a liability.

'I hope I shan't be expected to do all the cooking,' I had said to Ragnar at one of the early planning meetings in Oslo; and I had been relieved when his reply had been quick and decisive: 'Everyone takes turns.'

Our destination was Kirkwall, the tiny capital of the Orkneys, where we were scheduled to spend three days before visiting the Shetlands, Britain's most northerly islands. Weather permitting, we were hoping to make an unscheduled stop at Fair Isle, not however a place to visit under sail except in calm settled conditions.

On our first full day at sea, David's birthday, we saw an occasional fishing boat and a solitary gas rig, and let one of the pigeons out. It circled once, turned towards Bergen, then altered course towards Ålesund and disappeared.

By supper time, the sea was verging on 'rubbly', as a Cornish fisherman friend used to call it. Supper did not tempt me greatly, but then neither did it repel me. I parted with it a couple of hours later, thinking that I was the only person on board to have succumbed. It was not until much later that I learnt that I was the fourth.

We had reefs in and out of the sail throughout the evening and night. Long dodgers of dull-red sail cloth, stretched on heavy-duty wire from just below the top of the high sternpost to forward of the shrouds, and fastened several strakes down on the outside of the hull, provided some shelter for the open aft deck. Even so, one rogue wave found its way down the back of my neck. With spray breaking over the bows in a near-gale, *Gaia* shivered as she met the bigger seas, but rode them with considerably more grace than *Havella*, rolling along beside us.

The metal loo bucket on the foredeck become less and less appealing as the evening became rougher, but eventually it had to be braved.

From Bergen to Orkney, we had an Icelandic passenger. Valgeir, who was, Herdis had told us, 'world famous in Iceland' as a TV personality and pop musician, had been added to our watch, at the end of which he asked me if I had anything for seasickness. 'I have this bad feeling about going into the cabin,' he said. I gave him one of the earpatches which I have found work for me. These small round plasters, which release an anti-seasick drug gradually over a three-day period, must be put on a hairless patch of skin; they are known as earpatches because most people stick them behind their ears, although I once met some Germans who all put them on their navels, where they worked equally well.

My sleeping bag welcomed me warmly, and in spite of the noise of the water rushing past the hull, occasional crashes under the foot of the boat, and the creaks and groans of the timbers, the next thing I knew someone was saying: 'Six o'clock – watch time.' We were working a Norwegian system of six hours on, six hours off. This meant that the same people were always together on duty at the same times. Although in rough weather six hours could seem a very long time, with five of us on at a time it was unlikely that anyone would have to work non-stop throughout a watch.

Our morning watch greeted us with a calmer sea.

'That patch worked pretty well,' Valgeir told me.

David suggested filming the release of the second pigeon. Andrew and Nigel had been asleep when we released the first one.

'It's not there,' Andrew said.

'I let it out,' Ragnar confessed. 'It was wet and miserable. I like pigeons, and I thought you'd filmed the other one.'

The morning weather forecast threatened south-westerly winds of force eight, nine and even ten for the night – from gale through severe gale to storm. As 'admiral', Ragnar was faced with a difficult decision: whether to keep going, in the hope that we would reach Orkney before the storm; to make for Fair Isle and ride it out there; or to make straight for shelter in Shetland, which we should be able to reach by nightfall. He decided to keep his options open at first, by setting a halfway course for Fair Isle. But when the next forecast was still as bad the only possible option was to head for Shetland as fast as possible. *Havella* took us in tow.

Steering became a matter of 'Follow that boat'. We were pulled along at eight knots towards the islands hidden in the mizzle ahead of us. This put considerable strain on *Gaia*. Under her own sail power, the hull flexed with the seas; at first, I found it strange when I leant against the side to feel how much give there was. She rode and twisted over the waves, rather than ploughing into them like so many boats of modern construction. Instead of fighting the sea, she felt at one with it. Although I had had no opportunity to see her from a distance under sail, I had been impressed by the smooth movement both of *Oseberg*, and of the stubbier *Saga Siglar*. But towing at speed created conflict. It became impossible for the hull to adapt smoothly to the movement of the sea, so the motion became awkward, even violent, the bows crashing repeatedly on to the water.

Gaia would have been under even greater strain, however, if we had been caught out in a storm. Tank tests on a scale model at a Trondheim laboratory had shown that in the sort of seas which could be expected in storm-force winds there was a strong possibility that she might capsize or be swamped.

As we came into the lee of Sumburgh Head, the southernmost point of Shetland's mainland, Gunnar roared off in the gummiboat to investigate where we should come in. It was not long before *Gaia* and *Havella* were tied up at Grutness Point, at right angles to each other alongside a small harbour wall in a thick mizzle. A rusty crane stood on guard over us. To one side of the jetty, seabirds and Shetland ponies shared a field of boulders along the foreshore. To the other, a narrow road led in front of several derelict stone buildings, past a few inhabited stone houses, to Shetland's most southerly hotel, a building of remarkable ugliness. It overlooked Jarlshof, one of the most varied archaeological sites in Europe.

The Shetland scenery was soft and green compared with its Norwegian counterpart a couple of days sailing away.

19 May, Sunday, Grutness Point, Shetland, 21.00
Everyone else has gone off to the hotel for beer and showers, so we are in charge of *Gaia* for a few hours. Gunnar, who in David's opinion has the sort of bearded sea-dog good looks that should be advertising sardines, left with a wry comment: 'I don't know who is captain any more.' It is fortunate that he is easy-going, since otherwise this could be a problem. In theory Gunnar is skipper on *Gaia*, and Audun on *Havella*. But as 'admiral', Ragnar has the overall responsibility, and often countermands orders given by Gunnar or makes decisions without consulting him. Odd also tells everyone what to do.

It feels good to be safely tied up in a sheltered spot on such a wild night. We have just made ourselves smoked salmon sandwiches – one of the perks of being on a Norwegian ship. Largesse is distributed daily from deep freezes and lockers on *Havella*, weather permitting. *Gaia* only has enough food on board for a few days at a time. It is just possible that we may grow tired of boiled potatoes and carrots – served with almost every evening meal.

The question next morning was not whether it had been sensible to seek shelter, but whether the wind would moderate and go round within the next thirty-six hours, in time for us to make our official reception in Orkney. It was the sort of weather which would have blown the original Vikings straight back to Norway, since they did not have our option of being towed; but equally they did not have to keep to a timetable of official receptions and so would have been able to wait until they were sure of several days of settled weather before setting out. Their voyages west, and back east to Norway, could be timed to coincide with the period of gentle easterly winds which could be counted on in spring or early summer, and of westerlies in the autumn. Whether they waited a week, or a month, or even a year, did not matter; it was a leisurely existence, although with periods of intense activity.

We were moored within easy walking distance of Sumburgh airport. Small commercial aircraft linking the islands with the British mainland, and helicopters serving North Sea oil platforms, landed and took off at regular intervals in spite of the strong wind. David and I hired a car from the airport and explored the southern end of the island with Andrew and Nigel.

In the only shop for several miles, Andrew and I tracked down a few basic luxuries: Marmite, orange squash, black peppercorns and a grinder, chile powder, and cider vinegar. To make Gunnar feel at home, we bought him a tea towel with a design of puffins. 'Very good to eat,' he had told us about almost every seabird we had seen – and Icelandic puffins apparently made the best eating of all.

To get as near the top of the cliffs as possible, we drove along a single track road, through an open gate claiming that we were entering Ministry of Defence property. A tractor driver coming in the opposite direction waved cheerfully as he pulled at an angle on to the grass to let us pass. At the end of the track, the fencing round the old MOD establishment lay in twisted fragments. Two equally dilapidated long single-storey buildings, which appeared to have been used for long range radio communication, had been demoted to a farm store and were filled with great rolls of barbed wire.

Spray dampened the air even several hundred feet above the rocks. The car, parked on steep grass, was bounced by the wind. A family of seals played in the swirling foam below us. From time to time they raised their heads from the spume in curiosity. Wild white horses pranced out to sea. To our left, waves crashed high against the rocky outcrops and islets behind Sumburgh Head. On land, rabbits hopped happily among the sheep and lambs grazing on the gentler slopes. An amazing number of land and sea birds pecked, wheeled and dived around us.

In spite of the wild wind, it was a clear bright sunlit day, perfect for visiting Jarlshof, with its layers of Neolithic, Bronze and Iron Age, Viking and medieval remains. As I stood beside the low stone outline of the old Norse farmhouse, on a long grassy spit between a sheltered gently sloping beach and a steeper more exposed rocky shoreline, I tried to envisage what the place must have looked like to the first Vikings to land there. They probably came in peace – in search of fertile farmland, of which there has always been a shortage in Norway – but had to be wary of attack from the sea. It must have seemed a perfect site, both to the Vikings and to the people who had lived there before them, with a shallow sheltered bay where they could beach their boats; a steep headland to shield them from the prevailing wind; a vantage point over the sea in three directions; grass for grazing; turf and stone for building; fresh water; even Shetland ponies, which roamed the hills and moors long before the Vikings came to the island. The only thing lacking was wood; but Norwegian forests were only two days' sailing away.

But why had the Norse settlers then abandoned their flourishing farming settlement, after five hundred years? I could imagine them becoming increasingly irritated by the sand blown across their land and into their houses by repeated storms, and eventually feeling that enough was enough, deciding either to return to Norway or to join the waves of emigrants to the Faroes, or to Iceland, or even to Greenland.

Each consecutive layer of ruins at Jarlshof had in turn been covered by sand, and it was only when some of the top surface was blown off in a storm early this century that their existence was suspected. The last building, the old manor house ruin which Walter Scott had taken as a setting, and which had been abandoned not because of the sand but because of a family feud, was still standing. None of its inhabitants had know it as Jarlshof, a name invented by Sir Walter Scott long after they had all abandoned it to the sand, the sea and the wind.

The daisies flowering freely in the short grass were 'very Lovelock', as David put it: Lovelock had devised a computerized 'Daisyworld' metaphor for his theories about the earth's automatic climate control system.

The Shetland evening brought people from the neighbouring houses on foot, others by car, to look at the strange boat which had come in with the storm.

'Look – she lives in there,' a small girl said excitedly to her mother, who shushed her tactfully.

There were four of us on board that evening. A jazz tape competed with the whirr of the heater. Jon, quiet and shy, with deep auburn hair, rust-brown eyes, and a rusty voice, read Odd's *Ashley Book of Knots*, a tome so huge we agreed that it must be definitive, while David and Frode fought silently over the chessboard.

When the others came back from the pub, they brought a rumour that we might try to make Fair Isle in an overnight lull; but since according to the midnight shipping forecast the wind was again expected to reach more than fifty knots the idea, or the rumour, was abandoned.

From the warmth and privacy of my sleeping bag, I amused myself while the men prepared for the night by trying to identify their legs. One pair was smooth but as white as a washing powder advertisement, another pair thin and hairy, a third had particularly well-developed calf muscles but slim ankles.

It was so wild and wet when we woke that we exchanged congratulations about not having set out to sea. White caps covered the bay and the water outside as far as the eye could see. *Gaia* rocked and jerked impatiently.

The car was buffeted so violently as I drove a shopping party to Lerwick that the twenty-mile journey seemed twice as long. In good weather, the centre of Lerwick, the Shetland capital, is picturesque, with its narrow alleyways and solid stone buildings, but that day it was dour and sombre, uniformly grey except for the bright colours of a Viking ship on the coat of arms above the harbour.

Valgeir bought food for the supper he planned to cook, regardless of the cooking rota. Gunnar and Odd were in charge of various boat purchases, including hooks for safety harnesses. Nigel, who had fallen naturally into the role of ship's electrician, needed a switch. It didn't take me long to find everything on the list I had been given: needles and thread for sewing Gaia logos on to clothing, liqueur glasses for Norwegian aquavit, coat and cup hooks, two British courtesy flags and a waterproof flashlamp.

By the time all the shopping had been done, and the others had had a pint, or two or three, the wind had reached full storm force. Keeping the car on the road needed concentration. A red warning light was flashing where the road crossed the Sumburgh runway, so I stopped – and we waited, and waited.

'Why are we waiting?' the others asked.

'Because the notice says "Stop when red light shows".'

We waited a bit more – then, from the back of the car: 'It must be broken.'

As if to prove a point, a car crossed the road in the other direction, from Grutness Point.

'Shall we go?' I asked.

'Yes,' came the unanimous reply.

As I crossed the road, an aircraft swooped low over it to touch down on the runway only yards away.

Even in the lee of Sumburgh Head, *Gaia* was being thrown about and the wind was whipping the surface of the water into white-topped peaks. A local man who had braved the weather agreed that it was 'a wee bit breezy'. David was hanging on to the crane on the quay at the time, to stop his feet from being lifted off the ground. A Shetland fisherman told Ragnar that the weather was the worst he remembered. Perhaps Mother Earth – Gaia – was trying to tell us something.

'You must go to the lighthouse,' Ragnar had told us. 'Last time I was in Shetland, the people up there were very friendly.'

But that was many years ago. The light had since then become automatic, and the buildings were in that depressing stage between having recently been abandoned and dereliction. They were up for sale, but we felt that it would present a prospective purchaser with quite a challenge to find any use for them except that for which they had been built. The full power of the wind hit us while we were walking to the top of the headland. Several hundred feet up we still felt threatened by spray from the surf crashing on the rocks below.

'There is no way we are going to leave today, or tonight,' I noted in the late afternoon. The wind had continued to rise, and the sea with it. The forecast until dawn next day was hardly one to set out on: 'SW severe gale force nine, increasing storm force ten, westerly forty knots, gusts fifty to sixty knots, gradually veering NW and decreasing slowly after midnight to twenty-five knots, gusts thirty-five to forty knots by 0600 hrs.' The outlook for the following twenty-four hours, starting four hours before we were meant to be in Orkney for a formal reception, was however more encouraging: 'Wind NW force six gradually easing force five. Scattered showers. Visibility moderate to good.' But it would take a couple of days for the sea to subside.

'When I told Knut that we could not meet our deadline in Orkney, he said "Good".' Ragnar told us. 'Strange guy.'

'Maybe he feels things were going too smoothly,' we suggested.

Supper was interrupted for adjustments to lines and fenders. *Gaia* was being rubbed and bounced violently against the wooden pilings of the pontoon, and her soft wood was being severely chafed by her own lines. Eventually we secured her safely, with our strongest line round the crane on shore and with the addition of some huge spherical fenders borrowed from a fisherman's store.

I spent the evening splicing carbine hooks on to lifelines, although with some misgivings about their suitability, as they were the sort condemned by the inquiry into safety equipment after the Fastnet race in which several lives had been lost. They were, however, the only ones available in Lerwick. 'I wouldn't like to trust my life to them,' commented a fisherman's chandler who stocked them. Before leaving Shetland, David and I tracked down and bought the only four ready-made heavy duty lines, the rest ironically having been sold to visiting Norwegian yachtsmen.

We eventually set out on Wednesday evening, after seventy-two hours in Shetland, and ten hours after we should have sailed into Kirkwall. 'Better safe than sorry' and 'better late than never' were much-used clichés that evening. It was still rough, but the wind had moderated and was with us, and the sea was starting to subside. By the midnight watch change we were off Fair Isle. At times during the night we were doing eight knots with two reefs. There was much reefing and unreefing, which we cowardly Brits still considered foolhardy without safety lines. The Norwegians, who scampered across the cabin roof and swung from the rigging like nautical monkeys, scorned such admissions of fallibility.

The motion on *Gaia* was encouragingly comfortable, even in the gale-force gusts. I felt at ease with her, and with the rest of the crew, for whom our joint experiences so far had inspired trust, liking and respect. Provided we treated *Gaia* well, and continued to protect her from conditions she would not be able to cope with, I was confident that she would look after us and would continue to provide us with the most exhilarating sailing anyone could wish for.

9 Scottish Island Hospitality

Twelve hours after our rough departure, we were gliding between the soft low isles of Orkney at three and a half knots, still with one reef in the sail and one day late. Ragnar and Odd were discussing the price of milk over breakfast while David did radio tests which revealed that *Gaia* still had only one channel apart from the emergency frequency.

The weather could not have been better. If we had not put into Shetland, at the best we would by then have been back in Norway and *Gaia* would almost certainly have sustained some damage. What could have happened at the worst did not bear thinking about.

Shetland had looked green and soft in comparison with the west Norwegian coast; Orkney, being lower and more fertile, looked even greener and softer as we motored towards Kirkwall, leaving a dramatic Gothic castle and a lighthouse on a spit to starboard and a beach littered with strangely shaped pink sandstone rocks to port.

With a couple of small motor launches and a light aircraft in attendance, we hoisted sail to run into the harbour. Shepherded by the lifeboat, with Knut on board, *Gaia* made a slow and majestic entry, under sail until the last minute. Rikardur had gone ahead with the gummiboat to be ready to nudge us into position as we dropped the yard right inside the confined inner harbour, which I found nerve-racking with the wind behind us and no turning space. As we were piped in from the harbour wall, Ottar and I were waiting anxiously on the bows with fenders; that they were not needed was a tribute to the skilful timing of Ragnar and Gunnar.

Before we had even finished tying up, there were greetings and speeches and mayoral chains on shore. Half of us were still flaking and lashing the sail when the first visitors – the piper, Knut Kloster and his wife, the honorary Norwegian consul, and a clutch of local reporters – stepped aboard. Ragnar adopted his usual Viking-look pose for photographers, and David and I were interviewed for radio.

'It felt strange knowing that you were all at sea on *Gaia*,' Knut told us. 'I worried about you. It was as if you were all my family.'

Throughout the two afternoons we spent in Kirkwall, Orkney's village-sized capital, *Gaia* was a strange sight, her cabin roof hidden under flat boxes of miniature trees. These had been grown in Norway and flown over, accompanied by a Norwegian forestry girl, Bergljot Gundersen, who told us what they were: holly, green elder, spruce, mountain pine, rowan and juniper. On the first day, we gave them out to Orcadian adults, who queued on the slip, climbed aboard one at a time, walked round the boat, signed their names in a visitor's book, were given a sapling, and climbed back ashore.

Knut Kloster watched benevolently from the quay while, dressed in Viking tunics, we struck next day's Gaian blow for the environment by distributing another thousand saplings to children from ten schools. Provided they all remembered to plant them, and took note of Bergljot's advice about where to do so, some of the trees should escape the ravages of sheep, rabbits and strong salt-laden winds.

Somehow the chief organizer of our time in Orkney, Bill Spence, managed to cram everything planned for three days into two. Bill had been honorary Norwegian consul for thirteen years, after several years as vice consul. 'They told me being consul would take five minutes on Friday afternoons,' he said ruefully; in the previous few weeks our impending arrival had made it almost a full-time job.

For most of us, the highlight of our abbreviated visit to Orkney was a trip to the Highland Park distillery, where we saw every stage of whisky making – and were given generous samples to take away with us. At the end of the tour, we were offered a preliminary taste while we watched a wide-screen slide presentation of the Orkneys. From the start of the 1914–18 war until the Admiralty withdrew from its Orcadian naval base in 1957, the strategic significance of Scapa Flow had made the islands a part of modern European history. It was to Scapa Flow that the captured remnants of the German fleet were brought at the end of the First World War, and there that in a grand gesture of defiance the ships were scuttled by their defeated crews. The fifty square miles of sheltered waters were again a bleak British wartime naval base in the Second World War.

We had no time to visit Scapa Flow, or indeed any of the rest of Orkney's fifty-six islands, of which only eighteen were inhabited. On our one evening on the mainland, we were treated to a conducted tour, and a choral concert in Kirkwall's magnificent sandstone cathedral, dedicated to St Magnus. This was followed by a lavish buffet supper, accompanied by superb fiddle and accordion playing in the sailing club bar. The fiddler seemed equally at home playing a modern violin and a traditional double-stringed and elaborately decorated Norwegian hardanger fiddle.

Orcadians have a nostalgic affection for their Norse past. Many consider the Norse settlement which began in the ninth or tenth century and lasted for a few hundred years the high point of a rich history. According to a local guidebook, it was after Orkney was gradually drawn into the orbit of Scotland that 'most of the glory departed'.

The Orkneys have their own thirteenth-century *Orkneyinga Saga*, written by an anonymous Icelander, as well as featuring in Snorri Sturluson's *Heimskringla*. According to Snorri, the islands were settled in the days of Harald Hárfagri – Harald Fairhair – who gained his name by refusing to cut or comb his hair until he had won the woman he loved by becoming king of all Norway. It took him quite a while. His harsh rule was responsible for considerable emigration west from Norway. When some of the refugees took up residence in the Orkneys and Shetlands, King Harald gave chase, and founded the Earldom of Orkney, which included Shetland, Caithness and Sutherland.

Christianity was introduced through the persuasive missionary tactics of King Olaf Tryggvason. He started by imprisoning Sigurd, Earl of Orkney, whom he then allowed 'to ransom his life by letting himself be baptized, adopting the true faith, becoming his man, and introducing Christianity into all the Orkney islands'. As a hostage, King Olaf took Sigurd's son, Hund – the Whelp.

At least St Magnus, whose nephew Earl (later St) Rognvald founded Kirwall's cathedral, seems to have been saintlier than some of the Viking missionaries. There were omens before he was murdered by the supporters of a treacherous and ambitious cousin, Håkon, with whom he was supposed to share the Orkneys; and there were miracles afterwards: grass sprang up on the stony field where he was killed, for instance, and his grave was found to have healing powers.

A genuine red carpet was laid out at the top of the slipway before our departure, as a platform for a schoolgirl demonstration of Scottish dancing. An island band in full uniform marched in a mizzle to the other side of the harbour, piping as it went. *Gaia*, with Knut Kloster on board, was soon swinging along gently as she left the Orkneys via North Sound en route for Fair Isle. Henrich Nissen-Lie and his wife were on *Havella*.

The wind was so gentle that to increase speed we added the bonnet, a detachable rectangular panel fastened to the bottom of the square sail with a row of loops which it had been one of my first tasks on board to create. It was peaceful enough for 'special tea', heavily laced with local Scotch, before the midnight watch change. While Odd was making this brew, he discovered that we had run out of sugar to sweeten it, jumped into the gummiboat, untied and drifted back into the dark while he was still trying to start the outboard engine. He was soon out of sight astern.

Ten minutes later, David asked, 'Did Odd get there? Should we check with *Havella*?' No one else seemed to think this necessary. What worried us was that he had neither torch, pump, life jacket nor radio with him; but he eventually roared back out of the darkness with a packet of sugar.

The weather was gentle enough for a stop at Fair Isle, halfway between Orkney and Shetland and only three miles long by one and a half miles wide. We reached it well before breakfast. A couple of islanders appeared on the jetty half an hour later, peered down at us for a while and announced that someone would be out to greet us 'shortly'. In the meantime, we had the company of a million seabirds, whirling and squawking between their cliff-side nests and the sea. The only buildings in sight were either derelict, or boxes of an ugliness which insulted the beauty of their surroundings: steep sheep-cropped grass, and even steeper cliffs. Whitewashed stone crofts were, we were relieved to discover later, more typical of the island's architecture.

The farthermost of the buildings visible from the harbour was the Fair Isle bird observatory and hostel, which keep the island going economically as well perhaps as psychologically. They ensure a constant flow of people of varying ages and backgrounds, but all sharing one passionate interest: bird watching. Started forty years ago in two small buildings above the beach, it had later taken over an abandoned RAF wartime block – hence the ugliness – which was extended in the late 1960s to provide hostel board and lodging for visiting ornithologists. When I called there at breakfast time, forty people were sitting with their cereal and toast at several long tables. The warden and his wife, who lived in a self-contained first floor flat, were expecting their third child – one of two as yet unborn babies on the island.

The other prospective parents were Ian Best and his wife, a proper islander. Although he had been brought up on the island, Ian and his parents, John and Betty, were still considered 'incomers'. At lunchtime, we were entertained in the old laird's house, where the younger Bests were living until the new house they were building was ready. Like everything else on the island, this was a matter of self-help. Ian, who had set himself up as the local boatbuilder after spending three years training in Norway, showed us some of the small shallow double-ended open 'yoals' traditionally – but no longer – used for fishing.

A large mottled seal watched us lazily from rocks covered in wet slippery seaweed. John and Betty Best told us that the local seals often assembled on the beach below their house for an early morning serenade.

Islanders, ornithologists and crew danced together in the evening on a small sandy beach to the music of an accordion, a couple of fiddles, one played by Ian's wife, and two guitars. Light and warmth came from the bonfire on which a derelict boat was burning just above the waterline. The islanders provided barbecue food and *Gaia* contributed Norwegian beer. It was voted the best evening so far – because it was the most informal and relaxed. Ragnar looked ten years younger dancing on the beach, and for the first time I saw Frode looking happy and laughing.

The *Good Shepherd*, the twelve-passenger ferry linking Fair Isle to Shetland and so to the rest of the world, was dressed overall with a flag message: 'Skol, *Gaia*.' We failed to think of a suitably witty rejoinder. As usual, the *Good Shepherd* had been winched out of the water as the island's one minute harbour provided only limited shelter.

An encounter at the barbecue added a new task to our environmental mission: to record whale and dolphin sightings for an international whale – and dolphin – watching programme run by Pete Evans from Oxford. Pete, who was on Fair Isle on a project about starlings, claimed that whales were under greater threat from pollution than from hunting.

Although I had not seen any starlings, I had spent much of the day lying on my stomach looking down at the antics of a colony of puffins, comic little birds that looked as if their wings were run by clockwork. Patches of thrift and small purple flowers, as well as great white splodges of seabird droppings, spattered the cliff sides, which came and went all day as the mist retreated and rolled back in.

At midnight, eight of the island's adult population were sitting in *Gaia's* cabin, with several more outside in the cockpit. Ian Best was in deep conversation in Norwegian with Ottar.

The islanders' two major concerns were the impending loss of BBC radio services, and their anger with the Orcadian fishermen who they claimed were cleaning out Fair Isle's lobsters. They had even taken matters into their own hands by cutting some Orcadian lines, whereupon the local constable had been called in from Shetland, something which happened only rarely, and then only in the gravest possible situations. Life on Fair Isle was usually peaceful.

Half the population was under thirty. From three hundred and eighty in the middle of the last century, numbers had dropped below fifty before the observatory was opened, and had then risen to seventy. There were quite a few incomers, either spouses or dropouts from the rest of the world. Several times I heard: 'We came for a holiday – and we never left.' There did seem to be some special sort of island magic.

At least half of the island's population came to see us off. The engine was started, but used only to help *Gaia* clear the quay, then the yard was hoisted high enough to be manoeuvred forward of the mast, the lashing string pulled, and as the sail dropped there was applause from the quay. I felt proud to be a small part of a well-executed manoeuvre. By the time we were out of the tiny harbour, the sail was fully raised, adjusted and pulling. Within a few minutes, Fair Isle was hidden in the fog. So was *Havella*.

We were wrapped in a soft cocoon which made even the warm memories of the island we had just left seem unreal, like a half-remembered dream. With no visual reminders of where, or when, we were sailing, I stood for a while on the fore deck, gazing ahead into limbo, the air damp on my hair as I tried to imagine what the first Norse sailors to venture out of sight of land felt like – and then appreciating that, unlike them, I could go into a warm dry cabin and find out where I was by looking at an electronic chart.

There was great excitement for a few seconds when a couple of lorry tyres were mistaken for a whale. Usually by the second half of May there had been a number of whale sightings in the Shetland-Orkney sea area. That we had seen none we jokingly attributed to their common sense in keeping out of sight of a boat with crew members from two countries which would have liked to resume whaling.

Fulmars flew all the way with us. Occasionally flocks of frantically flapping puffins landed or took off – 'Very good to eat,' Gunnar reminded us, but forbidden food in the Scottish islands.

For several hours, there was nothing – apart from seabirds – to be seen through the murk. It was Nigel's turn to provide lunch. In spite of a Fair Isle hangover, he nobly fried thick slices of blood sausage which the Norwegians ate liberally sprinkled with sugar. Gunnar varied this by having his first course with salt, and adding sugar to his second helping as pudding.

The mist and mizzle had not lifted by the time we anchored south of the Shetland island of Mousa, under grass and cliffs where seabirds were nesting. Three seals were playing round the rocks. The weight and strain when we dropped anchor were taken round the mast, as for towing, with a fender as an anchor buoy. Even so, the rope tended to chafe the gunwale.

Within a few minutes, Knut had been transferred first to *Havella*, then to a small blue and white launch which took him ashore. Ragnar migrated back to *Havella*. It was my turn to cook supper. I turned the previous day's leftovers into potato cakes to go with frozen halibut which was that day's delivery from the mother ship. Demands for seconds of halibut and potato cake – '*Mer fisk! mer potet!*' – demonstrated either genuine hunger, or pleasure in the food, or both. The Norse rarely said 'please', for which there is no simple translation in Norwegian, but they were punctilious about saying '*takk for mat*' – 'thank you for the meal'. Andrew and Nigel set themselves the challenge of persuading Frode, with whom they were on good drinking terms, to say please and thank you.

To our relief, as choosing the film crew had been our responsibility, both Andrew and Nigel fitted in as well with the rest of the crew as with each other. The relationship between a cameraman and soundman is particularly important, as they have to work so closely together, and so when Andrew had suggested Nigel we had accepted his choice. They seemed in some ways an oddly assorted pair. Physically, they were very different. Andrew, who had very dark hair and eyes, could look handsome or petulant, depending on when he had last shaved, how short he was of sleep, whether or not he was hung over. A heavy smoker and a worrier, he found it difficult to sleep under way.

Nigel was fair-haired and short-sighted, and seemed generally more relaxed and easy-going, although he could on occasion sound surprisingly dogmatic. Although he did not look particularly athletic – especially when he was not wearing his glasses, which made him screw up his eyes so much that he took on the expression of an anxious hamster – he was an enthusiastic walker, climber and cyclist, which along with not smoking kept him physically far fitter than Andrew. In spite of their dissimilarity, 'the boys' were treated by everyone so much as a couple that to their understandable irritation their names were often confused, especially as they were in the same watch. They, and David and I, had initially been split up, but this had been changed when they pointed out that whenever they were working – as film rather than boat crew – they had to operate as a pair.

An overnight anchor watch was set. My two hours on duty, which started at 03.00, were so peaceful, and the unaccustomed solitude so pleasant, that I did not wake the next watch keeper. Although I did not find conditions on board at all cramped – being with ten people on a seventy-eight foot boat was far from claustrophobic compared with the half dozen I was used to on a boat less than half the length – I enjoyed the luxury of having the cabin to myself, and for once smokeless: apart from Nigel, David and I were the only non-smokers in the crew. Through the open top half of the cabin door I watched the gradual development of a slow soft dawn. A black and white bird, a Scottish sort of guillemot, sat on the stern rail for some time and let me approach it to within a few feet.

We reanchored in the morning under Mousa Broch, a circular two-thousand-year-old stone tower, one of Shetland's most solid and oldest historical monuments. No one knows who built it, or why, but on a couple of occasions it was apparently put to good use by lovelorn Vikings: first by a young couple who were shipwrecked while they were eloping from Norway to Iceland, in the year 900, making them fairly early would-be Icelanders; and then more than two centuries later by one Erlend and the woman he wanted to marry, Margaret, mother of the Earl of Orkney. The Earl granted permission for the marriage after an unsuccessful siege of the broch: 'not an easy place to attack', as the *Orkeyinga Saga* put it. With its single entrance, and tiny spiral staircase leading inside a thick windowless stone wall to the top of the broad-based tower, it must have been a claustrophobic place to live even for a short time.

Jon, and then Andrew, slipped climbing ashore on to slippery rocks. Above the broch, we scrambled over partially crumbled dry stone walls to explore a roofless two-storey house. Small but substantial, it must have been warm and comfortable a hundred years ago. A seagull was sitting on a nest in the corner of what used to be the kitchen.

Another seagull was brooding over an egg just below the steps to a small fenced-off shed between the broch and the house. Ragnar, Ottar, Odd and Jon planted a few Norwegian trees round the shed. The sitting gull gave a single anxious squawk when I trod too near it.

While we were ashore, a number of local boats, including some which had sailed from the farthest islands and *Dim Riv* – Lerwick's own Viking ship, a scaled-down Gokstad replica – had been waiting for a photo-call with *Gaia* arranged by Maurice Mullay, head of the tourist board. He was patient about Ragnar's decision to visit the broch first, rather than according to the schedule, although the change in plans caused delay and disappointment to the waiting crews.

The delay was further prolonged because on the last trip ashore the gummiboat was ripped on a rock. There was a long intermission while Maurice Mullay's launch picked people off the rocks and redistributed them. The crew of the local boats became so cold and bored that they too eventually went ashore to look at the broch. By then half *Gaia's* crew was back on board. The others were still on the rocks with the gummiboat, trying to mend it.

'Wouldn't it make more sense to bring the dinghy back on board and either fix it here, or get it fixed in Lerwick?' Maurice, who was waiting on *Gaia* with us, suggested. We were, however, beginning to acquire the ability to wait without becoming impatient which is an essential adjunct to the relaxed Norse it'll-be-all-right-on-the-night attitude, and knew that there was little point hassling them.

'There are two ways of reading a programme,' Ragnar commented, after re-reading the schedule. It was the first of several minor misunderstandings during our official visit to Shetland.

At last we were ready to move up Mousa Sound towards Lerwick. The wind direction meant that we would have to tack. Although she could easily outsail her escort, all the local traditional boats could both point up higher than *Gaia* and were more swiftly and easily tacked, except perhaps *Dim Riv*, the scaled-down Gokstad replica complete with brightly painted shields and a dragon's head.

We dropped sail to motor into Lerwick harbour, looking a motley lot as we had not changed into Viking gear, partly because we were cold – it was a raw day and the tunics would not have been warm enough – and partly because everyone was fed up with the delays, the misunderstandings, and, most of all, with the punctured dinghy.

'Three cheers for *Gaia*!' came from a colourful contingent of Shetland 'Up-Helly-Aa' neo-Vikings, magnificent in winged helmets and bearing decorated shields. 'Up-Helly-Aa' – from 'Uphalliday', meaning the end of the holiday – is a rumbustious neo-Viking festival invented in Victorian times and held annually at the end of January. The culmination of the annual procession of 'guizer' – mummers – dressed in Wagneresque Viking costumes, and carrying flaming torches, is the ceremonial burning of a large-scale model Viking ship. The mummers then proceed from pub to pub and dram to dram until dawn. In the words of the Up-Helly-Aa song written by its prime instigator, a blind Lerwick poet and scholar, it harks back to the times when 'grand old Vikings ruled upon the ocean vast'. Shetlanders are urged:

Where the fight for freedom rages,

Be bold and strong as they!

The Up-Helly-Aa-ers in their helmets got little response from a crew more concerned with adjusting lines and fenders. It was, for those waiting for us, a disappointing arrival. For David and me there was a welcome bonus with the appearance of Christopher and Valentine Thornhill, fellow Royal Cruising Club members, who came aboard for a wee dram.

The Lerwick Boat Club had invited us all to an evening's informal entertainment. By the time David and I arrived, a little late, speeches were under way, and the club bar was packed and smoky. Ragnar, Odd and Steinar left as soon as the speeches were over; the rest of the crew were already in a bar in town. The men from *Dim Riv* were disappointed not to have a chance to talk about Viking sailing techniques to the Norse experts; and our fellow crew members missed the treat of a violinist of Grapelli standard, accompanied by accordion and guitar, and a buffet supper of immensely generous variety and proportions.

We walked back to the hotel at midnight with the Nissen-Lies. Knut had not been at all happy with the way the crew had comported itself so far in Shetland, Henrich told us; nor was he, and it was not difficult to understand why. We were asked to pass on a request that we should all wear our Viking tunics for the departure. Henrich's chief concern, however, was about what he considered the laxness of some of the safety practices under way. He gave us an example. 'The other night, in the dark and miles from anywhere, I was in the wheelhouse on *Havella* when suddenly with no warning a figure appeared on deck. He had tied his dinghy to the rail in the fog and had climbed aboard unnoticed. It was incredibly dangerous.' The figure was Odd fetching the sugar.

Neo-Viking reputations were partially restored next morning by a good turn-out for an exchange of speeches and gifts at the Town Hall. Kirstin Nissen-Lie and I received brown and grey shell-pattern scarves, the men ties. Some of Shetland's traditional fine lacy shawls and hand-knitted sweaters were on display at a temporary craft show upstairs. None of these could compete, however, with the permanent stained glass windows, each telling a story from Scottish history. My favourites were the twin windows of King James III of Scotland and his wife Margaret, the former Norwegian princess, whose dowry – the Shetland and Orkney Isles – had been mortgaged to the Scots.

Even in Viking days there were never many trees on Shetland; the soil has always been thinner and poorer than in Orkney, and the wind just as strong and salt-laden. However, a consignment of Norwegian saplings flown into Shetland should eventually – weather, sheep and ponies permitting – grow into a small Vinland forest on the outskirts of Lerwick. Ragnar and Knut each planted a symbolic sapling. 'You'll spoil that tree,' Knut was told as he carefully removed stones and broke up soil round the hole for his.

'What time are we leaving?' I asked Øyvard at ten o'clock the next morning.

He looked at his watch: 'Ten o'clock, give or take. This time it's give.'

There was no sign of Ragnar. Water was being pumped from *Havella* to *Gaia*; our mother ship's desalination plant kept our tanks full of sweet fresh water. A wind generator had been fitted, and a couple of new black plastic buckets bought. 'They aren't toilets,' Ottar told me when I commented that they looked more comfortable than the metal bucket. Gunnar had dived soon after dawn to do some essential underwater repairs, and the dinghy had been mended. But our schedule in both Kirkwall and Lerwick had been so full that there had been little time for maintenance and there were still many tasks undone or uncompleted; the VHF radio, for instance, had neither been replaced nor repaired.

Jon was in considerable pain from an infected gash on his leg. 'It happened yesterday, when I went ashore, but then I felt nothing,' he said. By the evening he had been unable to walk, which was one reason he had not attended an official farewell dinner given by the Icelandic and Norwegian governments; the other two reasons were that he was on boat watch duty, and that he preferred whenever possible to avoid large social gatherings. To allow him to rest his leg in the comparative luxury of *Havella*, he and Rikardur were to swop places on the way to our next official stop, the Faroes, just over two hundred nautical miles from Shetland.

By the time we left, nearly two hours late, most of the people who had gathered to see us off had become tired of waiting. It was not an impressive harbour exit. Only Gunnar, David and I had donned Viking tunics. Ragnar came on board at the last minute and took the tiller. There was some lengthy fending and pushing off, but disaster was averted and we hoisted sail near enough to the harbour mouth for the few remaining onlookers to see.

For a while after the rest of our escort of small boats had turned back the Thornhills sailed alongside us in tandem, then they too dropped behind. But Christopher and Valentine were not easily beaten – first they poled out their genoa, then it slithered down and preparations were made for a spinnaker chase. Gunnar, at the helm, ordered sail adjustments, but in vain. 'I don't like it,' he said as they caught us up.

'You've proved your point!' David shouted across as *Sai See* passed us, courtesy of a red and white spinnaker which gave her an advantage over our single sail.

29 May, Wednesday, on passage; 20.30
Foula has just emerged from the fog, majestic in its isolation. The cliffs tower up from the sea to well over mountain height – 1370 and 1220 feet for the Sneug (nothing at all snug about it) and the Kame respectively. Maybe these cliffs make it the legendary Thule seen, according to Tacitus, by Agricola's fleet.

'Terrible place to live,' comments Ragnar. Like us, he has sailed past Foula before, but has never been able to go in there. Not much more than two miles by three, it has no sheltered harbour, and is separated by twenty miles of open Atlantic from the nearest Shetland habitation, and that in itself is pretty remote.

A quarter of a century ago, Eric Linklater called it 'an old folks home remote in the pitiless Atlantic'. He expected the population to die out, but according to the latest edition of his *Orkney and Shetland* there are now more than forty people living on Foula. Until 1880 it had a population of well over two hundred and fifty, who fished from seven traditional rowing boats called sixareens because of the number of oars. The people who live there now don't like visitors, since like the Tristan da Cunhans they mix so little with other people that they have no immunity to germs.

Ragnar is poring over Pacific charts planning *Gaia's* progress round the world after Washington. Odd is on the helm. A few minutes ago *Havella* came so close that Odd told David to call her on the VHF and tell her to steer to port – what a foolish collision that would have been! Although with a good wind *Gaia* sails superbly she does not respond quickly to the helm, and so must keep her distance.

10   Unofficially in the Faroes

30 May, Thursday, 13.00, on passage between Shetland and Faroes.
The morning has been as foggy as the night and evening. At 6.00 am, when our watch came on, it was raw and dank, as if we were sailing in limbo. My breath was white, and it did not take long on the tiller for my hands to be painful with cold. We took it in turns to do tiller stints – an hour at a time was long enough for anyone – and are making good time, keeping up six to seven knots even close-hauled.

In the two-hundred mile gap between Shetland and the Faroes, we sighted our first whale. A distant fin and rounded dark back broke the surface of the water three times, then vanished. Fulmars circled and wheeled around us as if they were part of the air currents. Although it often looked as if their wing tips would dip into the waves, somehow they never did. The Vikings called them 'heste', 'horses of the sea', except at sea, where it was considered unlucky to mention horses, so they were given a second name: *tjalk*.

For a while we had as passengers two small brown birds, which we tentatively identified as godwits. Frode adapted a box as a well-ventilated resting place for the second, which he treated with a gentleness belying his macho image. After a couple of hours, fortified with food and water, it had recovered its strength enough to flutter off happily towards the Faroes, fifty miles ahead. For the original Vikings, without the benefit of charts and log, this would have been a useful clue about the course to steer for land. The variety and number of seabirds increased the nearer we came to the Faroes – another Viking aid to navigation. By a strange trick of the light, the sunset looked just like the sail of a Viking ship on fire; a thousand years ago this might have been interpreted as an omen.

Ragnar called a cabin conference under way, with everyone sitting round the cabin table except Rikardur, who was on tiller duty.

97

'What language shall we speak – Norwegian, Icelandic or English?' Gunnar asked, in Norwegian. We could by then follow some Norwegian, but far from enough; David spoke for all four Brits when he pleaded for an occasional clue.

Everyone laughed when Ottar pointed out that we had had four weeks to learn Norwegian. 'If you can't speak it by now, it's not our fault,' he said lugubriously. We were aware that we were still missing a lot, and especially the light-hearted banter which enlivened every watch.

Ragnar, whose skin looked crumpled with tiredness, took pity on us, and spoke English. 'OK, so we have started, and things are falling into place. But there are still a lot of things which can be done better and be better organized. What is of course a problem is that when we are on shore I am not much on board here – there are a lot of things to do. What Gunnar and Odd and I have agreed is not actually so much different from what it has been so far, but maybe we should make it even clearer. Gunnar will have the responsibility of the ship and the sailing, the hull, rigging, dinghy, life-saving equipment, all that part of it, while Odd will have the responsibility for the "inner services" – provisions, order, information. Together they will work out a watch list for every harbour, make a list of work to be done, things to be bought and so forth. And when I am not here, Gunnar is the skipper.'

'I think that's all about that, and clear,' Gunnar agreed. His English was less fluent than Ragnar's, and he had the additional problem that Norwegian too was a foreign language. 'So, we shall talk a little bit about work in harbour. When we come to the Faroes, we have to tighten the forestay and check everything. And we shall test the survival suits –'

'We're going to throw you in and leave you there for two hours,' Ragnar threatened. '*Havella* is going to pick you up, or try to! It may be a long swim because of the currents and the main winds. I advise you to head for Norway.'

As the laughter subsided, he added: 'We have safety harnesses, but we're not clever enough to use them – this must change. And one more thing. When we are having a pee, that has to be done through the bucket and not overboard. It's OK to do it that way when we are in harbour but not when we are at sea.'

'That's my fault – I started it,' Gunnar admitted. Everyone laughed with him.

'Are you happy in general with the organization?' Odd asked. Since our only serious reservation had been about safety, and in particular about the use of harnesses, David and I were able to say that we were, although we found the reliance on electronics worrying.

'What happens if *Gaia's* electronics pack up?' David later asked Gunnar privately.

'Then I use a sextant. It is in my drawer,' Gunnar said. He had, he told us, always relied on electronic navigation, but in any case he claimed that he had an instinctive in-built navigational ability. Maybe that was how the Vikings navigated. But the one procedure we missed from our own boat was our simple dead reckoning, using a trailing log and with regular position marks on a paper chart, as well as details of course and speed in columns in an exercise book, alongside any general remarks which seemed relevant or interesting.

Gunnar and Odd were keeping an official record, and each of us on *Gaia* was keeping a private diary; Ottar and Frode in particular wrote copiously, and David and I kept our own joint log. But it seemed a pity that there was no general account which we could all read, and in which we could all make entries when we were on watch. The lack of detail of the electronic log was also frustrating for the areas for which *Gaia* had neither detailed paper charts nor information about tidal streams. This was all available on *Havella*, however, and navigational decisions were discussed over the VHF.

Log entry on passage, Shetland to Faroes
Gaia is horsing along at 6.6 knots with a biting northerly breeze. We are listening to Benny Goodman and eating apple cake freshly baked (from a packet) by Ottar the boatbuilder. A mile astern *Havella* is rolling in the swell while we ride it elegantly. Down below there is a great groaning and creaking as the hull flexes with each sea, but the motion is not alarming and the off-duty watch members are in their bunks snoring loudly. We have all dealt with broiled salmon steaks, potatoes and carrots like gannets, and complimented the duty cook: today it was the 'admiral's' turn.

The Faroes, which in fair weather can be seen from far off, rising from the sea as steeply and spectacularly as Foula, were still shrouded in damp cold mist as we made a dawn approach to Suduroy, the most southerly of the eighteen islands. The mist had lifted by the time we had tied up under the stern of a Russian tug at Tvøroyri, the only town on the island but itself little more than a straggling village.

To arrive at the start of a day of blue sky and clear visibility, even if there was a north-easterly nip in the air, was a bonus. The Faroes have the reputation of having rain at least five days a week. As the mist cleared, the deep shadows cast by the early morning sun darkened the brightly painted boxlike houses huddling together at the bottom of steep coarse grass below even steeper rock. On our previous visit to the archipelago, we had spent a day haymaking in a village so overcast by cliffs and mountains that from October to April it was never touched by the sun.

While the others went back to their bunks, David and I made an early morning tour of the town. Within a few minutes, we had left the small central core of shops and houses below us and were on a narrow road leading steeply uphill. There were broad bands of basalt in the rock which towered above us like a long dragon's back against the skyline. Sheep and lambs, sometimes one family per household, sometimes two or three, were fenced into small oddly shaped sloping paddocks.

There are said to be twice as many sheep as people on the islands; and 'Faroe' is an anglicization of Føroyar, from old Norse 'faar oy' – sheep island. The sheep found there by the first Norse settlers, farmers in search of land rather than pillagers looking for plunder, were probably introduced by Irish monks – who wisely left the islands to the Vikings. No one knows if anyone lived on the islands before the monks, nor who the monks were, where they came from, where they retreated to, indeed whether there were any monks at all.

A ninth-century Irish monk called Dicueil wrote about a group of islands thought to be the Faroes: 'A certain holy man informed me that in two summer days and the night between, sailing in a little boat of two thwarts, he came to land on one of them. . . . Some of these islands are very small; nearly all of them are separated one from the other by narrow sounds. On these islands hermits who have sailed from Scotia [Ireland] have lived for roughly a hundred years. But, even as they have been constantly uninhabited since the world's beginning, so now, because of Norse pirates, they are empty of anchorites, but full of innumerable sheep and a great many different kinds of seafowl.'

Dicueil claimed that the islands could be reached 'from the northernmost British Isles in two days' and two nights' direct sailing, with full sails and an undropping fair wind'. The Vikings reckoned on three days and two nights, sixty hours. It took us forty-two hours, although a full week had been allocated on our schedule for the crossing from Shetland to the Faroes, and in unfavourable conditions we might well have needed this, or have had to wait as long for a fair wind.

'This is not an official visit, so we can relax,' Ragnar had said on his way to bed on *Havella*. Official or not, by the time David and I had walked once round the town, thirty schoolchildren and a couple of teachers were standing on *Havella*, looking down on *Gaia*. As soon as news of our arrival had reached the local school, all the children had been given two hours off to visit the Viking ship. Everyone on board both boats was still asleep.

'I was a bit surprised when the hatch was lifted several times,' Steinar said when he emerged, bleary-eyed, from the depths of *Havella*, 'and especially when some children looked down and said "Oh, you're still asleep." '

Throughout our time at Tvøroyri, uninvited guests continued to step aboard at almost any time of the day or night. We would be sitting in the cabin with the half door open, and a head would appear; or with the door fully shut, and when we went outside there would be several people on deck. The Faroese seemed to think this perfectly normal.

The guidebook suggested that after walking along the one main street there was nothing left to do but read a book. This could well be true for people on holiday, but on a boat there are always things to be done. I spent a wet and happy hour hosing and scrubbing decks that afternoon with Odd, who had dispatched David to dispose of a bucket of dirty engine oil. He commented on the tatty state of some of the rope ends: 'They must be whipped,' he said.

'That's something I can do,' I replied, 'I haven't done it for a long time, but I'm sure I can remind myself.'

'You can look it up in the Ashley knot book,' Odd suggested, 'or better still, get one of the others to show you the first time.'

Deck hosing had obviously given him an appetite as afterwards he started frying potatoes and bacon.

'It's a sinful day today,' he said cheerfully, putting Danish pastries on a plate. Jon and Frode were the only others on board. Although his leg was still painful, Jon was back on *Gaia* in a non-working capacity.

We had two women visitors that afternoon. One, who had a baby in a pushchair, was English. A cello teacher at the local music school, she came from Essex, had been in Tvøroyri for five years, and was married to a Faroese.

'I am terribly homesick,' she admitted. 'I look forward to my annual visit home after the end of the school term here.'

Her friend was a Norwegian music teacher. Out of forty-five music staff, fifteen were Faroese, a few Norwegian, five British and the rest Danish. The school operated outside school hours, with salaries paid by the council but with the pupils paying for their tuition. Playing with an orchestra in the Faroese capital, Torshavn, involved the staff in a two-hour ferry journey each way and an overnight there.

Instrumental music has no tradition in the Faroes, since until recently the human voice was the only instrument. The music school had been running for five years, and was still feeling its way. The cool wind of worsening Faroese fortunes was, we were told, a threat to its improvement, and even to its continuation. In spite of an apparently high standard of living, the Faroese economy was in decline and severe cutbacks were being made, with even more economies needed. Education, along with all other domestic policies and finance, was a Faroese responsibility under the home rule granted by Denmark in 1948. Although Denmark was still in control of defence, foreign relations, banking, insurance and justice, the Faroes had underlined their independence from their mother country by staying out of the EEC.

When the visitors left, Odd announced his intention of cleaning the cabin, and sent David, who was officially on domestic duty, to retrieve the bucket which he had disposed of along with the oil; it was wanted after all. I started to tidy the bookshelf.

'I will do that, Judy,' Odd said sharply. The reaction to my offer of washing-up or drying-up was equally curt.

So, effectively barred from the cabin, I decided to start whipping some of the frayed ropes. All I could find to whip with was the sail mending thread.

'Is this what I should use for whipping?' I asked Odd.

'I don't think so – ask Frode.'

'No, it isn't,' Frode said, in the tone of voice of someone who thinks the person asking is too stupid to deserve an answer. 'What do you want it for?'

'To whip some of the untidy rope ends.'

'What ropes?'

'Whichever want doing most – you tell me.'

Odd then chipped in, telling me that we – the Brits – should not be on board in harbour, and should not do any boat jobs.

'You cannot do the jobs,' Frode added belligerently.

'Many we can't, I know,' I agreed, 'but we would like to help when we can. Whipping is something I can do.'

'Then just do it,' Frode shouted, slamming the cabin door and storming out.

There was silence. Odd carried on washing-up. 'Frode has a temper,' he said after a while.

'I have a temper too,' I answered, 'but I would prefer not to lose it.'

'I understand your wish to be involved,' Odd said after another silence. 'But Ragnar promised us that you would only be on the boat at sea, and not in harbour.'

The implication that this had been discussed with the others, and that none of them wanted us around, was hurtful. I felt near to tears – and what an admission of failure that would have been.

'But this is our home as much as anyone else's for the next few months,' I pointed out. 'And if we can't come on the boat in harbour at all, then we aren't part of things on board.'

'Ragnar made it quite clear in Bergen that was what he wanted,' Odd said.

'Ragnar told us we should sleep ashore so that the rest of the crew could have some privacy and invite people on board,' I agreed, 'but I did not think that meant being banned from the boat during the day. And where are we supposed to eat, if that is the case?'

'I don't know, you have to discuss that with Ragnar. We can't lay down the law here.'

'Don't let the buggers get you down,' David advised; and it was not worth spoiling a wonderful adventure by feeling resentful. Both Odd and Frode clearly found it difficult to live in a confined space with a lot of people, and I had the impression that Frode did not like having a woman on board anyway. We were however all stuck with each other, so we might as well make the most of it.

In the large modern school buildings in which we were entertained on that first evening in Tvøroyri, there was more than ample space for its four hundred pupils. As well as an outdoor playground, there was a sizeable covered indoor recreation room, complete with facilities for playing all sorts of sports under cover which I would normally have expected to be played only outdoors.

We were ushered by a local MP, the mayor and the harbour master into the school dining room, used for festivities and receptions rather than for daily school meals. A long table had been laid with candles, flowers, bottled beer and soft drinks, and large vacuum flasks of coffee. As soon as we had finished one plate of sandwiches – with a strong emphasis on fish – it was replaced with another; the supply seemed never-ending, and particularly generous for such an impromptu reception.

When we were taken back to the boats afterwards by coach, it would have seemed natural to go on board *Gaia* with the others. But Frode's brief display of temper and Odd's longer, calmer criticism were inhibiting. As David and I turned to walk back to the hotel, we met the harbour master at the foot of the gangplank to the Russian ship. 'Would you like to go on board?' he asked. And so the three of us spent the rest of the evening, and much of the night, with the Russian captain, Valentin.

'I will show you round my ship,' he promised, 'but first, we drink a toast.'

A bottle of vodka was opened.

'No politics – we are all friends here, and we forget politics,' Valentin insisted. We agreed, and drank toasts to friendship, and to 'no politics'. We were not the ones to introduce politics but, apart from the occasional repetition of the initial toasts, they, and Valentin, dominated the ensuing conversation. We toasted the Russian president, Boris Yeltsin, repeatedly, and each other almost as often, with suitably elaborate phrases. In the lulls we asked questions about the ship. Although Valentin's broken English became increasingly fragmented, we understood that it was two years old and that when it was built in Finland it was the largest ocean-going tug in the world. It was currently employed as a support ship for the Russian fishing fleet, which had several ships in and near Faroese waters. The principal licensed Russian catch was of blue whiting, or coley, for which there was little demand elsewhere.

There were two empty vodka bottles on the captain's table by the time our conducted tour started. 'It is a very clean ship,' he said proudly, 'clean enough to eat from any surface.' To prove his point, he ran a spotless handkerchief down the railing along the stairs on the way to the engine room.

Afterwards, we were taken back to his quarters for more toasts with more vodka. A stewardess was hustled and even shouted at.

'Thank you so much, we really must go,' we said, not for the first time.

'No, you cannot go, she is bringing you food.'

A feast appeared. It was well after midnight, and we had already had one feast that evening, but we could not refuse. The stewardess, who was instructed to join us but was ill at ease, abstained from vodka, which continued to flow freely.

'Once in Finland I was arrested for having vodka on board,' Valentin told us. The injustice obviously still rankled. 'I tell them I must have vodka for my guests, it is part of my job. But they kept me in a police cell all night.'

The sixteen bottles he had mentioned as being a reasonable ration for a shore stop had been considerably depleted by the time we left, not long before dawn. The harbour master, who was worried about driving two miles to his home, spent the night on board.

His colleague the customs officer lent us a car next day so that we could explore the island. There was only one main road, with half a dozen short diversions which soon came to dead ends. In one afternoon, we drove through or past all but five of the island's sixteen villages. They differed only marginally in size and steepness. The focal point in most was a fish factory, plainer but more noticeable than the churches.

The landscape was grandiose, equally rugged inland and along the coastal cliffs – and particularly at the southern end of the island, along the high west coast cliffs on the way to the village of Sumba and the lighthouse of Akraberg, which looked as if it might fall off the end of the world. We leant carefully out and down to see the myriads of squawking seabirds nesting on the cliff face. Little clumps of pink seathrift clung to patches of soil in rock clefts.

Halfway back to Tvøroyri, we stopped at the tiny harbour of Vágur, at the top of one of twenty-one authorized Faroese whaling bays. We had been told that two weeks before our arrival Vágur had had a whale hunt – *grindadráp*, or *grind* – a *grind* being a school of pilot whales, individually *grindahvalur*. The Faroese consider their non-commercial *grind*, during which pilot whales are rounded up at sea, driven into a bay for slaughter, and shared among the local people according to ancient rules, to be a vital part of their cultural heritage. Since the Faroes now enjoy a high standard of living with regular imports of alternative fresh food, outsiders find it difficult to share this interpretation of the frequent but irregular mass slaughter in shallow bays from which the whales cannot escape.

During our absence, the Russian stewardess and her friend had taken up our invitation to visit *Gaia*. Communication was difficult – the only common language being English, of which the girl we had met spoke little, and her friend none. There was to be a Saturday evening Faroese dance on the island, and after the two girls had spent the first part of the evening on *Gaia*, it seemed a logical extension of international goodwill to invite them to it. Gunnar put the request officially to the Russian second in command. A few minutes later, one of the men from the Soviet ship unceremoniously ordered the girls to return, with much shouting. The tug's gangplank was drawn up behind them.

After our Russian evening the night before, David and I opted out of the dance. Andrew put in a brief appearance next morning at a late hotel breakfast, and then retired to bed. Nigel was not seen until much later, and then only briefly.

Alcohol had, we gathered, flowed freely, from full-strength beer bought openly to a variety of hip flasks and a Thermos flask of coffee mixed with vodka and beer. All ages danced, old-fashioned ballroom style, until the light end of the early hours. Judging from the effect on our fellow crew members, anyone who attends weekend dances as a regular part of Faroese life must need a couple of days a week for recovery ready for the next social onslaught.

In an attempt to curb alcoholic excesses, during the last century alcohol was banned in the Faroes; we were told it had all too often led to a Faroese form of going berserk: men in their cups paid in kind, with land, to have them refilled. Life was so tough in the early 1800s that it was not uncommon for farmers to barter land for groceries – but it was taking the barter system too far when the price of a hangover was all too often the family home. Since prohibition had little effect on alcoholism, it had been abandoned, but alcohol was still rationed. Although the subject had, we gathered, been raised in Parliament more than once, there were still neither pubs nor hotel bars, and it was impossible to have an alcoholic beverage other than very light local beer with a meal out. Even the stronger beer brewed locally could only be bought after a complicated procedure of form filling and advance payment at a post office. All other alcohol had to be imported, by licence. Resident adults were entitled to a quarterly ration, provided they had paid their taxes. There were, of course, ways of getting round even the strictest restrictions – like buying vodka from Russian seamen – and a certain amount of derestriction seems almost inevitable if, as we were told time after time, the Faroese seriously wish to extend tourism.

'We are all going to church,' we had been informed by Rikardur after supper on Saturday, but that was before the dance had sabotaged Sunday. David and I were the only 'Gaians' at morning service, at the end of which there was a multiple christening. A wooden boat, a copy of an old sailing fishing smack, hung from the roof. The one time when all Faroese churches were left unlocked was, we were told by the mayor, on whale hunting days – 'because whales are so important for us'.

It seemed unlikely that anyone else on *Gaia* would want any lunch, but as I was officially on duty I thought I should show willing, in spite of what Odd had said. In the meantime, after giving the subject serious consideration, he had made a point of telling me that we could after all eat on board during shore stops. The cabin was closed against the sun. Inside, Ottar was sitting looking almost alive with a cup of coffee. He had gone to bed at about three, he told me, but he thought that the others had stayed up talking and drinking all night. Jon was fast asleep stretched out on one bench. Gunnar was sitting on the other, equally fast asleep with his head on the table.

'I think it is not necessary to put food out,' Ottar said. We ate at the hotel.

Later, David looked with Audun and Øyvard at the video sequence Audun had shot of *Gaia* on the way from Lerwick. It was only a few seconds long, but well composed and steadily held. *Gaia* dipped and rose in the slight swell.

'Later on we are bound to get big seas, then she'll disappear,' David commented.

'Not completely, I hope,' I put in.

'If she does – just make sure you keep filming,' David said.

It snowed – not in the harbour, but visibly on the high ground – during supper, for which everyone was present but many still seemed less than half-conscious. Most of our evening was spent trying to trace *Vinland*, the Swiss-built Viking ship replica which the Norse had feared might present a threat by making the North Atlantic crossing faster than *Gaia*. She had been scheduled to reach Bergen after our ceremonial departure, but then to sail directly to Iceland. As she was already a week overdue in Bergen, Harald Bjerke initiated a *pan* call asking if anyone had seen her. This alerted Norwegian journalists; they contacted Ragnar, who asked us if we had the Swiss phone number. Eventually, after several phone calls in various directions, it transpired that *Vinland* was in Amsterdam. This was a relief, and we were pleased to be able to pass on the news in *Havella's* comfortable depths to Odd. He had temporarily replaced Steinar, who had flown back to Norway for a few days, and was in a particularly friendly and jovial mood. Ragnar was audible in the forecabin, where he was coughing and sneezing miserably in his bunk with a heavy cold.

He recovered enough to order us all to go swimming next afternoon, and to swim with us – to test the survival suits, and perhaps ourselves.

It was not nearly as bad as I had feared, although the suits, one-piece garments incorporating boots, but with separate gloves and inner hoods, took a bit of getting into. Then, when they were zipped up to the neck, it was important to double up so that all the air was forced out, holding the neckline away from the body with one hand to allow it to escape.

All the men jumped in, most of them holding their noses. Since I am a coward about water, I climbed down on to a fender and slithered in. Swimming was strange – the swimmers looked and felt like damp space men, making large floating gestures and not getting anywhere much on our fronts. At least on our backs we went vaguely in the right direction. Climbing back on board *Havella* was awkward, but possible.

Ragnar, Gunnar, Odd and Frode performed an impressive Viking synchro swimming display. It was almost the first time I had seen Ragnar without a cigarette; but even for such an avid smoker, jumping overboard in a survival suit with a lighted roll-your-own was too much of a challenge.

There was to be an early start next morning – and 'early' was for the first time really early. We were motoring out of harbour by 5.00 am. *Havella* then took us in tow, in a lumpy sea with wind against tide. The currents round the Faroes are strong, and not to be trifled with. Some of the strongest are caused by the parting of the sea round Lítla (little) and Stóra (big) Dímun, past both of which we were towed. Lítla Dímun, the smallest island in the archipelago, is a steep hump rising up from three-hundred-foot sheer cliffs to a grass summit nearly a thousand feet above sea level. Its half a square mile hardly seems fit to live on, but it is said to have been inhabited by Irish monks, whose dark brown sheep were still there when the first Vikings arrived. One family spends part of the year – with sheep – on its bigger sister. Stóra Dímun, which is still small at nearly three times the size, now has a helicopter service.

After the Dímuns, we passed the least rugged of the islands, Sandoy, so-called because of its dunes. Our destination was the tiny settlement of Kirkjubøur just above the south-west tip of the largest island, Streymoy.

'This is a private visit,' Ragnar told us. We had been invited to visit Påll and Trondur Patursson, twin brothers whose family had farmed at Kirkjubøur for fifteen generations. Påll, who had taken over the farm, lived with his wife Sólva and their children in the old farmhouse built on the site of a tenth-century Viking bishopric. Having their home in a national monument had its drawbacks. Although Påll and Sólva received no government grants towards the upkeep of the property, they were expected to open all except their private accommodation to the public, and to host official banquets at frequent intervals in the old timbered hall.

Trondur, who had built himself a new house and artist's studio a few hundred yards uphill of the Viking homestead, had sailed on Tim Severin's leather boat, *Brendan*, in the wake of the mythical ninth-century Irish monk who may or may not have reached North America before Leif Eiriksson.

We were within sight of Kirkjubøur when Ragnar issued an instruction from *Havella* that anything visible which did not look Viking was to be dismantled or disguised instantly. As a preliminary to our private visit, a young Norwegian singer called Sissel Kyrkjebø was about to come on board, with a couple of film crews who were making a pop video, using Kirkjubøur as a background because of the link between the names, although Sissel's family did not claim any direct genealogical connection. We motored past our destination, so that we could sail back towards it.

Ragnar rejoined *Gaia*, wearing his Viking tunic; Sissel, muffled up in a woolly hat and scarf, was brought aboard with the two film crews and a Faroese schoolgirl from an island choir. The two girls posed together, and Sissel posed alone and with Ragnar, to be filmed and photographed from every angle. In spite of the adulation we were assured was her due, she seemed unspoiled, unassumingly open and friendly. She did not sing on the boat, but we listened while she was being recorded in Kirkjubøur's roofless grey stone Viking cathedral. She sounded as sweet as she looked, with a clear pure voice which had gained her a wide following in Norway. It was doing so in the Faroes, judging by her reception a couple of evenings later in Torshavn's grass-roofed cultural centre, the Nordic House, where she shared a concert platform with a Norwegian harmonica player and composer, Sigmund Groven, and two Faroese choirs.

From the water, there seemed no obvious reason for a settlement at Kirkjubøur, which straggled obliquely uphill from the original church site beneath uninvitingly steep cliffs. But the Vikings who built houses, a bishopric and church and erected the outer walls of a cathedral there knew what they were doing. Its harbour was a natural trap for driftwood. In these treeless islands, which relied on wooden boats for communication, trade and to a large extent food, this was an invaluable commodity.

Local driftwood was used by Trondur Patursson to make furniture for his house half a mile away from the harbour. Sitting round a large plain wooden table in its main room, he and his wife Borgny offered us home-made and Faroese-brewed beer, and invited us to try the local delicacies of dried fish, smoked dried lamb and whale blubber. I liked the lamb, but found the smell and taste of the blubber, already a couple of years old, too strong, even when a little was eaten with a piece of the dried fish.

'This is the picture the British all love to see,' Borgny told us, pointing out a framed colour photograph showing Trondur thigh deep in blood in the act of dispatching one of several pilot whales. It may have been the whale whose blubber we had just been offered: I did not ask. We had said nothing about whaling, but because we were British Borgny assumed that we were opposed to it and launched into an empassioned defence. She felt particularly strongly about the hypocrisy of British and American critics. 'How can people who kill children [by napalm bombing in Vietnam] condemn the Faroese for killing whales?' she asked.

Later in the evening, her son Brandur took the same photograph of Trondur down from the wall and talked with equal passion about the rightness of whaling. He was clearly proud of the photo and looked forward to taking his own place in the whale hunt when he was older. It was difficult to imagine the pale thoughtful teenager, who was about to go by ferry on a school trip to Iceland, glorying in killing, even with the justification that it was for food.

I was relieved that Brandur's sister Diana, as dark-haired and beautiful as her mother, did not mention whaling. She was more concerned about being out of work because of cutbacks. Having lost her job in local government, she felt that her training and experience were useless and so had gone back to college. After a year's study in Torshavn, she planned to study economics and marketing in Copenhagen for two years, and then return to the Faroes 'to put a bomb under selling'. 'Our crafts are not properly developed or exploited,' she explained, 'nor is tourism.'

Before walking back down the hill with us for supper at the old bishopric, where Sólva was serving a first sitting for Sissel and her entourage, Trondur showed us his studio. His most recent work, and so that about which he was most informative and enthusiastic, was in thick, heavy, layered stained glass. He moved some of his favourite finished designs so that the natural light through the open door would show us the richness of the colours. The blues were particularly vibrant. Huge semi-figurative panels leant against walls; smaller panels were stacked on tables. Among his earlier work I preferred figurative sketches and watercolours to later large garish paintings inspired by Faroese nature. Although the studio was on the side of the hill, there were no windows overlooking the sound and the islands over which the clouds cast constantly changing shadows. 'Perhaps the view would be distracting,' Odd suggested.

Toasting glasses were passed around with hospitable frequency, first by Trondur and Borgny, and then at the bottom of the hill in Påll and Sólva's *roykstova* – literally smoke room, from the atmosphere caused by the open fire of a traditional Faroese living room. Kirkjubøur's *roykstova* was part of the so-called timbered rooms open to the public. According to local legend, these were built in Norway, then dismantled and carried by ship part of the way to an unknown new destination. The kit house reached its present site, probably some time in the fourteenth century, when the ship was wrecked or attacked by pirates: the details are vague. The massive log structure, re-erected on top of the basement of the earlier bishop's palace, had originally included a much bigger and higher medieval hall.

The warmth of Sólva's welcome was undimmed by the work caused by having to cater for a second sitting of thirty people, with a formal government dinner for forty to prepare for the next day. It was late in the evening by the time we – the crews of *Gaia* and *Havella*, the Patursson brothers and their wives, some of Påll and Sólva's children, and several of their employees on the farm and house – sat down to eat traditional boiled Faroese lamb. The Norwegian couple who looked after the cows and helped in the house had come to Kirkjubøur from Gøteborg, on the west coast of Sweden; the wife had spent ten months in Britain before that, and spoke fluent Glaswegian.

The cows could not, she told us, be allowed outside until July, and then only for a couple of months; even in the short Faroese summer the average temperature was unlikely to exceed 10°C. For the rest of the year, they stood with huge hoops round their necks in a first floor barn. The calves were free to wander within the confines of the barn but did not stray far from their mothers.

Our first environmental mission to the Faroes had been carried out on our arrival at Kirkjubøur, when Ragnar presented the cask of twenty frozen Norwegian cow embryos to Påll and another senior representative of Faroese dairy farming. Faroese cattle were by then already largely of Norwegian origin, but through straightforward artificial insemination rather than through implantation of embryos.

As there was no hotel at Kirkjubøur we were staying on *Gaia* at night – which did not appear to present any problems. When we arrived back on board at midnight, we discovered that *Havella* had borrowed the electric plug from *Gaia*. This caused much to-ing and fro-ing by gummiboat, during which the last dregs of everyone's whisky supplies were consumed and Ottar inadvertently coined a new name for the pigeon holes in which we stored small personal belongings in *Gaia's* main cabin: these were known from then on as 'chicken holes'.

Gunnar stayed up through two-thirds of my anchor watch. He had not been sleeping well, and talked for a long time about various things which were worrying him. As the only Icelandic on *Gaia*, he was very conscious of being seriously outnumbered by the Norwegians: more significantly, he felt that his responsibility as skipper was frequently undermined. 'I lie awake and think of these things,' he told me. 'I plan to have it out with Ragnar, and maybe if I do not like what he says I shall leave.' I very much hoped that he would not find this necessary, although I could appreciate that being skipper and not being skipper put him in a difficult position, and that he was particularly concerned about his professional pride when we reached Iceland. 'People in Iceland know that I am skipper,' he said, 'and they will not like it if they see that I am not really skipper.'

A strange but beautiful light filtered from the moon through clouds which by morning had deposited more snow on the high ground. After four hours of fitful sleep, I walked up the hill hoping to accept Borgny's offer of a shower. The house was unlocked, but deserted, the pervasive smell of whale blubber lingering over its elegant simplicity.

Some of the crew were energetic enough to climb up the mountain side to a small cave way above the narrow steeply sloping strip of grazing land between the sound and the cliff face stretching almost sheer above it. A Kirkjubøur milkmaid who had found brief favour with a king of Norway is claimed to have kept their illegitimate son hidden in the cave. The story has a happy ending: she found a husband, and eventually, after a long struggle, the boy himself became king of Norway.

'The cave was tiny – I can't see how anyone could have lived in it, even a child: and there really wasn't much to see,' David reported. Andrew and I, who had declined to climb with the others, felt that our laziness was vindicated. I was in no way tempted to emulate the Faroese who traditionally added sea-birds and eggs to their diet by scaling the cliffs in search of free food. Even for locals, the cliffs could be dangerous. A few months before our visit, one of the Kirkjubøur farmhands had fallen nearly two hundred feet to the rocks. When he came round, in hospital in Torshavn, the first thing he said was: 'I was on a tractor' – which was a write-off. He was lucky to survive, although he still needed a crutch to walk.

Odd gave David and me carte blanche to sort out the space intended as the heads so that there was at least room to use the bucket under cover, rather than on deck. Although as the only woman on board I had been determined neither to ask for nor to expect any concessions, I was relieved to have some privacy at last – and so, as they admitted, were the men. A few days later, a bolt was added to the inside of the door.

Havella had excellent facilities. There were two flushing sea toilets and fresh hot and cold water to a wash basin and shower in her main heads, a forecabin that slept two and a luxurious saloon with maroon velvet upholstery. Everyone's spare gear was stowed in her second heads, between an aft cabin with four bunks (she had sleeping accommodation for ten altogether) and an engine room equipped with a washing machine and dryer. There was still a general them-and-us feeling between the two boats, with a certain amount of amicable rivalry. While Odd was temporarily on *Havella*, he became one of 'them', and seemed more relaxed when he visited us on *Gaia* than when he was living on board. We made jokes about how he was being seduced by the soft life of luxury on *Havella*, but what he probably appreciated most was that with fewer people there was more individual space.

By the time we left Kirkjubøur for our official entry to the Faroese capital, Torshavn, we had been in the archipelago for a week and had already been the recipients of so much unofficial hospitality that our official welcome had a lot to live up to. Relationships on board had dipped, but had risen again, and we had all appreciated having some free time before resuming our duties and being constantly on public display.

11 A Whale of a time in the Faroes

Gaia was escorted towards Torshavn by three restored sailing smacks, stately under full sail. They had however been left behind by the time we motored into the harbour, accompanied by dozens of assorted smaller boats. Many of these were very much along traditional local double-ended Viking lines, but without sails. Sailing has never caught on as a sport in the Faroes: the sea is too serious, too dangerous – a place to earn a living, catch food, all too often to die, but not a playground.

Until 1872, when the first sloop was introduced from Britain to improve the efficiency of the Faroese fishing fleet, open rowing boats were used for fishing and whaling. The first auxiliary engines were installed in the sloops in 1930. During the war, the Faroese fleet provided nearly a quarter of all fish eaten in Britain, with the loss of twenty-five boats and one hundred and thirty-two fishermen. Churchill's promise that the courageous support of the Faroese would never be forgotten had however a hollow ring: less than half a century later, all that most people in Britain seemed to know about the Faroes was that they still hunted whales there, and their name in the shipping weather forecast.

Flags, music, speeches and exchanges of compliments and gifts greeted us as we came alongside. There were more speeches and presentations at an official reception in the government building in the oldest part of the town, Tinganes. Old houses, built of wood although none grows on the islands, some with sagging turf roofs, cluster tightly together along alleys too narrow for cars on a small spit of land between the old and new harbour.

Reciprocal thanks and congratulations continued the following evening, first at a large and sumptuous cocktail party given jointly by the Norwegian and Icelandic governments, and then at a formal dinner at which, as guests of honour of the Faroese government, we were equally generously catered for. Many of the Faroese speeches were given in Danish, spoken slowly and carefully since it was the speakers' second language. This made it much easier for the British contingent to follow.

At the official dinner, I was again subjected to passionate Faroese defences of whaling. It was disconcerting throughout our stay in Torshavn to find ourselves repeatedly under attack about what was assumed to be our attitude to the pilot whale hunt, even when we ourselves did not raise the subject. The Norwegian and Icelandic crew members were considered pro-whaling allies.

The question put to us most often was: 'What right have other people to tell us what to do?' It is only a generation since the Faroese relied on whale blubber and meat for survival; environmentalists are now trying to impose on them an instant change in attitude which has evolved gradually elsewhere. The Faroes have, however, never had the luxury of agricultural and industrial choice. Their traditional harvest came from the sea – and the more people tell them to change their ways, the more fiercely they are likely to resist. Ironically, outside interference has consolidated solidarity and those Faroese previously opposed to or concerned about the whale hunt have closed ranks to resist pressure from organizations such as Greenpeace and the Environmental Investigation Agency (EIA).

An EIA team spent several months in the Faroes in the mid-1980s. Its leader, Allan Thornton, will not be satisfied until the Faroese agree to end their pilot whale hunt, the *grindadráp*. 'Can you justify such a basic sport hunt by modern wealthy Scandinavians?' he asks indignantly. 'What right do the Faroese have to kill whales? They do not own the whales.'

Several people told me that Greenpeace had withdrawn its objections to the Faroese whale hunt, a statement which I found surprising, but had for the time being to accept as it also appeared in print in a recently published book. It was emphatically denied at the organization's London office.

'Greenpeace opposes Faroese whaling on the grounds that the size and status of the stock is unknown,' I was told by Andy Ottoway, a senior campaigner. 'We are for the phase-out of a hunt which we consider unjustified and unnecessary.'

Pollution, rather than the empassioned campaigning of the anti-whaling lobby, may yet limit and in the long term eventually stop the hunting of pilot whales. Faroese government health warnings have been issued about the danger of frequent consumption of the meat and blubber because of high levels of mercury and PCBs – pollution caused, it is pointed out, by Britain and other European countries.

I wished that I could have discussed the whaling question objectively with my fellow Gaians, but if we mentioned it at all, the Norse still thought we were trying to be controversial. Nigel, whose wife was a vegetarian, was just as intransigent on the anti-whaling side of the fence.

After we had tactfully moved away from the subject of whaling, my Icelandic dinner neighbour admitted, 'I don't understand what the whole Gaia thing is about.' This inadvertently brought us back to whaling via my attempt to explain. All conversation was brought to an end, however, when Faroese and foreign guests alike were invited to join in a ring dance.

The Faroese are proud of their medieval ring dancing, which survives only in their islands and which was until this century their only form of music. Participants link arms in a circle, or a serpentine when there are too many for a circle. Learning the steps presented no great difficulty even to non-dancers like Andrew. All members of the ring move together, two steps to the left, one back to the right, swaying and knee-bending. Progress is slow and solemn, or lively and bouncy, depending on which of hundreds of long ballads is accompanying the dance.

The songs themselves are the Faroese equivalent of the Icelandic sagas, a way of keeping the old stories alive and handing them down through the generations. Those we heard all seemed to share a chorus based on the repetition of something sounding like 'dansa i ring, dansa i ring'. Although the Faroes have their own fourteenth-century saga, *Færeyínga Saga*, by an Icelandic writer who knew the islands by hearsay, it is only a hundred years since they acquired an independent written language. The official language was Danish until home rule gave Faroese equal status in 1948. So the ring dance ballads are their entire literary tradition.

A special demonstration was laid on for us at Torshavn's eight-year-old Nordic House, which had been conceived and built as a Faroese, Danish, Norwegian, Swedish and Finnish cooperative cultural venture, from its glass-sided steel-framed grass-roofed design and structure to its internal wood fittings and furnishings to its everyday running and maintenance.

The dancers were splendid in their colourful national costume, with individual variations of colour and pattern. The women wore aprons over long skirts, with tightly fitted laced bodices, belts and shoes with silver clasps and buckles and shawls fastened with elaborate silver brooches. The men were almost as colourful, with silver buckled shoes, stockings, knee-length breeches with tassels and a side row of silver buttons, coloured decorative waistcoats and woollen jackets with a dozen silver buttons down each straight front edge. Like the language, the national costume has only evolved recently, although it is based on traditional Sunday best clothing.

Halfway through a dance, one of the women left the circle and sat down to rest. I realized at the same time as a couple of ring-dancers that she was more than just tired. The dancing stopped, an ambulance was called, and she was carried into the Nordic House. By the time the ambulance arrived, the dancers had resumed their singing swaying circle. The invalid, who had had a heart attack, died in hospital later that evening.

'I'm so sorry . . .' I said later to one of her fellow dancers.

'There is no need to feel sorry,' she replied. 'It was a wonderful way to go, doing what she loved most.'

The Faroese still have an acceptance of death which stems from the toughness of their traditional life. The overwhelming impression after a visit to their national art gallery, Listaskálin, was of death and disaster at sea, of dark colours relieved only by the gore of the whale hunt. As official neo-Vikings, we benefitted from the knowledge of a leading Faroese art historian, Bardur Jakupsson.

The first, most famous, and most influential of all Faroese artists was Sámal Elias Joensen Mikines, born in 1906 on the island of Mykines. His pictures show a melancholy considered typical of the Faroe Islands, and of what our guide called the 'mainstream of Faroese art' – though he admitted that was still in its infancy. Much of Mikines' painting was inspired by life on his home island, where a sizeable fishing community had shrunk since the war to a population of fifteen, and where while he was growing up one in four of the men had died in disasters at sea or on the cliffs. Many others, including three of his siblings, had succumbed to 'the island disease', tuberculosis.

Even, or perhaps especially, at the gallery, it was impossible to escape from whaling. Trondur Patursson was represented by 'Atlas', a square column of driftwood holding up part of the skull of a sperm whale mounted on glass. Among the few other sculptures on display – 'As a painter you can live on the Faroe Islands,' Jakupsson told us, 'as a sculptor it is more difficult' – was a white three-dimensional representation of three hatchet-faced men, each with a foot on a whale, knees bent, chin in hands.

It was however Mikines who depicted the *grindadráp* most vividly, his wild colours intensifying its emotional and physical drama. A whaling enthusiast could no doubt interpret his paintings as a glorification of the life and death struggle of the whale hunt – and an animal rights environmentalist could see in the same paintings the most passionate rejection.

Fishing, traditionally equally important to the Faroese way of life, does not attract the same violent polarization, although it too is under threat because of declining fish stocks. At Faroe Sea Food, a sales cooperative employing seventy people in its main building, owned by the producers living round the islands, and with subsidiaries at Grimsby in England as well as in Denmark, we were treated to a fish buffet lunch after our visit to the art gallery. Founded in 1948 to export salt fish, its trade had later embraced all sorts of fresh, frozen and salted fish on behalf of well over a hundred members. A sixth of the total population of the islands depended directly on the fish co-op, many more indirectly.

Because of the growing shortage of fish, the government wanted boats taken out of its fishing fleet. Some had already been sold to Canada and New Zealand. It was considered essential for the Faroes' economic future to make fishing pay as well as it used to, rather than to look for an alternative form of income. One solution suggested was to close fishing for a couple of weeks, with longer bans in certain areas. Fish farming was proving less of a help than had been anticipated.

Feelings between the Faroes and Iceland were according to our hosts less than amicable. 'The Icelandics claim that the migration routes of their wild salmon are through the Faroes, and so they want to be able to fish for them here,' we were told. 'An agreement has been drawn up, but not yet ratified, whereby Iceland would pay the Faroes to stop Faroese boats from fishing salmon in the North Atlantic.'

The answer seemed to be that it was 'cheaper and easier to buy fish than to fish fish', so the Faroese were already buying fish from Alaska, Russia, Canada, Iceland and Norway – but mostly from Alaska – to process for export.

We paid a brief visit later to a government fish farm, where fish were being bred experimentally to try to increase their rate of growth. In one of a series of tanks under cover on land, huge halibut did their best to bite any hand that fed them. Salmon in circular pens on the edge of the sound between the islands of Streymoy and Eysturoy jumped and twisted as if in vain efforts to escape, although we were told that they were merely trying to catch food pellets in the air.

Not far along the road from the fish farm, our guide, a student called Randi, pointed out an ugly rectangular single storey building. 'That is the NATO station,' she said with a hint of distaste. 'It was planted there by the Danes, in the late fifties. The Faroese people didn't like to have it. But we were not asked. It just came like a thief in the night.'

Although the British, or as Randi called them the English, had also come uninvited, their arrival a week after the German occupation of Denmark had been welcomed. 'There are very good relations between the Faroese and the English,' Randi told us. Many British men had taken Faroese wives during the war.

As we skirted the edge of a steep valley, we listened to Randi's story about its history. 'It's called the Valley of the Fallen People, and it's the site of the only civil war in the Faroes. In the eleventh century there was a battle for the cathedral at Kirkjubøur. The people on the south islands didn't want to pay taxes for the cathedral. This resulted in two battles – one was here. The southern islanders won, and that's why the cathedral was never finished. The grass is said to be red because of the blood; many people have seen this.'

Apparently otherwise rational people have observed the phenomenon of the red grass, although that day it looked a perfectly normal green.

At the risk of seeming controversial, we asked Randi her views on whaling. She described a traditional hunt: 'When the signal is given that whales have been seen, everyone stops work. The whales are driven into a narrow bay, and they make their own tidal wave which carries them right on to the beach. Then the water goes down and they are stranded. Killing them is very skilled – it's done with a special knife so that they die as quickly as possible. The meat is shared out between all the people in that area; everyone gets some. That's the way it's always been done, it's part of our culture, and it isn't commercial, and the pilot whale isn't an endangered species.'

The destination of our bus tour was Saksun, a tiny place overshadowed by mountains at the head of a minute, steep and narrow fjord, the entrance to which has been blocked since a severe storm some years ago. An old farmstead has been turned into a small museum. Only twenty years ago, its tiny low-ceilinged, turf-roofed rooms were still in family use. Like all old Faroese houses, the main construction was of wood, which seemed to me particularly obtuse in a cluster of islands where the only trees were those planted recently in sheltered positions in Torshavn.

As part of our environmental mission, Ragnar planted a symbolic sapling at a site selected for a small Norwegian plantation, near Torshavn's new shopping centre. In spite of the quality of the shops, the skeletal building of glass and brightly coloured tubes looked strangely impermanent and could have been anywhere in the western world. Although the city had grown considerably in the fifty or so years since the Faroese novelist William Heinesen described it as 'only a scrap of a town, between sea and mountain moor', I could not help hoping that its modern suburbs would be outlived by its oldest and most picturesque buildings, tightly packed on the tiny steeply twisting alleyways of Tinganes above twin harbours.

Gaia and *Havella* were moored in the newer harbour, where a demonstration of rowing by both male and female racing teams enlivened our Saturday afternoon. David, Andrew, Nigel and I followed this on the local radio launch, from which a live running commentary was broadcast to all those Faroese unable to gather in the sun to watch. A couple of windsurfers did their best to keep out of the way of the racers. We considered them intrepid to the point of foolhardiness to attempt their sport in the Faroese climate and currents.

Our shore accommodation in Torshavn was at the old harbour in the Seaman's Mission, where in spite of a ban on alcohol on the premises we were kept awake one night by a raucous party in a neighbouring room. There was a slight contretemps between the Brits and the Norse when Andrew and Nigel discovered that not only were they expected to share a room as usual (contrary to what they were used to on film trips) but that on this occasion it had only one double bed. A room with single beds was eventually made available.

A rash announcement had been made on behalf of the ten smoking neo-Vikings: both *Gaia* and *Havella* were to become non-smoking boats from the moment we left Torshavn – well, maybe not quite instantly. When we left, at 4.00 pm on a Sunday afternoon, after a speech by Ragnar and another by the prime minister of the Faroes, the deadline was pushed back to midnight. Nigel, David and I on *Gaia*, and Øyvard on *Havella*, looked forward to smoke-free cabins, but with some apprehension about what giving up would do to the tempers of the converts.

Although we left with several hours of foul tide ahead of us, it was good to be under way again, even on a grey lumpy sea. Round the headlands as we passed between the islands of Streymoy and Sandoy the effect of wind against tide was dramatic, with steep seas which Gunnar watched anxiously over his shoulder as they threatened to swamp us. Audun, a professional seaman with considerable experience of sailing in the Arctic and Antarctic, said later that this was the most dangerous part of the voyage.

Gaia coped well, although the gummiboat – which as usual we were towing – charged at and round her stern, and for a while seemed certain either to finish on top of us or to capsize. It would perhaps have been more sensible to stow it when we set out. Instead, Odd had half an hour of damp excitement as he was bounced violently up and down alongside *Gaia* trying to remove the outboard. Eventually he succeeded, the dinghy was hauled aboard and stowed along the port side deck, and Ottar set to work with a saw to make a space for the outboard under the forward decking.

The Brits happened to meet on the starboard side deck while he was doing this. 'It'll be all right on the night,' David remarked.

'That's all very well,' Nigel said. 'Which night? And what about the day?'

Not being an experienced sailor, Andrew had never before encountered the violent effect on the sea of wind against tide. 'I was bloody terrified just now,' he admitted. 'I couldn't think why everyone wasn't getting into life jackets.'

By then, we were under tow, and grateful that we were on *Gaia*, as *Havella* was rolling even more violently than usual. Once we were clear of Hestur and Koltur, horse and colt, two small steep wedge-shaped islands rising dramatically from the sound west of Kirkjubøur, the sea settled down and we were able to hoist sail, with two pre-set reefs. I felt a sense of pride in doing my share with what I considered smugly was quiet efficiency. Odd produced supper of fillet steaks, spuds and salad, which contrary to what I had anticipated a couple of hours earlier I enjoyed.

The evening scenery was unforgettable, with views of the stacks and cliffs and steep escarpments of Vágur and Mykines, and the atmosphere on board was relaxed and amicable. With a liberal sprinkling of Anglo-Saxon, Ragnar aired his views on a long list of criticisms he had received by fax from Oslo about details like dirty fenders and frayed ropes – which were still unwhipped. He was especially irritated that no one had said anything about the Gaia message in the Faroes.

Halfway through the evening, David suddenly remembered some amazingly bawdy National Service words to a chorus of 'Oh what a horrible song, sing me another one'. He, Ragnar, Ottar and Odd sang verse after verse enthusiastically while I sat sewing and singing more sedately on the liferaft in the late evening light. Our Gaia pennant finished the watch a metre shorter, at Ragnar's request, to stop the end catching in the rigging.

It was still light enough to read or write or sew outside at the midnight watch change, although by then the visual magic of the Faroes was beginning to recede.

'Is there any whisky left under you?' Odd asked as he put out mugs for a midnight brew of special tea; I was sitting on the starboard bench under which the Orkney samples had been stowed.

'Not a hope – I think we've all looked at least twice,' Andrew said. Ten days in the Faroes can have this effect even on the most abstemious and soberminded crew.

Before our watch turned in, there was a midnight feast of whale blubber, a Faroese gift which Ragnar and Odd appreciated more than some of the rest of us.

'Do you eat this from choice?' David asked. There were enthusiastic 'yes' noises from those who did. David chewed a bit more, then asked: 'If we are supposed to be sending a message to the world about the environment, what are we doing eating whale blubber?'

'Whales are part of the environment,' Ragnar answered, still chewing. 'It's not an endangered species.'

'For the Faroese, it's like harvesting part of the nature that they have,' Odd added.

A midnight ceremony was made of Ragnar's last cigarette, although none of the rest of us believed that he would succeed in giving up.

'You just take one day – and one day – and one day –' he said.

'And this is the day?' David asked.

'We'll give it a try,' Ragnar promised, coughing as he took his last luxurious drag. All the other smokers claimed to be giving up too.

12 Volcanic Island

Gaia treated us to the most consistently exciting sailing so far between the Faroes and Iceland. A north-easterly wind took us from Torshavn to the volcanic island of Heimaey, off the south-western Icelandic coast, at an average speed of nearly seven knots; less than sixty hours for a little over four hundred nautical miles.

10 June, under way, Torshavn to Reykjavik, 19.30
Drizzly start, a bit lumpy, sailing well, reefed. Forecast: force five, easterly and then north-easterly – sounds OK.

Faroese fishing boat sighted.

Out with the reef. On with the engine and then the bonnet. Off with the engine, on with the generator.

Food delivery from *Havella*: fender thrown across attached to black plastic sack. First time *Gaia* missed it. Better luck second time.

I had an excellent deep late-afternoon sleep – how much sleep can one person manage?

We have been doing nearly eight knots but wind and speed are now dropping.

23.00
So far no one has lapsed by smoking. But there is some extra eating going on. Ottar made two cakes from a packet an hour ago – there is none left already.

Motoring, Odd at helm. David and I did our turn earlier.

11 June, under way towards Heimeay, 12.45
We are doing over nine knots, sailing, under a blue sky. The motion is fine, apart from occasional lurches, one of which caused Andrew to drop his full lunch plate.

123

We have tried out the 'Viking' wooden latitude measurer –
whether these were in fact used by the Vikings is a matter of dispute
among experts. Alan Binns thinks not, unlike the Dane who brought
it and a wooden sun compass to us in Bergen.

The latitude measurer is a wooden disc with a circle drawn on it
and a vertical stick through a hole in the middle. The height of the
stick is adjusted so that when the contraption is floated in a bucket of
water at midday it will cast a shadow on to the circle, which
represents the desired latitude. If the shadow falls outside the circle
the ship is too far to the north – and if it falls inside the circle it is too
far south. It is all pretty basic but seems to work, although it needs
sun, which cannot be guaranteed in the North Atlantic. But land
need never be out of sight for more than a day or two at a time. The
white loom of Iceland, and in some conditions a sort of ice-mirage,
can be seen from far away – and Greenland is so huge that it is pretty
difficult to miss. The Vikings had all sorts of other clues about where
they were, and where land was, and where the wind was coming
from, which most of us miss nowadays (the temperature of the wind
and type of cloud formation, for instance).

Now that we have found that we are approximately at latitude 62 –
the Vikings are not thought to have been able to measure longitude –
we are going back to the electronics. Since we know that the Vikings
sailed this route, at least a bit at a time, we don't need to prove
anything, but we do need to keep to our schedule as VIPs with
receptions awaiting us. We should be in Heimaey before this time
tomorrow unless the wind changes, with several days in hand before
our next official appearance, in Reykjavik.

A single whale was spotted half a mile away. It blew twice but then
left the area.

When we reached 9.9 knots just now, with wind force six, it felt
wild, too fast for safety, so the sail area was decreased, bonnet
removed, one reef in. The danger is that if we broach, we could lose
control.

17.00

Wind E seven; over eight knots with one reef; much pulling of prias –
the lines controlling the shape of the sail's belly – to slow down a bit.
At this speed we'll be in Heimaey in the early hours.

There was a sudden excitement just before supper, when the rope
which forms the forward link of the jaw holding the yard to the mast

broke. The sail had to come down at speed – or the nearest thing possible. The Norwegians scampered across the heaving cabin roof to make a new jaw lashing. The sail was then rehoisted. All remarkably fast and efficient.

20.00

Gaia is horsing along at eight knots, plus or minus a bit, with rich green seas mounting up. Odd is asleep in the main cabin under a blanket. Ottar is making pancakes. Frode is sharpening knives outside.

The south coast of Iceland is stretched long and dark to starboard. It is many hours since we first saw the distant white of snow and ice mountains. Now there is a little snow showing behind the coastline, which is tough and not indented with harbours for shelter.

22.00

To starboard there are steep cliffs, quite close, with some caves, and behind them a huge icy snowhump of a mountain, with streaks of snow elsewhere on the high ground. Ahead, off the port bow, some huge freestanding rocks look like two of the Isle of Wight's Needles, with another bridged like Old Harry.

12 June, under way off Heimaey, 01.30

The Westman Islands are clear and large on the bows, at about nine miles. The wind has dropped, although there is still quite a swell, and we are motor-sailing. Gunnar, who is delighted to be nearly home, is on the tiller. Only Odd has turned in after our watch, although David has fallen asleep at the table with his head on a book.

To starboard, the Icelandic southern coast is still a dramatic combination of cliffs and mountains, with a lot of snow on the high ground.

Ragnar is sitting in the cabin reading aloud from a book of poetry in a good rich declaiming voice. This is in true Viking tradition. I can only understand bits – like something which sounds like: 'kom heim under storm into havet . . .' ('come home through the storm into harbour . . .').

Gunnar has had several VHF calls from home this evening.

02.30

We are still motoring with sail towards Heimaey, which is now very close. It must be a strange place to live. No one lives on the other fourteen Westman Islands, Vestmannaeyjar in Icelandic. Their name comes from the legend that a group of 'Westmen', Irish slaves, fled there after killing their Viking master, brother of Iceland's much-vaunted first settler. Not a story with a happy ending: after a fortnight's freedom they were found and killed.

Heimaey, which means Home Island, is still smoking (we can see the smoke) from a volcanic eruption nearly twenty years ago. Surtsey, only twelve miles away, didn't exist at all until it was spewed up by a volcanic eruption in the 1960s. It was named after Surtur, the Norse fire god who is expected to set fire to the earth when the gods fall.

We were still several miles offshore when suddenly an inflatable dinghy with six people on board was keeping up with us with a powerful outboard. Others joined it, coming from all directions until the sea seemed alive with little boats bouncing up and down all round us.

'Who are they? Do you know them all?' David asked them.

'They are all my friends,' Gunnar answered, beaming and throwing his arms wide as if to embrace them all together. 'I know them every one.'

We had not expected such a welcome at 3.00 am. The sky was streaked with the red glow of dawn as we were shepherded towards the narrow opening to the harbour, although the night had never been fully dark; as the Irish monk Dicueil put it, no darkness occurs on either side of the summer solstice, so that 'whatever task a man wishes to perform, even to picking the lice from his shirt, he can manage as precisely as in broad daylight'.

Even without an escort, the entry would have been dramatic. To port, we passed close to the dark browns and blacks of naked jumbled lava; to starboard, the cliff face looked as if a giant insect had nibbled away at it, eating out huge misshapen holes alongside untidy white splodges and streaks left by innumerable seabirds. *Havella* motored in sedately ahead of *Gaia*, whose high prow was briefly silhouetted against the cliffs; even at such a nocturnal hour seabirds were swooping loudly.

As soon as we were alongside, Gunnar, his breath white in the cold air and his eyes looking even bluer and more deepset than usual, was presented with a large basket of multi-coloured flowers on the quay. Then he was hugging his daughter, a long-haired blonde fourteen-year-old; his mother – small against his bulk, her hair darker and smoother than his, but there was a strong family resemblance – and various other friends and relations.

'Do Norwegian men get given flowers?' I asked Jon.

'Not at three o'clock in the morning,' he replied.

An Icelandic TV reporter grabbed Gunnar. It made a change from Ragnar always being interviewed, and it had also been a change for Gunnar to be at the helm during an entry. This was his place, and so the glory was for once his too. More and more cars arrived on the quay until it seemed as if half the population had woken up to greet him.

With amazing hospitality for the middle of the night, Gunnar's mother invited us all home for pancakes: thin ham on pancakes, pancakes with vegetable salad, waffles with jam and whipped cream, and coffee.

Back on board, Odd had one of his periodic tidying-up fits, which always tended to leave a lot of things in strange places – like dumped on the deck, with a threat that if they were still there in two hours time they would be thrown away. Then he joined the rest of the sleepers, leaving Jon, David and me awake on board and Andrew out walking in the rain, which had started not long after our arrival.

It was raining so heavily that neither David and I, nor Jon, felt inclined to explore ashore, but nor did we want to sleep. There was something particularly pleasant about sitting talking in a warm dry cabin when the rain was loud on its roof and there was no immediate danger of having to do anything.

'How did you come to be on *Gaia*?' I asked Jon.

'I don't know,' he answered, 'I don't know what I'm doing here.'

There were times when we had all wondered what we were doing there – but perhaps not in the way Jon meant, which was that he did not feel that he had any special competence to offer. His previous employer had cut back on employees, leaving him out of work for several months. So he had signed on. Svein, Ragnar's boatman at Håholmen, had been given his name from a list of people available for work; and so Jon, a former central heating engineer, had started at Håholmen in October, at the time when agreements for Vinland Revisited were being discussed and drawn up. He was then first asked to join *Oseberg*, and moved to *Gaia* shortly before the start from Trondheim: 'I was surprised, because I have not much experience in sailing, only for short times in little boats,' he said.

'So far, is it what you expected?' I asked him.

'Some of it,' he said, 'but I thought there would be more work, and there is a lot more free time than I expected.'

Andrew returned, dripping, from his walk round the town and retired to his bunk. Under way he hardly managed to sleep at all, so he had some catching up to do. David decided that the *Saga* he was reading was soporific so also removed himself to his sleeping bag. I did not feel at all tired.

By the time Jon and I hoisted the flags, dead on 8 o'clock as instructed by Odd before he went to sleep, the rain had eased to a drizzle. Jon went for a walk, leaving me alone in the cabin. It was so unusually quiet that I was aware of every small outside noise, and realized that the automatic pump was being activated by the water level in the shallow bilges unusually frequently.

When David and I eventually wandered ashore, we bumped into Steinar: 'I was told to book you hotel rooms in every place,' he said, 'but now Ragnar says he isn't sure so I don't know what I must do.'

'Whichever you want, we don't mind,' we replied.

We walked towards the volcano. Topsoil had been spread over the slopes immediately above the town, and grass planted. Even from the top of this, not very high up, we could see across the whole town, a collection of boxy buildings with brightly coloured roofs along straight roads on a triangle of flat ground surrounded by steep volcanic hills. It was the one nearest the town which had erupted without warning – a potent expression of the inexorable power of Gaia.

Beyond the new grass, occasional patches of lichen gave a softening greenish tinge to lava which had solidified into tortured waves after spewing out during a January night in 1973. Four hundred houses, nearly a third of the total, as well as a number of other buildings had been buried, and as many more damaged. Miraculously, there were no deaths, and the lava stopped just short of the harbour – whether naturally, or deterred by the cold sea water hosed onto it, it was impossible to say. The local fishing fleet, Iceland's biggest and most prosperous, served as a nocturnal ferry service to the safety of the mainland; it was only by chance that the entire fleet was in harbour.

Of the original population of five thousand three hundred, by the end of the year two thousand had returned. Most of the rest followed in dribs and drabs, until there were nearly as many people living on the island as before.

To us, unaccustomed to a landscape with such a potential for sudden violence, the whole area affected by the eruption looked sinister and threatening. We scrambled through a valley of sharp twisted towers and ridges, where a river of lava on its way towards the harbour entrance had twisted as it cooled into monstrous natural sculptures. The slopes of the old mountainside, and of the bowl of the crater, were covered with scree, which made walking almost impossible. Most of the lava slag was bare, smoking dramatically after the rain. I was surprised at the variety of colours: some was black as I had expected, but there were many different shades of brown, red, ochre. By the time the volcano calmed down, the island was considerably larger than before the eruption. The new land, which was still as barren as the lunar landscape it resembled, gave additional protection to the harbour, which had previously been exposed to the south-east.

When we returned to *Gaia*, Steinar shouted across to us from *Havella*: 'You can stay on board here.' Odd seemed surprised.

If the cost of beer in Heimaey's pub was anything to go by, that of staying or eating in its hotels would have been astronomical. Although we set out that evening two or three at a time, we all ended up in the same place, at a bar a few hundred yards from the harbour. A group of local fishermen, all in their early twenties, were downing beers as if they were millionaires, to celebrate their return from a good trip. A glass boot in front of one of them was refilled several times during the course of the evening.

Jon, David and I left before midnight, considerably earlier than the others but we had spent less of the morning asleep. It was still light, although with a dull lifeless nocturnal light, and the roads were busy: the young men of Heimaey seemed to spend most of their free time driving round and round the few miles of tarmac road in large expensive cars, which consumed much of the money they earned as the best paid fishermen in Iceland. Their affluence was well deserved: in spite of its small population, the island accounted for more than half of Iceland's lucrative fish exports.

At 3.30 am I heard Nigel giggling as he struggled into his sleeping bag, 'It's easier when you're drunk,' he told anyone who wanted to know.

While the Norse carried on next day with boat maintenance tasks, like dismantling, adjusting and rehanging the steering oar, and tarring the rigging, Nigel struggled simultaneously with a hangover and with the wiring of navigational instruments which were supposed to tell us in the cockpit the speed and angle to the wind of the boat, and the strength and direction of the wind. David and I were entrusted with hull and deck oiling. The more often this could be done the better, and the last oil and turps mixture had been applied in Norway.

Andrew, who had cooked what he called 'gummi stew' for supper, spent the morning turning the unchewable leftovers into a far more palatable curry. The general Norse eating pattern of a cold collation at breakfast followed by more breakfast at lunchtime, and one hot meal in the evening, was broken for curry in the cockpit at midday. The crews of the two boats usually ate separately, but joined forces in the sun on *Gaia* at Andrew's invitation.

The Norwegian crew members took *Gaia* out in the afternoon for a photo call cruise. While Andrew and David filmed from a helicopter, with Valgeir and an Icelandic photographer, Nigel and I went to the Volcanic Film Show. Although the full colour eruption must at the time have seemed like a firework display from Valhalla, it was almost more awe-inspiring to see the immensity of the task of cleaning up afterwards, and the tenacity of the people who repaired the damage. In the most expensive of the local hotels David and I saw a display of black and white photographs which gave an even more powerful impression of the scale of the disaster in a series of pictures recording both the destruction and the reconstruction. The young man at the desk, who had been thirteen at the time, remembered it vividly.

'Didn't you have nightmares afterwards?' I asked him.

'No, never, no one did,' he said. 'It has not affected people. It was like a bad storm, but more so – and very beautiful. We felt grateful to see it because it was so beautiful. Perhaps people did not have nightmares because no one died that night.'

Gunnar led us in the evening down into the crater. From a distance, the smoking slope looked deceptively smooth, but above us the edge of its bowl was jagged against the skyline. I could feel the heat through the soles of my shoes.

Squatting down surrounded by blowing smoke, Gunnar scooped out a few huge fistfuls of lava: 'You just take a hole down. You don't have to go far down, then you can't lay your hand in it, it's so hot.'

I did lay my hand in it, and pulled it back swiftly. 'It certainly is hot. Can you cook in it?'

'Yes, you can put bread in a tin in it, and the bread is baked in a short time.'

'Is it safe here?' David asked.

'Yes, of course.'

'Why do you say of course?'

'Because there hasn't been an eruption here for many years.'

'There might be another one though,' David suggested pessimistically. 'There hadn't been one for many years before, either,' I added.

'When it comes, then it comes in another place,' Gunnar said emphatically, 'never again here.'

'How long will it stay hot?'

'Who knows? Maybe twenty years from now, maybe thirty years.'

'How far down is it hot?'

'Down to the devil.'

It was easy to understand how survival of a volcanic eruption might strengthen belief in God and in the devil, and I had already noticed that Gunnar had a Bible on board.

It was Ottar's turn to cook supper, which was a friendly jokey meal, with the teasing exchange of insults which seemed to be part of Nordic friendships.

Gaia lurched and was rocked violently when a fishing boat made its way out of harbour.

'What's that?' someone asked.

'A duck,' Frode answered solemnly. This, like Ottar's 'chicken hole' and Gunnar's 'very good to eat', became a crew catch phrase.

Somehow neither David nor I had found time that day to follow the example of the others by swimming and showering at the island's public baths. Although we were too late for the evening swimming session by the end of supper, we just made it into the showers before the pool was closed. On our way back to the harbour, we made a detour to the north-west corner of the island. Much of this seemed to be devoted to the municipal rubbish dump, which was being progressively reclaimed and added to a golf course complete with club house. This, and a neighbouring camp site, had taken over the valley where Heimaey's first Viking settler is thought to have had his farmstead, in the relatively fertile bowl of an extinct volcano.

A man we thought from a distance might be Gunnar (it wasn't) was abseiling down a cliff face several hundred feet high. His companions looked like matchstick people, high above him – and us – on a slope so steep it seemed surprising the grass did not fall off. A white curtain of birds fell from the cliff face and divided into a million individually soaring white specks. A huge cave was alive with birds, all squawking and shrieking as they swooped in and out of its darkness.

We talked about Gaia as we walked, and about our sense that Heimaey's society reflected the impermanence and potential violence of its setting. The discussion continued on board with Jon.

'Do you think anybody on this boat is interested in Gaia – in the idea of Gaia?' David asked.

'Yes, but it's a very big question,' Jon said. 'Everybody's interested and sees the problem.'

'This place – Heimaey – is a microcosm,' David suggested. 'Everybody gets the biggest most expensive car possible. They are using resources.'

'There isn't so much here to destroy,' Jon pointed out.

'They are catching fish, hunting a natural species on a very big scale.'

'But they always have, and they will do as long as they can.'

'There is a problem with fishing, with cod, in the North Altantic. These people are coining it in, sucking up the fish from the sea in very large numbers. On the other hand there is no other big industry here – they have to have fish, so if the fish go, they go . . .'

In the middle of the night I was woken by shouting: it sounded as if several people were fighting immediately above *Gaia* on the quay. An altercation in a pub between Frode and the boyfriend of a girl he had spoken to had escalated, and Rikardur and Andrew had eventually intervened to prevent what both were convinced was about to develop into a serious fight. They persuaded Frode back on board, where one of them restrained him verbally while the other attempted to deflect the wrath of his opponent, who was soon embroiled in a fight on shore with some of his fellow islanders.

One of those coincidences which sometimes makes the world seem very small was discovered on Heimaey by the two Icelandics. As far as they knew, Gunnar and Rikardur had met for the first time through Vinland Revisited. It was only when they were exchanging memories of student life that they realized that for a couple of years they had been classmates at Heimaey's nautical college.

'You remember old so-and-so?' – one of their teachers.

'He got so drunk that we put him in a bath tub and carried him round the town after the end of term party . . .'

'We went from one house to another, and at each house we left him outside in the bath, then carried him on to the next one afterwards . . .'

'And he didn't know anything about it . . .'

'I was one of the people carrying the bath –'

'So was I.'

Rikardur, who came from the mainland, had arrived as a student not long after the general return to the island. He had made the most of the aftermath of the eruption by buying a bus and taking tourists off the ferry on lava-viewing tours.

Odd seemed to have accepted having us on board in harbour, and asked me what I felt about the domestic routines on board. So far, one person had been in charge of cleaning and lunch every day, and another of the evening meal, a difficult rota to keep track of, especially when interrupted by official functions ashore. On one occasion I had inadvertently upset Frode by taking his lunch duty. Hoisting and striking flags had been done by anyone who happened to think of it. At a crew discussion over breakfast, the general feeling was that it would be easier to have one person in charge each day of all domestic duties. These were to include hoisting and striking flags, responsibility for all meals, and daily cleaning of both day and sleeping cabins.

'There must be better routine and discipline on board,' Odd lectured us jovially. 'Everything must be left clean and tidy at night, and everyone must be up and ready for work on time, at nine o'clock.'

'When are we going to taste these wonderful puffins you're always telling us are so good to eat?' we had kept asking Gunnar. The nine hundred and twenty-seven he had caught in one day was not a record, he insisted whenever David referred to him as 'Iceland's puffin netting champion': 'The record is more than one thousand.' On our last day in Heimaey, we were all invited by the mayor and council to lunch at a local hotel restaurant – and as first course were served a puffin each. It looked like a braised heart in a rich brown sauce, and tasted like a cross between pigeon and liver – not fishy, as I had expected, and very tender.

'This is not how we usually cook puffin,' the mayor apologized. 'Usually we boil it and then fry it, and then it is not tough like this.'

Herdis joined us in Heimaey, although as she was staying at Gunnar's mother's house we saw little of her after our first warm greeting. Rosa appeared during our last evening, which for most of the crew was spent at a disco, as was much of the night. Their presence greatly improved the ratio both of Icelandics to Norwegians, and of women to men.

Nigel, on domestic duty on the day of our departure, had been given an alarm clock set for 6.30 am so that we would be ready to leave promptly at 8.00 am. Frode was unwakeable. So was Rosa, who was asleep in the main cabin under a blanket. There was no sign of Gunnar or Herdis. *Havella*, we were told, would wait for them. *Gaia* left without them, with Ragnar on the tiller and a Canadian film crew on board.

By 8.20 am, *Havella* was following us out. Gunnar and Herdis were delivered by gummiboat. Puffins whirred desperately off the surface of the sea as we passed. The sky was a brilliant blue, the sea a rich green – I have never seen it so green anywhere as off the south coast of Iceland. Just outside the harbour, under the steep bird cliff headland, three dolphins showed, disappeared, humped and showed again.

We sailed south for a while for the benefit of Ragnar and the Canadian TV team since otherwise the sun would not have been on the helmsman's face.

It was good to have some female company on board, although I did not mind being with a boatload of men. When I went up to the foredeck to start attacking the fenders with white spirit, so that 'Oslo' would have no cause for complaint about *Gaia* being scruffy, I was joined first by Herdis, then by Rosa, so that with no intention of falling into a female role all three of us found that we had done so. It did not matter. The fenders were indeed dirty, and it was as pleasant a way of spending a sunny afternoon at sea as any other.

15 June under motor off Iceland, 20.00
Ragnar and Odd disappeared by gummiboat some hours ago, with the Canadian TV crew. We assume they are on *Havella*. The Canadians were to be landed ashore at the mainland ferry port.

No one knows when Ragnar and Odd will rejoin our crew, which is in any case up to numbers with the two girls instead of them. The wind and sea have dropped. It is a perfect peaceful evening.

A few minutes ago we downed sail and started motoring. Gunnar has cut the engine and has announced: 'Nu shall ve fiske.' This has interrupted a game of chess in which David was about to beat Frode again. Instead, Frode is taking photos of Gunnar, Nigel, David and Rosa fishing for cod over the gunwale in the stern. Nothing caught so far.

'Ve ha fisk!' The first, brought in by Frode and David, is eight to ten kilos. The Icelandic girls call it a sea salmon but say it is not good to eat: 'My mother makes fish cakes with these,' Rosa says. Then – David again – up come two smaller cod; but Rosa drops one over the side while she is washing it, so now we are trying for more. 'We shall show *Havella*,' Gunnar says, '*Gaia* is best.' A sprinkling of small fishing boats is a good sign: they must know where there are likely to be fish.

The seabirds, mainly silent soft-breasted fulmar, certainly realize

we are on to a good thing here. It is only three hours since we were
eating breaded filleted fish distributed from *Havella*'s freezer.

'British people aren't allowed to fish here,' Gunnar jokes. 'Watch
out – you'll start another cod war!' we warn David.

By the time the fishing lines were being reeled in, we had half a dozen
assorted fish: two large sea salmon, two red fish, two cod, perhaps a
total weight of thirty kilos. As David reeled in his line, he exclaimed:
'Get the boathook ready – I've got another one – it's a bigger one – shit!
– it's big, a big weight.'

'Maybe a kveite – a halibut,' someone suggested.

'It could be a lorry tyre,' was another suggestion.

Then – 'It's three – three cod – and big ones too.'

'Now we go,' Gunnar said. 'We have enough fish.'

'Judy, start making fish cakes,' Ottar ordered.

David let his line out again so that he could rewind it neatly as he
pulled it back in. 'But no more fish,' he was warned.

Gunnar set to filleting the big cod, and Herdis the small red fish, as
we motored on into the evening: 20.00 and full daylight. David and
Frode flung buckets of water around to clean the blood from the deck.

Just before midnight we were told over the VHF to take down or
camouflage everything non-Viking which would be visible from the air,
including all crew members wearing bright orange Norwegian all-in-
one sailing suits. 'A small plane will come out to film us,' Rosa, who
answered the call from *Havella* – still out of sight – told us. At midnight,
the plane appeared, circled us a few times, presumably filmed, and
disappeared. Aerial filming at midnight . . .

As the light of day changed to the light of night, we were approaching
a long point protruding from the south-west corner of Iceland.
Keflavik, where we were to rendezvous with various crews' wives who
were flying to join us for our official Icelandic stop, was on the other side
of the narrow land strip, which it would take us several hours to round.

Havella reappeared and took *Gaia* in tow for the entry to Keflavik. As we
approached the end of the spit, *Havella* altered course. On board *Gaia*, it
looked as if she was preparing to drop the tow. The line slackened in a
wide sweep, then suddenly became taut. It was no longer possible to
keep pulling it in. Somehow Rosa and Herdis were between the line and
the hull when it became clear that something was wrong.

'Cut it – cut it!' Jon's knife sawed quickly through the rope just in
time to save the two girls from being crushed.

Later it transpired that *Havella* had not dropped the tow at all.
Confusion reigned that hour between *Havella* and *Gaia*, and through a
further misunderstanding we found ourselves not in Keflavik's main
harbour, but in a small fishing harbour miles from anywhere except a
vast anonymous sprawl of modern apartment blocks and an equally
anonymous row of factories.

Andrew and Nigel left *Gaia* by taxi for Reykjavik to meet their wives,
who had already arrived by air, with Andrew's six-month-old baby
Sophie. The rest of us pottered about aimlessly for a couple of hours,
then were driven by minibus across a vast expanse of the sort of lava
lunar landscape we had become familiar with on Heimaey to the Blue
Lagoon.

The communal women's changing room had the same poster as in
every swimming pool in Iceland, telling us all to strip and shower
before donning bathing costumes; big red arrows pointed helpfully at
the places most in need of washing. The men were given similar
instruction by poster in their changing room.

The lagoon itself looked like a space fiction set. Steam roared
constantly from the surrealist spouts and chimneys of a power station at
which the ground's natural energy was harnessed. The water, which
had a strong sulphurous smell and was almost as salty as and more
buoyant than sea water, was not so much blue as milky white. It was
cool at the entry point, becoming warm and hot in moving patches. At
its hottest it felt as if there might be no escape from being boiled alive.
The ground, invisible beneath the thick milkiness, was uneven,
sometimes with quite steep shelves of rock, and everywhere with the
thick underwater slime of a white gritty deposit which was being
liberally used as a face mask.

'We could be standing on bodies,' Øyvard suggested cheerfully.

We motored out of the deserted fishing harbour just before midnight
to spend the night on the way to Akranes, on the other side of the huge
bay to the west of Reykjavik, so that the wind would be behind us for
next day's ceremonial entry. As we were not on the night watch, David
and I woke to find ourselves tied up in Akranes, where we were joined
by Eggert – whom we had last seen on *Oseberg* in Norway, and who
made Icelandic–Norwegian numbers on *Gaia* temporarily and diplomatically equal. As Kari had joined Ragnar for the official Icelandic
visit, with Herdis and Rosa the male-female ratio was also considerably
improved.

After a half hour walk and a cup of coffee ashore, we felt we had sampled what Akranes had to offer tourists, although it looked clean and pleasant enough. Rosa gathered everyone's Viking tunics and took them ashore to be ironed. Herdis had spent hours under way reorganizing the galley. Both were determined that *Gaia* and her crew should look their best for the national day entry to their capital. Activity on board was directed chiefly to dressing *Gaia* and *Havella* overall. But as soon as this had been worked out *Gaia*'s flags were dropped: she was to be filmed in genuine Viking guise before dressing again for the final moments of the entry.

13   Iceland – Showing the Flag

It took the first serious Norse settler in Iceland, Ingólfur Arnason, three years to find the place he called Reykjavik – Smoky Bay. Fortunately, as we did not have to follow the procedure of throwing over symbolic 'high seat pillars' and waiting for the gods to wash them ashore at a propitious stopping place, our journey from Akranes to Reykjavik was more straightforward. Iceland's National Day was blessed with a fair gentle wind, a calm sea, a brilliant blue sky and sixty-mile visibility of such clarity that we felt we could almost touch the purple humps of distant mountains.

The reason for going into Akranes – to ensure a good sailing wind into Reykjavik – certainly paid off, and we were able to sail right into the harbour. Our welcoming flotilla included the fishery protection vessel *Tyr*, also dressed overall.

'She looks far more festive than when I last saw her, in the cod war,' commented David, who had been a TV reporter aboard a Royal Navy frigate which had collided with her.

Gaia made a triumphant entry, holding sail until the very last minute as we came alongside a pontoon of assorted dignitaries. Among the crowd lining the quay were many children waving their national flag, which some had even had painted on their faces. Icelanders on their National Day were in festive mood, as had been the Bergenese on Norway's Independence Day, exactly one month earlier.

For once, time had been allowed for us to tidy the sail before the shore reception started officially. Valgeir, looking smooth and smart, was master of the welcoming ceremonies. For these we donned Viking tunics and lined up on shore with our backs to *Gaia* facing several rows of seated dignitaries for an hour – quite long enough, as in spite of the June sun there was a chill in the wind.

Since the speeches were mostly in Icelandic, with an odd spattering of Norwegian, we Brits could make out little except the general welcoming drift. Knut delighted the Icelanders by speaking for a page or two in their language, to the quiet amusement, it seemed, of his wife. And, as we had been told was always the case, the Icelandic President, Vigdis Finnbogadottir, delighted everyone both by her appearance – dressed all in cream, with a few pieces of chunky gold jewellery – and by what she said.

As the choice of the name 'Gaia' was hers, it was of course eminently suitable that she should conduct the official christening. Knut passed her a wooden bowl of one-thousand-year-old Norwegian glacier water, mixed with water from Iceland. She spooned it generously on to *Gaia*'s starboard bow, then clasped one of Ragnar's hands warmly in both of hers. In a symbolic gesture, *Gaia*'s ensigns were run down and rehoisted with Iceland's on the starboard side in pride of place. Although the transfer of registration from Norwegian to Icelandic was not yet formalized, we were to consider ourselves from then under the Icelandic flag, and our vessel in Icelandic ownership as the property of World City Discovery's new Reykjavik branch.

After the speeches came the music, starting with the Norwegian composer Gustav Lorentzen leading a children's choir in his composition 'Kids Have Rights'. He sang the verses, and the children whistled the links and sang the three-word title chorus. Valgeir assisted the accompaniment of a three piece band (including a piccolo player in a traditional woollen hat which reminded me of a striped night cap) with what looked like half a tambourine. A Nordic girl violinist played music which sounded vaguely Greek, quietly accompanied by two male electric guitarists – one sporting a vast oiled curled moustache.

President Vigdis Finnbogadottir and other dignitaries were then shown round *Gaia* by Ragnar, with much filming of presidential hands caressing the carved tiller, as well as interviews for local newspapers and radio. Gunnar was fetched and introduced: Ragnar had been on the helm as we came in, as well as being the focal neo-Viking ashore. Eventually there was time for a presidential interview by David, for which permission had been granted by post before we left England.

Still wearing his Viking tunic, he asked the obvious questions. It was neither a long, nor a probing, nor even a very interesting interview. I am including it in full, since asking a courteous question about whaling on Iceland's National Day was interpreted as deliberate provocation, both by those Icelandics and Norwegians present, and afterwards by many who were not.

DL: Madam President, why have you suggested that this boat should be called *Gaia*?

VF: Because when the owner – the original owner, Knut Kloster – suggested that the boat should have an ecological message to underline that although the countries are still there, they have changed on the surface, I thought that a symbolic name like Gaia would be not so bad – and it was accepted – because we of the Western cultures, we know that more or less our cultures originally are based on the Greek cultures. So we are more or less familiar with the fact that in the Greek mythology Gaia was the symbol of the Mother Earth. We have the same in the Norse mythology, that Freya and Frigga were Gaia's sisters, but I think that Gaia is better because people are not as familiar with Norse mythology as they are with Greek.

[Freya was the Norse goddess of love and beauty, the twin sister of Frey, god of vegetation and prosperity; their father was Njord, god of summer and the sea; Frigga, as the wife of Odin, Allfather and god of wisdom, war and death, was the mother of the gods, and goddess of the sky, marriage and fertility.]

DL: What is the environmental message which you think this expedition is trying to give?

VF: Mainly to remind people that the surface of the countries has changed in these thousand years – it's not the same – and as soon as we start thinking of the changes, we perhaps start remembering something, realizing that we have perhaps taken too much and it is of paramount importance that we do something about all this *now*, and not tomorrow. Start today – it might be too late otherwise.

DL: How do you reconcile concern with the environment with Iceland's determination to resume commercial whaling?

VF: Has Iceland resumed commercial whaling?

DL: – *determination* to resume –

VF: Those are your words, not mine. I have not heard about that.

DL: I wondered how you reconciled concern for the environment, concern which so many people have, with Iceland's wish to start whaling again.

VF: You know, whaling is such an emotional question that it is difficult to find the core of the matter because there are so many emotional opinions about that. And I can assure you that the Icelanders have studied marine biology in your country and in other countries – because we do not study marine biology here. Why should *your* universities abroad teach Iceland to kill the last whale?

DL: But many people might see a contradiction in your talking about the environment from a country which has alarmed a lot of environmentalists by its attitude towards whaling.

VF: Now you are saying something that – *you* think that whaling is anti-ecological. You are asking a leading question.

DL: No, I was suggesting to you that some people might see a contradiction between your statement that you are keen on the environment with Iceland's policy towards whaling.

VF: Yes, of course, because it's an emotional question. Let's see how things develop. It's an emotional question when people are so much against it, that's a fact.

DL: As far as you're concerned, it's an environmental expedition?

VF: Yes.

A few hours later, we and the rest of the crew, plus the seated VIPs from the welcoming reception, were guests at an official Vinland Revisited banquet at Bessastaðir, the elegant presidential residence on a peninsula outside the city. David and the President greeted each other defensively. 'That was below the belt –' she started. 'It was a fair question –' David said at the same time. He introduced me, and my hand was taken and held during a brief exchange.

Maybe it would have been diplomatic to talk about the weather – since Iceland certainly seemed to have had a change of climate since my previous wet blustery visit – but instead I talked about what I assumed was still on her mind as it was on ours after the unsatisfactory confrontation on *Gaia*: whales, and the differing British and Icelandic attitudes to whaling. We felt that the subject had to be raised, not so that we could state anti-whaling views, but because of the anomaly others might see in two pro-whaling countries backing a project in support of the environment – of which the whale had become such an emotive symbol.

My hand was released after we had exchanged a few sentences. 'You are dismissed,' the President said regally.

At the start of her after-banquet speech, she said that earlier in the day she had been asked 'a certain question' – glancing in David's direction – to which she had since given some thought, and which had focused her thinking on the general Gaian environmental issue. These matters were, she indicated, too serious to be used by one nation to score points over another; everyone internationally was equally responsible for the environmental future of the world, and equally guilty of the damage which had already been suffered by Gaia.

Next day, several members of the Vinland Revisited Committee present in Reykjavik debated at length the propriety of David's question. As we only learnt of this later, and unofficially, David had no opportunity to defend himself against the accusation that he had made an 'undignified attack' on the President at the christening ceremony. 'That's what made her upset, and that's what we talked about afterwards,' Knut told me several months later. 'Not the whaling question.'

The question about whaling was nevertheless the one which David was apparently not supposed to have asked – or at least not on that occasion. It would no doubt have been considered inflammatory if we had quoted what James Lovelock, on whose hypothesis our project was supposed to be based, wrote about whales in his first book about Gaia: 'If we hunt them heedlessly to extinction, it must surely be a form of genocide.'

We – the British contingent – had become used to our presence never being mentioned, although we made up two-fifths of *Gaia*'s crew, and to having to explain to everyone we met what we were doing on a Viking ship. The Icelandic presidential dinner was the occasion of the first public acknowledgement of our existence, by the British Ambassador, Sir Richard Best, who proposed a toast in our honour. 'About bloody time someone acknowledged us,' Andrew muttered.

The dinner was also the first at which Sue and Sophie Dearden, Andrew's wife and baby, and Nigel's wife Sandra, were present. Permission for Sophie's presence had been officially requested and granted. Even at the tender age of six months, she rose admirably to the occasion, charming everyone, and causing considerable amusement by looking so astonishingly like her father.

Sophie was soon a firm favourite at the hotel we Brits had all been booked into, along with the Bjerkes, the Nissen-Lies and Øyvard and his wife. Suitably named the Hótel Leifur Eiríksson (the Icelandic version of Leif Eiriksson) it looked onto a larger-than-life statue of the Icelandic hero, standing on a massive plinth in front of the city's largest and most modern church. The hotel had only been open a few days when we arrived, and was still being finished. One day there was no electricity, another no water, and neither bar nor restaurant were ready; but these details were insignificant when set against the generally friendly helpful atmosphere, and the convenience of being at the same time within easy walking distance of anywhere in the centre of Reykjavik, and peacefully just outside the city centre.

'A week in Reykjavik will be far too long,' Ragnar had commented before we arrived. He and Kari disappeared for a few days on their own halfway through the week. For the rest of us, it was so full that although we saw each other only at official functions we were all in our different ways busy the whole time. Down in the harbour, *Gaia*'s sleeping cabin was winched off so that Ottar and Gunnar could investigate, and cure, the leak suspected when the pump started to work overtime.

There were inevitably a number of official functions to attend, and very enjoyable they were too. Our second evening in Reykjavik started with a cocktail party as the guests of the leading mayoral candidate at the Höfði House, since the 1986 summit meeting better known as 'the Reagan-Gorbachev house', followed by a dinner at the city's smartest hotel. The British Ambassador and his wife invited the British members of the crew of *Gaia* for drinks the following evening. Among half a dozen other guests were our old friends Tony and Katie Jonsson. Tony, being half-British and having been the only RAF Icelandic Spitfire pilot in the Battle of Britain, had twice been presented to Queen Elizabeth II on a recent British royal visit to Iceland.

We had to rush away from the Embassy to be on time for a dinner given by the Export Council of Iceland on Viðey – Wood Island – where we waited, and waited, and waited, on the first floor of Viðeyjarstofa, Iceland's oldest house to have survived unchanged. Built in 1751, it had been turned into a restaurant and conference centre; it was an idyllic setting yet within a few minutes of Reykjavik by ferry.

'They will be here in a few minutes – half an hour – an hour – maybe half an hour,' we were told at intervals. At least the wait gave us time to explore the island. It was, however, so small that this did not take long, and the wind was so cold that we were not tempted to linger outside on its soft grass slopes, especially with the Deardens' baby in her pushchair dressed, as we were, for an indoor social occasion.

There was another large dinner party on the first floor that evening. The other diners were, we gathered from eavesdropping on the speeches (given in English) an international group of electrical engineers. The conference they had been attending in Reykjavik had been considering ways of harnessing Iceland's vast natural power resources for wider European use. It seemed a very Gaian topic.

At last, two hours late, the rest of our party arrived. The chartered aircraft which had taken American journalists and selected Vinland Revisited representatives on a one-day Export Council PR trip to Greenland had been delayed. Their destination was to have been Eirik the Red's settlement, Brattahlið, on a south-western fjord. Because of strong crosswinds they had however been diverted to Kulusuk, the airfield serving Ammassalik on the east coast. 'A rubbish dump with people living on it,' was Gunnar's unflattering description of Ammassalik, which he and Ragnar had visited briefly by helicopter.

At the British Embassy, Tony Jonsson had given us a copy of a letter he had written to an Icelandic newspaper criticizing the Norwegian domination of Vinland Revisited. 'The Norwegians have been very energetic in claiming for themselves our Leifur Eiríksson, and because of this it is fairly certain that nine out of ten North Americans who have heard of him, think that he is a Norwegian,' Tony had complained. 'In the few instances when the Norwegians have not ventured to make a direct claim to him they have described him with the English word Norse, and seldom – if ever – called him an Icelander. And now the attack is to be intensified! To be sure they [the Norwegians] have found themselves forced to invite the Icelanders to take part in the afore-mentioned expedition [Vinland Revisited]. What generosity! Two Icelandic men and two Icelandic women are to be graciously allowed to stride along!'

Tony felt that Iceland should share the blame for the discrepancy in national representation in the crew: 'The Norwegians are going to contribute most of the money . . . and have therefore acquired the right to take charge. The question is whether we Icelanders shouldn't have put more money into the kitty and thereby have more say in running things? . . . I am not going to blame the Norwegians for "manning their oars", but shouldn't the Icelanders have at least as many oars as they do? . . . Should not the Icelanders, descendants of the Vinland discoverers, have been more numerous among the crew?'

Tony's resentment about what many Icelandics considered a Norwegian take-over bid for their national hero was widely shared. In an effort to diffuse the acrimony, the Export Council host, Ingjaldur Hannibalsson, suggested in an after-dinner speech at Viðey that Ronald Reagan's description of Leif Eiriksson as 'the son of Iceland and grandson of Norway' should be adopted. It seemed a fair compromise, as Leif's father, Eirik Rauðe – Eirik the Red – had been exiled first from Norway, and then from Iceland, in both cases because

okstad ship, Viking Ship Hall, Oslo; and putting final
uches to the replica of the Gokstad ship, Bjørkedal, west
orway

Top: launch of Gokstad replica, Bjørkedal, April 1990 and *above*; the Viking fleet – l to r *Oseberg, Saga Siglar, Gaia* – at Håholmen

Top: *Gaia* and *Oseberg*, west Norway.
Above left: Icelandic crew members wearing plastic horned helmets, Bergen, on Norwegian Independence Day.
Left: distribution of Norwegian saplings from *Gaia* in Kirkwall, Orkney.
Above: meeting of 'Christopher Columbus' and 'Leif Eiriksson' on board *Gaia*, west Norway

Clockwise from top:
Ragnar Thorseth; Jon Folde,
with Gunnar Marel Eggertsson
in background; Dr Helge Ingstad
and Anne Stine Ingstad; Andrew
Dearden and Nigel Chatters (l),
filming off East Greenland;
Frode Sætre, gummiboat king;
Frode Sætre and Rikardur
Petursson; Gunnar Marel
Eggertsson

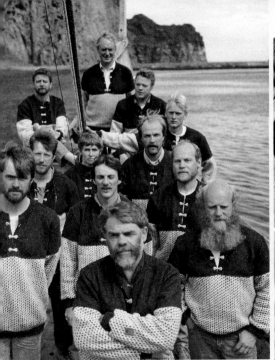

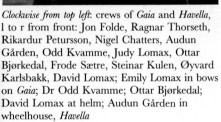

Clockwise from top left: crews of *Gaia* and *Havella*, l to r from front: Jon Folde, Ragnar Thorseth, Rikardur Petursson, Nigel Chatters, Audun Gården, Odd Kvamme, Judy Lomax, Ottar Bjørkedal, Frode Sætre, Steinar Kulen, Øyvard Karlsbakk, David Lomax; Emily Lomax in bows on *Gaia*; Dr Odd Kvamme; Ottar Bjørkedal; David Lomax at helm; Audun Gården in wheelhouse, *Havella*

Right: *Gaia*, *Havella* and *The Good Shepherd* in harbour, Fair Isle

Below: Ragnar Thorseth, President Vigdis Finnbogadottir of Iceland, Knut Kloster, on *Gaia*, Reykjavik

Foot: rowing skiffs, Torshavn, Faroes

Below: Faroese pilot
whale hunt.
(Environmental
Investigation Agency,
July 1986)

Gaia off Heimaey,
Westman Islands,
Iceland

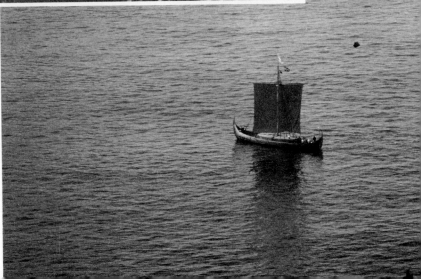

Below: whale and whalers, sculpture,
Torshavn, Faroes

Above: greeting to Lerwick by
member of Shetland's Jarl Squad

Right: statue of Leif Eiriksson,
Reykjavik

avella, support ship, off east Greenland and *inset*: fending off ice in fog, east Greenland

Jon Folde letting out
a reef

Above: Greenlandic costume. Julianehåb (Qaqortoq), south west Greenland

Top: traditional Greenlandic kayaks, Narsaq, south west Greenland

Right: seals, detail of 'Creation' mural by Greenlandic painter Aka Hoegh

Below: seal flensing, Ammassalik, east Greenland

Foot: *Gaia* and ice berg, south west Greenland

Ice through rigging, south west Greenland and *foot*: crew barbecue, south west Greenland

Gaia from *Havella* in rough weather in the Labrador sea and *below*: *Gaia's* steerboard

Arrival in 'Vinland': *Gaia* approaching l'Anse-aux-Meadows

Top: welcome to l'Anse-aux-Meadows
Left: reconstruction of Norse houses at
l'Anse-aux-Meadows.
Above: Dildo, Newfoundland: Gunnar, Jon, and Ottar
with skipper of a mini-*Gaia*

Left: the Viking fleet, New York

Below: Colonial uniforms, Newport, Rhode island

Foot: arrival at Museum of the Atlantic wharf, Halifax, Nova Scotia

Right: racing at sunset in Chesapeake Bay: *Oseberg* from *Gaia* and *below*: girl in Indian costume aboard *Gaia* in Washington.

Foot: President George Bush on board *Gaia* in Washington

of some killings, although Leif himself had lived almost all his life in Greenland. What I found intriguing was that a compromise statement should have been considered necessary, especially as Leif and his followers had failed to establish any long-term presence on the new continent.

Perhaps to make up for their shortage of numbers – the population of Iceland is only a quarter of a million, three-fifths of whom live in Reykjavik – Icelanders are intensely patriotic, and extremely well versed in the literary and historical wealth of their sagas. We had inadvertently, we discovered, been guilty of the crime of misusing the word Norse to include Norwegians and Icelanders. 'It means only Norwegian,' Jónas Kristjánsson, director of the Árni Magnusson Institute in Reykjavik and a world expert on the sagas, told David. They were looking at the first use of the word Vinland in the fourteenth-century *Flateyjarbók*, one of the manuscripts rescued by Árni Magnusson from a Copenhagen fire which destroyed most of Iceland's literary heritage.

As no alternative was suggested, I have continued to say 'Norse' when I mean Norwegian and Icelandic jointly. Iceland was after all originally settled by Norwegian 'Norse', and is the only Nordic country where the old Norse language has survived almost unchanged. Since the Danes returned the surviving medieval Icelandic manuscripts, it is also in Reykjavik that Norse mythology, legend and history can best be traced.

Apart from the President, no one we met while we were in Reykjavik showed any obvious interest in the environmental symbolism of the name she had chosen for our ship. Most people wanted to talk about the Vikings and their heritage, and what one of their ships was like to sail. The only neo-Viking environmental action allied to Vinland Revisited was another symbolic tree-planting by Ragnar. As Iceland has banned the import of plants as well as animals, he could not plant a Norwegian tree, but it was perhaps about time that a Norwegian Viking representative made amends for the destruction caused by his ancestors. When the Vikings arrived in Iceland, they destroyed the country's natural forests by cutting down trees whenever they needed wood for boat- or house-building or repairs. The forests they destroyed have never regrown. New forests have recently been planted, and an 'adopt a tree' scheme initiated. But tree growth is slow, and it will be a long time before they lose their stunted look.

In Norway, the midsummer festival of St Hans is a major celebration, with all-night bonfires and carousing. I had expected something similar in Iceland. At first, when I was told that midsummer was not celebrated much, I was disappointed; then Katie gave me an excellent explanation: wood was too rare and valuable to be wasted on a bonfire. Instead, on the longest day of the year, as one day became the next with no intervening setting or rising of the sun, Tony and Katie drove David and me through rolling acres of purple lupins on the outskirts of Reykjavik. The lupins, in full flower under the soft eery light of midnight, had been introduced from Alaska because of the enriching effect they have on the poorest soil, seeming almost to create soil where there was none before. In a few years, they have spread with wild abandon, transforming a barren wilderness of lava where previously nothing would grow. It was a wonderful way of seeing the second half of the year in, except that the soporific motion of the car kept enticing me to doze off: I had been finding Iceland in its midsummer fortnight exhausting. Conditioned as I was not to feel tired unless it was dark, the non-stop daylight kept me alert and wakeful even when I knew I needed to sleep.

I was more likely to fall off, than doze off, on my next excursion into the lupin and lava fields; I spent a pleasantly energetic afternoon riding through them with Jon, Ottar, Frode, Rikardur, and Steinar. David, who considers horses of any size dangerous at both ends and unpredictable in the middle, refused to burden one of the Icelandic riding school miniatures hired by Valgeir with his great height and weight. 'They are not ponies – they are horses,' I was told firmly when I was misled by their small stature into referring to them incorrectly.

Frode was inadvertently first away, at great speed, as if his horse were a land-based gummiboat. When at last it turned round and returned, of its own accord and equally fast, one of the instructors gave Frode a few minutes of instant tuition, after which he looked considerably less precarious.

My mount, which I had thought looked too small and skinny to give me any trouble, soon proved me wrong by demonstrating that it had two speeds: fast, and very fast. I concentrated on staying on, and steering, and was carried alternately at a fast smooth running trot, and at a gallop which was far from smooth, until the horse decided it might as well keep with the others.

'I never want to do this again,' Steinar told me as he rode towards the corral at the end of the afternoon.

Icelandic horses, which unlike other breeds can be trained to have a fifth gait – the *tölt*, a sort of fast smooth run somewhere between the trot and the canter – have the reputation of being immensely strong and hardy. They are now no longer used as transport or as working farm horses, except occasionally to round up sheep in the autumn, but are still bred for leisure and food. Horse meat, banned as pagan by the early Icelandic Christians, is exported, chiefly to France. We saw horse pelts on sale in many of the tourist shops in the town, including the one where Katie Jonsson worked.

The horse was introduced by the early Norse settlers, along with sheep, cattle, Christianity and a form of government which has been hailed as the first example of Western democracy, at least by those who do not claim this distinction for the ancient Greeks.

For the first sixty years of settlement, there was no formal government in Iceland. But the settlers were a disputatious lot, and it soon became obvious that some form of law and order was essential. As one of the chief reasons for emigration from the Norwegian motherland was to escape the tyranny of the king it was decided to dispense with royalty. From the year AD 900 on, there was an occasional *thing*, or local assembly; but the first *Althing* – Althing, or national assembly – was held in 930, on a broad plain bordering Ingólfur Arnasson's land, fifty kilometres from Reykjavik. Both because of its setting, and because of its availability (it had been confiscated from its owner, who had been found guilty of murder) it was an ideal site for what soon became established as an annual fortnight's combined parliamentary assembly and midsummer fair.

It was at Thingvellir, Assembly Plain, that to avert the escalation of conflict between the adherents of the old and new religions a pagan lawgiver decreed in the year 1000 that all Icelanders should become nominal Christians, although they might still adhere to their pagan beliefs and practices in private. The parliamentary experiment lasted for three hundred years, with as much success as a democracy as could be expected when those sitting in judgement were also those seeking wealth and influence. When the country was torn apart by the corruption and ruthlessness of the Sturlung and other self-seeking ruling families, it was at a parliamentary assembly at Thingvellir that Iceland was reluctantly sucked into greater Norway. For centuries the country was dependent – first on Norway, then on Denmark.

Full Icelandic independence was only re-established in 1944. This too was symbolically signed and celebrated at Thingvellir, which is now a national park. We visited it, with Tony and Katie Jonsson, on

Midsummer's Day, which nine hundred years earlier would have fallen in the middle of the annual parliamentary assembly. Wild flowers added splashes of colour to the banks of a small sparkling river which runs across the plain from Iceland's largest lake. At the early parliamentary gatherings, the river provided fresh water, and the lake fish, for the assembled Icelanders. The gods thought to control natural phenomena must have seemed very close to the early pagans as they looked across the plain to the steam escaping from the core of the earth, or looked down into a rift where the continental plates are slowly pulling apart. Even now, with our scientific explanations of these extraordinary phenomena, Thingvellir is one of many places in Iceland where the scenery still inspires awe.

A flag pole marks the Law Rock, from which for three hundred years the Law Speaker, appointed for three years at a time by the goðar, the priest-chieftains for Iceland's twelve administrative districts, recited one-third of the law every year before reading and writing were introduced. Behind and above the flag pole, the walls of a ravine of basalt and lava form a dramatic boundary to the huge flat grassy expanse of the plain. It is a magic place, unspoilt by tourist attractions except for one hotel. There are never anything like as many people there now as there were for the old Althing, for which almost the entire population gathered, even those from the east coast for whom it meant a seventeen-day cross-country trek in each direction.

Thingvellir is surrounded on all sides by mountains, one the home of its guardian spirit, another, to the north, the volcano from which lava was spewed across its plain, which we left through a steaming geo-thermal area. I found the power station harnessing some of its immense power even more impressive than the unharnessed geysers of Geysir. In both places, and in many others, Iceland's geological youth and instability make it seem as if the earth is bleeding when it throws up its scalding jets of steam and water.

The notion that anything we mere mortals could do would have any effect on Gaia seemed presumptuous alongside her raw energy, which could scald us and boil us alive, open up and swallow us, bury us in steaming lava – and whether this affected one of us, or hundreds, or thousands, or even the entire puny dispensable human race, was irrelevant. I would have liked to talk about these intimations of Gaian strength and human mortality with Knut, but the opportunity did not arise. Harald and Henrich, whom we often saw as we were all in the same hotel, were more concerned with the logistics of the operation than with its Gaian aspects.

Somehow the violence of the ancient Nordic mythology seems more in keeping with the primeval Icelandic landscape than the Christian faith for which Norse paganism was abandoned. The old religion has recently been resurrected, and I had been looking forward to a promised crew invitation from the Icelandic Druids, as they called themselves in English. But we were unaware that there were two invitations waiting on board for us, so the entire British contingent missed meeting the Druids, and must have seemed equally rude not to have been at a reception at the Norwegian Embassy. We were lucky not to be sacked for missing official engagements, as Rosa was by letter. The general feeling among the crew was that Rosa had been badly treated, and had been let down by the Icelandic Foreign Ministry, which we were told neither supported her nor even asked for an explanation for her dismissal.

It was decreed by the Oslo management that the crews of *Gaia* and *Havella* should smarten up for official occasions on shore, and so a few days before we left Reykjavik we were sent to be measured for navy blue blazers, on to the breast pockets of which Vinland Revisited logos were to be sewn. Reykjavik, one of the most expensive cities in the world, was hardly the most economical place for the purchase of so many blazers. We wore them for the first time on our last evening ashore, at a special Vinland Revisited farewell reception at our hotel. There we were invited to sample the Icelandic delicacy of specially rotted ancient shark meat; in case some of us did not like this, dried lamb was also provided.

A suggestion by a young Icelandic furrier that we should continue the voyage dressed in sealskin had been rejected. It would, he insisted, have been so much more in keeping with the historical and environmental spirit of the expedition. His arguments, which turned those of the majority of environmentalists upside down, had a certain logic: sealskin was a natural fabric; the creation of synthetic fabrics caused pollution and waste; sealskin would outlive synthetic fabrics; and the Vikings used skins.

Long before setting out on *Gaia*, we had had some correspondence with an American couple who were hoping to sail to Greenland. Bob and Beth Lux, who reached Reykjavik on their yacht not long before we were due to leave on *Gaia*, planned to set out again a few days after us. We made mutual promises to do our best to keep in touch.

Whether we were in fact going to be able to set out for Greenland on

Gaia at all was for a few days hanging in the balance. The compromise of transferring ownership of the ship to an Icelandic subsidiary of World City Discovery, and of re-registering her in Reykjavik, was fraught with unexpected bureaucratic difficulties. Before being allowed to leave as skipper of an Icelandic vessel – Gunnar was officially mate – Ragnar was supposed to comply with Icelandic medical and navigational requirements. Whether he would pass a stiff medical examination only a fortnight after giving up smoking, after nearly thirty years of several packets of cigarettes a day, was a matter of interested speculation. As for the navigational qualifications, he had previously sailed with a special Norwegian dispensation since he had never taken any formal exams, though earlier in the year he had sat and had passed his coastal skipper's examination. So he was technically not qualified to be master of a ship on an ocean crossing. The only two people on the two ships with the full qualifications were Audun and Gunnar, but we could hardly envisage Ragnar relinquishing his leadership.

Whether he had a particular piece of paper or not did not bother us personally: after all, David and I had sailed many thousands of miles in our own boat without ever acquiring any qualifications. But since we were on an official dual-nationality expedition, as well as all being paid crew and so putting the whole operation on a professional footing, we could appreciate the problem facing the Icelandic authorities. Quite how the matter was resolved we never found out; it was clearly a sensitive subject, and one which we felt it diplomatic not to raise. But we were allowed to leave Reykjavik on time.

The Druids whose invitation we had missed came on board just before our departure. They presented us each with a pendant depicting Yggdrasil, the Norse tree of life, an ash linking the three cosmic regions of Asgard, realm of the gods, Midgard, the dwelling place of living mortals, and Niflheim, to which mortals must go after death, with the nine worlds. According to Crossley-Holland's *Norse Myths*, Yggdrasil was already a full-grown tree at the time of the creation: 'Burning ice, biting flame, that is how life began. . . . And all that has happened, and all the regions of the world, lie under the branches of the ash Yggdrasil, greatest and best of trees. . . . It gives life to itself, it gives life to the unborn. The winds whirl round it and Yggdrasil croons and groans. Yggdrasil always was and will be.'

A graven image of Njord had been placed on guard above *Gaia* in Reykjavik. We left Reykjavik under the protection of a smaller version, presented by the Druids. The Viking equivalent of St Christopher,

Njord, the senior Vanir or fertility god, father of the twins Frey and Freya, master of the sea and winds and guardian of ships and seafarers, sat in the stern as we motored across the bay to Keflavik, a squat phallic symbol carved in wood with a disdainful expression on its face. We saw two small whales on the way, and entered them dutifully in our whale-spotting book.

It was as usual a relief to be under way when we left Keflavik late in the evening. The toughest, and the longest, leg of the voyage lay ahead. *Gaia* quivered and flexed with the strain of once again being towed, even across a calm windless sea.

There was an unspoken shared sense of nervous anticipation as we set out to cross a notoriously dangerous and unpredictable stretch of water, in which we were certain to encounter ice and unlikely to meet any shipping. Our destination was Nuuk, Greenland's west coast capital; but first we had to round Cape Farewell, the North Atlantic equivalent of Cape Horn. No weather forecast could guarantee us fair weather the whole way, so we all knew that we and *Gaia* were about to face our greatest test.

14 'Ice & Cold
& Countless Wonders'

Instead of setting a south-westerly course direct for Cape Farewell, Ragnar took us due west. His strategy was that this would carry us round the top of a depression forecast for later in the week, and that the north-westerly winds which would follow it would carry us on a broad reach down Greenland's east coast.

For the first thirty-six hours, *Gaia* was towed at six knots, sometimes swinging gently but often protesting with an uncomfortable motion and alarming creaks. The normal flexing of the hull was exaggerated by the unnatural movement.

By our second early morning watch change, thirty-six hours out from Keflavik, we were all tired of being towed and welcomed Ragnar's decision to heave to and await weather developments. The gummiboat was hoisted in after Gunnar had bobbed up and down alongside *Gaia* struggling to remove the outboard. A small jib was set; the Vikings may have used a triangular foresail but there is no proof. For most of the day, we drifted under a dull grey sky, with nothing to see except the short rolling seas and *Havella*. At least the motion was better when at last the sail started to draw and we were moving under natural power, although our north-westerly course was taking us even further from Cape Farewell.

'What the hell am I doing here?' I asked myself at the evening watch change.

It was a wild night. To start with we charged north-west at six knots, every nautical mile increasing the distance from our destination. Then the wind strengthened to force seven, near gale, from the south-west – the direction in which we were eventually hoping to go. Approximately sixty miles east of Greenland's east coast pack ice, and four hundred miles north-east of Cape Farewell, we altered course to the south-east, back towards Reykjavik.

28 June, Wednesday, 23.00; 64 12 West, 31 48 North

At the end of a long cold day we are three miles further away from our way-point than at the same time yesterday. We seem to be heading in the general direction of Morocco, with Cape Farewell about 100° to starboard up-wind across a very lumpy swell. With two reefs and wind gusting to force seven, *Gaia* seems to ride everything quite comfortably.

There was a minor crisis this evening when the electric bilge pump packed up. Nigel's expertise and instruments were summoned to diagnose what was wrong and make up new fuses. Ottar scooped water out of the bilges with a bucket which Andrew then emptied overboard, while Ragnar and Odd on their hands and knees with screwdrivers tried to find the fault. The original Vikings would of course always have had to bail with buckets.

It is amazing how easily one can adapt to this six-hours-on/six-hours-off routine, although it can be disorientating. When David emerged from his bunk at 18.00, he thought it was dawn and was helping himself to breakfast while Frode was preparing salmon steaks for supper.

The forecast, picked up by Øyvard on *Havella*, predicts that the wind will drop and go round to the south-east but not until Sunday – so we will have to bear a bit more of this creaking and lurching.

29 June, Thursday, 09.30; 63 50 North, 31 18 West

Yet another horrid grey day with no overnight progress towards Cape Farewell.

There is still bird life in this otherwise empty sea – mainly fulmars, with occasional black guillemots and gannets, and a few puffins.

11.00

We are under motor again – our own, not *Havella*'s – and have gone about. Now heading towards Ammassalik at four knots in a wallowy grey sea and sky, still four hundred-odd miles from Cape Farewell.

Ragnar's plan is to take a tow from *Havella* as soon as the sea and wind drop a bit more, and make for the coast in the hope of getting shelter 'behind the ice'. Although none of us has actually said so, I suspect that I am not the only one to wish I were someone else, somewhere else, and to feel miserable at the prospect of being at sea for much longer than we originally thought without actually getting anywhere.

12.30
Andrew at the frying pan with huge slices of blood sausage knows the best way to a Norwegian seaman's heart. We are being towed at six knots in a temporary calm towards Cape Farewell at last. A much better position – except that a new low, lower than the last, is forecast to come lurking in this no-man's water where we seem destined to spend the rest of our lives. So we are trying to reach the far side of it before it hits us, which is exactly what the tactics were with the last towing several days ago.

Our afternoon off-watch snooze has been somewhat thwarted as the cabin floor where we sleep had to be removed in search of a leak.

A little while ago there was a VHF call from Steinar on *Havella*: 'Good afternoon. In view of the pleasant weather we intend to take a promenade on deck with cigars.'

30 June, Sunday, 10.30; 63 12 North, 37 01 West
Another forecast via Øyvard threatens winds up to forty knots from the south-east. Ahead there is a grey band of mizzle.

There is much talk over the VHF between Ragnar and *Havella* about the weather, and about what to do.

'Bad news,' Ragnar says when he finally puts the receiver back. 'We are going north again.'

Even wearing thermal underwear under several layers of sweaters and trousers, and with a sheepskin hat pulled over my ears and sheepskin gloves, my hands and feet are numb after an hour outside on watch.

16.30
The sun came out with the first sighting of ice, an hour and a half ago. We are peacefully still under fast tow towards a long line of glistening ice, or maybe it is snow on mountains. I've seen several pairs of puffins, as well as innumerable ubiquitous fulmar.

The stark cold beauty ahead is drawing us towards it. The electronics tell us that we are being towed at over eight knots towards a position marked on the chart off the long cold uninhabited east coast. The ice is now about nine miles away.

18.30
The tow was dropped as we approached the line of offshore pack ice. Fenders were put over, and *Havella* made as if to come alongside to

replenish our food stocks. Better was then thought of this, and she set off through the pack, which to the south was relatively sparse, no more than four-tenths.

Gaia followed the mother ship sedately, with Frode in the gummiboat bunting bits of brash aside, and Odd and Ottar doing likewise with oars on the bows; we have half a dozen long Viking-style oars on board, this is the first time they've been used.

We are now alongside *Havella* in a little ice-free pool, although it is surrounded by broken brash off the pack. Seabirds sit and watch us curiously from the ice. Most of this is purest white, but there are a few brilliant translucent blues and greens as well. Diesel and water are being taken on board *Gaia* by hose from *Havella*.

20.00; 63 09 North, 39 57 West

Supper was interrupted by much sudden pushing off of ice with boathooks and oars, but too late: a large chunk had already forced the rudder up so hard that the leather strop and wooden chock attachment at the top were broken.

Havella and *Gaia* then split up and moved out into clearer water. We are floating a few hundred yards from the crumbled brash edge of the pack, with lots of seabirds – mainly fulmar, of course – around us. They are feeding in two lines of tide or current which meet here.

It is difficult to imagine that within forty-eight hours this place could be hell for us. There is blue sky and a light chill breeze. It is one of those magic Greenland days; but there is no way we will get right in behind the ice for shelter from the impending storm.

In the meantime, this is a peaceful and pleasant pause. Ottar and Co. are busy repairing the ice damage on the aft deck. It just underlines how careful we have to be in ice with *Gaia*. Odd is in one of his odd moods, tidying up and taking any joke seriously, deadpan.

1 July, Monday 08.00

Me: 'Is it July 1st?'

Ottar: 'Yes.'

Me: 'What day is it?'

Ottar: 'Sunday.'

Ottar again, after a pause: 'No, it's not Sunday – it's Monday. Sorry.'

We are still adrift in a silent sea. It feels quite warm, but all things are relative and for the first day in July 4°C would not elsewhere seem a suitable temperature for a calm and sunny summer's day.

It is incredibly beautiful. From a distance, the stark white of ice and snow was pristine against the blue sky and dark sea. Then as we came nearer the thin even whiter line of pack ice etched beneath the mountains divided into individual markers, jagged multi-shaped floes, white with an occasional garish splash of blue. Close up, the colours are more varied, with clear turquoises and many shades of white; and the clarity and purity of the pack makes the solid white of the mountains look almost grubby. All the time, the pack ice rumbles and grinds and grumbles to itself like the distant sound of motorway traffic on a hot day.

The meeting of the east Greenland current coming down from the Arctic at one to two knots, and the last of the Gulf stream going north at much the same speed, caused swirls and fragments in suspension in the tide lines on the surface at the temperature change. Fast moving cirrus cloud high in the sky gave a warning of what we must expect.

Andrew, who admitted that for the first three days out of Reykjavik he was thoroughly miserable, left a note on the Thermos: 'Gone to Bed. In the unlikely event that I should be required I don't think you will need the radar or sat nav to find me. Love Andrew.'

On the morning watch, I shut myself in the heads cupboard with some hot seawater to try to get clean. David performed his ablutions on the foredeck. Everyone else had been invited to shower on *Havella*, where luxurious hot fresh water and general comfort made cleanliness more inviting. We assumed that not including us in the invitation was deliberate, but realized afterwards that it was an unintentional omission.

The Ice Reconnaissance Twin Otter zoomed over to look at us as well as at the ice. Ragnar (confusingly purporting to be on *Gaia* rather than *Havella*) chatted on the VHF with the Danish pilot in Danwegian. The gist according to Jon was that the ice was pretty awe-inspiring all along the coast and impossible for Viking ships to penetrate, and that trying to get into Ammassalik, two hundred miles to the north, was a Bad Idea.

There was a considerable amount of doing nothing during the afternoon, to the extent even of bare feet and somnolence on deck. Sleeping bags were aired, and maybe a few idle thoughts. After patching several minor holes in the sail, I assisted in the airing of my sleeping bag by getting inside it on the coachroof and snoozing with a book.

The 'admiral' came aboard briefly, spread a clean chart on the engine box, told us that there was a forecast of fifty knots of wind, pointed out Ammassalik, and asked:

'So which do you prefer – to be here in that wind, or to be in Ammassalik?'

It was not a question to which he wanted an answer, but a way of informing us that we were to proceed under tow to Ammassalik, to ensure that *Gaia* was not caught out in a storm. A contributory factor in the decision may have been that *Havella* needed refuelling. Her tanks held five tons of diesel, which she was using up fast with all the high-speed towing.

It was a calm sunlit evening. Those off-watch showed no sign of wishing to retire, and sat around with those on duty, chatting, reading, taking the occasional look to make sure we were still Following That Boat.

'It will take us twenty hours,' Ragnar had told us optimistically, 'with some help from *Havella* – but I don't want to see any more about towing in the bloody film.' He folded his chart and departed for *Havella*. For the first time, everyone knew where we were going, or trying to go, and why.

'Do you think we would be round Cape Farewell by now if we had taken a more southerly, rather than westerly, course to start with, when we left Iceland?' I asked Gunnar.

'Yes,' he said.

'The fact is,' David pointed out, 'that even with all this – the towing and the engine and the electronics – it's still bloody difficult, and the farther we go the greater our admiration for the Vikings and the way they did it.'

It was not far off *middag* time when we set out, and David's turn to cook. He poached generous fillets of the cod he had caught off Heimaey – and which had since been stored in the deep freeze on *Havella* – in herbs and milk, from which he made a sophisticated white sauce. It was only when it was served that it was discovered that the milk stored in cartons beneath the deck had been contaminated by gasoline. We eventually made do with plain boiled saithe (coalfish).

'People think we are having a hard time,' Ottar said, '– and we are having a hard time, when our milk is spoilt with gas.'

'Not a problem which bothered the Vikings too much,' I agreed, 'but if it had done they might have gone berserk.'

'They didn't have much choice of food – they had dried fish –'

'– and more dried fish, and even more dried fish . . .'

After supper Frode broke out into poetry reading. This, although at first we found it surprising, was not uncommon. The poems he read were invariably those of Jakob Sande, a modern Norwegian folk writer.

2 July, Tuesday, midnight; 63 27 North, 38 39 West, heading 050

Ragnar and Odd are aboard a Norwegian long-line fishing boat, *Torita* from Ålesund, the first ship we have seen since leaving Keflavik. Fulmars have gathered hopefully on the oily grey swell under a mackerel sky. While we have been waiting, we have eaten two chocolate cakes I've just made.

There was something particularly unreal about the scene this evening. There we were, being towed across a smooth flat sea at over seven knots to avoid a storm which wasn't happening – yet, at least. The ice of the shoreline is out of sight, except for a thin white line on the horizon which might be ice, or might be snow, or might be sky. The sky itself is one of those mixtures beloved by the makers of complex jigsaw puzzles; and after midnight it is still light enough to write and read by.

It seems impossible that tomorrow there can be fifty knots of wind. But nothing of course is impossible. Today has been a good day. Now for a good night.

07.00

The overnight watch report that they have had to shove off ice and reverse and do all sorts of manoeuvres. It is now mizzling in fog.

'There were times when I thought this is definitely not on,' Nigel told us. 'When even Frode wants to be someone else you know it's bad.'

13.00

Our watch was enlivened by much fending off of ice in freezing fog. It is grey and damp, with visibility varying between less than the length of the towrope and a mile. At times *Havella* is invisible. Even in the middle of the day, breath vaporizes and merges with the fog.

We are now sailing due north, as part of a dog leg through brash round the pack ice. Ragnar's estimate of twenty hours was wildly optimistic. We are still one hundred and sixteen miles south of Ammassalik, which if we keep up this speed – 7.5 knots – without any more deviations the GPS tells us we shall reach in fifteen hrs and twenty mins.

Odd, who is sometimes chatty on watch, and sometimes makes it clear that he does not feel like talking, has been telling us about his way of relaxing: going hunting. Hunting what? Everything: elk, reindeer, ducks, geese. He was a paratrooper during his National Service, training partly in Norway, partly in the US, and often being dropped into remote areas and having to survive for three weeks at a time. As a doctor he does not, he says, have much to do, since there are so many fit people on the island where he has his practice, so he has been on a course in explosives and sabotage. Then, of course, there is his acupuncture, fairly recently acquired.

Ragnar has just addressed the troops from *Havella* to report the latest weather forecast. Apparently there is now a full south-west storm off Cape Farewell and a severe gale where we were lying yesterday.

13.30

Having satisfactorily completed the washing-up, Ottar announced that he would make a good wife.

'What are we having for dinner today, Mrs Bjørkedal?' Nigel asked. (The answer is halibut donated at midnight by the Norwegian trawler.) A new phrase has entered the ship's vocabulary: 'Wife of the day'.

17.50

Our afternoon snooze was rudely interrupted by the loud crump of ice on wood, which got us out of our sleeping bags in record time. For the next hour we joined the rival watch on the bows, using oars and boathooks to push away bits of ice brash enough to get in our way in the freezing fog. There was no wind, only the chill factor of our own forward motion.

Havella, at the other end of the tow line, was never more than a ghostly darker grey shadow in the overall grey. Often we were in a grey world of our own, isolated except for the umbilical rope stretching ahead. At other times, when *Havella* slowed down from her standard seven-point-something towing speed, the umbilical hung down from *Gaia's* bows in a huge submerged loop.

Frode was wheeling and zooming around, pushing brash ice aside with the gummiboat, even riding it up on to the occasional floe. If he had flipped or punctured it, it would have been incredibly difficult to retrieve him.

When we were in open but fogbound water again, I started thinking about breakfast and whether there was any bacon left. Then I realized that we were approaching the 18.00 watch change, not the early morning swop. Ottar is now frying the halibut we were given this morning – or was it yesterday morning? Time has ceased to have any meaning.

3 July, Wednesday, 07.45

We have again been fending off ice for a couple of hours. The tow has been dropped, which makes this much easier, although *Havella* keeps disappearing and has to be tracked by foghorn. It is impossible to steer a steady course with all this ice to evade. Our current position is 65 33 North, 27 38 West. No wind. Fog. Rain. Ice. Summer?

Audun on *Havella* spends much of the time up in the crow's nest ice-spotting. It is raining through the freezing fog and very cold. Sometimes the ice is fairly scattered and small, but there have been some full-sized bergs as well. For quite a while there was maybe four- tenths coverage, the most it would be safe to take *Gaia* into, and even then only very slowly and with much pushing off by pole and gummiboat.

'We need a breakfast reward,' Odd said. It was warmer down below than up above, and so I was happy to make coffee, and fry all our remaining bacon, eggs, sausage, cold potato and tomatoes.

'Land!' Low under the cloud there is a solid line of ice-strewn rock – a good excuse for a reward.

We hoisted our ensigns and a huge Greenlandic courtesy flag. Gradually the land became higher, steeper, more solid; then we were in a fjord, and at last rounded a corner into the harbour. The *Magnus Jensen*, a red and white Danish cargo ship, had arrived just ahead of us with the first supplies for seven months.

From the water, Ammassalik looked far more picturesque than Gunnar's unflattering description had led us to expect. Little multi-coloured box-like houses were clustered on several steep rocky hillsides. The tiny town of Ammassalik, on an island of the same name and the largest of a group of small settlements linked only by dog-sled or boat, is the administrative centre of the east coast of Greenland, which is otherwise virtually unpopulated except for a few hundred people at Scoresbysund to the north, well inside the Arctic Circle. Tourist day trips by air from Iceland to the airport of Kulusuk, on another island a few miles away across the Ammassalik Fjord, have had little impact on the area, which is even more isolated from the west coast of Greenland than from the rest of the world.

Ammassalik, known locally as Tasiilaq, has been linked with a saga describing an abortive attempt to establish a settlement at Gunn-bjornsker – Gunnbjorn's Skerries – some time before Eirik the Red discovered Greenland's more hospitable south-western fjords. It appeared in a prophetic dream to one of the would-be settlers: 'I can see death in a dread place, yours and mine, north west over the waves, with ice and cold and countless wonders.' The dream came true: there was such violent quarrelling within the group that only two men survived to return to Iceland.

In 1884, when a Dane, Gustav Holm, led an expedition to the area, it was inhabited by four hundred and sixteen Inuits. There are now five thousand people on the island, fifteen hundred of them in Ammassalik itself.

'At first, I thought there were easy ways to solve the problems,' a Danish tourist officer told me. But there are no quick answers to the high rates of birth, suicide, VD, murder and alcoholism, all of which are apparently even higher than in the rest of the country. Because of its isolation, it is difficult to persuade professionally trained west Green-landers to work in Ammassalik.

Another Dane, who had spent several years in Alaska studying for his doctorate in environmental studies, was running a museum in an old church which had been replaced by a square modern building.

'I have a good life here,' he said, 'with my own dog team and kayak. I am about to go sealing. Whaling and sealing have a greater importance here for survival than in other places.'

This was not difficult to believe. There was obviously no scope for farming, and although supplies were being unloaded as fast as possible from the *Magnus Jensen*, the food shelves in the two small local supermarkets were almost empty.

David and I volunteered to stay on board as evening boat guards – *Gaia* and *Havella* were rafted up together at anchor a hundred yards from the shore – so that the others could visit Ammassalik's bar-cum-club. We were looking forward to having *Gaia* to ourselves when Gunnar brought a Greenlandic guest on board.

'Maybe 1993 me come back to England – maybe no,' the visitor told me. 'Me no work – my heart – now sixty-three – me wife am die 1982 – me have house Denmark.'

He presented me with a bead necklace and Gunnar with a brooch, then held out a glass. 'Whisky?' he asked hopefully. He was already far from sober.

'I thought he was different,' Gunnar said apologetically. He returned to the boat just before midnight, with two Greenlandic women, one more sober and more inclined to stay so than the other. The less sober of the two decided sometime in the early hours to climb into Jon's narrow top bunk. He tried to reason with her, tried to move her out, and eventually gave in and moved out himself. Audun took her ashore at breakfast time. For several hours during the morning, David and I were marooned on *Gaia* and on more than one occasion had to contend with intoxicated boarders.

As it was my turn to be wife of the day, I decided to try some local fare. A group of four, whom we assumed to be father and son, mother and daughter, were swiftly and skilfully skinning and flensing seals on the rocks. The carcasses awaiting butchering lay dead-eyed on their backs, anchored by cords through their nostrils. While I was negotiating the purchase of a side of ribs for supper, the girl thrust a great chunk of raw liver into her mouth.

David and I found the seal meat delicious, with a strong rich flavour, although it could have done with longer cooking than there had been time for. We were in the minority, which we found surprising given the general Norse support of whaling and sealing.

'I am just going to wash my face to try to wake it up,' Ottar announced as we motored away from our anchorage in the morning. I had dressed in layers of ice-dodging clothes. Although the fjord itself was relatively clear, with only an isolated large greeny-bluish berg, there was still plenty of pack outside, but at least visibility was good.

'This is how I like ice,' David said, 'photogenic without being frightening.' We positioned ourselves as look-outs in the bows.

It was not long before Audun was seen ahead on *Havella* climbing up the rigging ladder to the canvas crow's nest lookout. Even at its thickest, the ice was fairly scattered but sometimes big enough to be spectacular, especially against the granite and snow of the shoreside mountains and the purer white of the ice cap above and behind them. One large floe looked from a distance like a bright red motor boat; closer inspection as we passed within yards of it revealed that a seal's blood from a shooting had soaked into the ice.

A few hundred yards further on, several large lazy seals scarcely bothered to lift their heads as we passed.

'How can they tell that we are gunless Gaians?' I wondered.

'I expect they know it's going to rain tomorrow,' Ottar suggested, 'so they have to enjoy the sun today.'

While Nigel was washing up after lunch, he and David and I talked about the Gaia theory. 'My own feeling in places like Ammassalik is that if the world is a living entity, it could very well get rid of man altogether,' I commented.

'Are you assuming that it is a living entity?' Nigel asked.

'I don't know – but if it is, and has a self-regulating ability, it seems to me that if there is a need for regulation it would be all too easy for the removal of people to be a part of it.'

'Mankind is relegated to just one part, no more important than all the rest, by Lovelock's Gaia theory,' David pointed out. 'That's why he has fallen out with the Church, or at least with the fundamentalist elements.'

The discussion was interrupted by a call for ice watchers. When we had emerged from the pack into open sea, marked only by an occasional isolated berg the size of an apartment block, Ottar leant back on the port bench in the cabin with a cigarette, a mug of coffee and a Jack Higgins paperback translated into Norwegian. 'I like being a Viking,' he announced.

By the evening, it was raining heavily; but the forecast for the next few days, certainly for long enough to take us comfortably round Cape Farewell, was at last for helpful north-easterly winds. Ragnar had decided that we should forget about Nuuk, or Godthåb, to give it its old Danish name. The Greenlandic capital had been on the schedule more because it was the one place in Greenland which it was almost always possible to get into, than because it held any great attraction. Instead, ice permitting – and it looked as if it would – we were to visit south-west Greenland, where Eirik the Red established the first Viking settlement.

At the end of our evening watch, Ragnar was singing cheerfully about four bells and waving a whisky bottle in the air while he waited for the kettle to boil. The atmosphere on board was particularly relaxed and friendly. There had been times when we had not felt at ease with Ragnar, and had sensed that he resented our presence, but we felt as if he had at last accepted us. This illusion was about to be shattered.

It had been agreed from the beginning that Andrew and Nigel would have some time off when we reached l'Anse-aux-Meadows in Newfoundland, and would rejoin *Gaia* in Halifax to continue to Washington. David and I were under contract as boat crew for the entire time, however. After David had been on the tiller for a couple of hours in the early morning drizzle, he was joined by Ragnar, who informed him that while Andrew and Nigel were away we were also to leave the boat. There were, he said, many people who would want to come on board; the crew agreed that it would be a good idea if we had a break too, and we should respect the decision because we had had Emily with us for the first trip down the coast. 'No discussion.'

'Who will pay for extra accommodation, food and transport for us between l'Anse-aux-Meadows and Halifax?' David asked.

'Pay it yourself,' Ragnar answered.

Nothing of consequence that would need to be filmed would happen between Newfoundland and Halifax, he told David, adding that if we did not have a cameraman or soundman on board, there was no reason for us to be on board.

What I found most hurtful was the implication that the whole crew had talked about us behind our backs, and did not want us on board at all. Maybe it was true – I did not really want to find out. David was more angry than hurt.

Odd, who was obviously in Ragnar's confidence, acted to some extent as a go-between, raising the subject himself, asking what we felt about it, apologizing for the Norwegians' blunt and undiplomatic way of putting things, and saying diplomatically that he thought we had all fitted in very well. We pointed out the logistic and financial problems which obeying Ragnar's order would cause us, and which quite apart from the personal insult made it such a bombshell. He did not seem to think that what we said was unreasonable. 'I think that Ragnar is the sort of person who only trusts himself,' he commented.

After giving Cape Farewell a wide enough berth to be clear of pack ice, we encountered more ice in freezing fog when we started to close the coast.

'We have seen three distant small whales, otherwise sod all,' David wrote. 'We have been towed for so long now it feels as if we are in a pointed wooden barge.'

'Do you know what the plan is?' he asked Odd at some point during the many course changes in freezing fog and ice after we had rounded the Cape. I felt as if we had been condemned to spend eternity under tow at eight knots in limbo. 'To get in as soon as possible,' Odd replied, '– at least that's what I hope.'

Then at last we pierced the fog and emerged inland of the pack ice under blue skies, except for an occasional streak of white fog or cloud across the base of mountains, rocks and bergs. Cape Desolation did not look desolate at all. It was warm enough to remove several layers of clothing, a perfect Greenland day. Peering for ice through freezing fog was already a thing of the past.

Sleeping bags and mattresses were brought out to air, and *Gaia* looked like a gypsy ship as she was towed through the Matelob, a narrow steep sided sound, at seven knots, although *Havella* slowed to one knot for some narrows. We found it frustrating that there were no coastal charts on *Gaia*.

'Tomorrow is the day for blood tests again,' Odd informed us.

'If there's any blood left to test,' someone grumbled. Greenlandic mosquitoes were in full biting mood.

David, who had been reading the Greenlandic guide book, reminded me that the rocks were supposed to be the oldest on earth: 'Three and a half billion years old . . . and all scarred from glacial power which has left little rocks balanced on the top of others when the ice melted. The power of Gaia is obvious here too.'

The ice cap, looking deceptively smooth, seemed to stretch to eternity above dark multicoloured rock and mountains on which patches of snow still lingered.

Jon took his duty day seriously and did a major spring clean, washing every saucepan, tidying books, shaking and airing rugs. When the call to hoist sail came, suddenly, as usual, the aft deck and coachroof were littered with carpets and pots and pans. We had by then been under constant tow, except for a few short stints under our own motor power in the ice, for four and a half days.

After an hour, the order to down sail was given as suddenly as the one to raise it. The tow was then reattached, and off we were yanked at the usual speed.

'Where are we going?' I asked Gunnar.

'Julianehåb.'

'All the way there tonight? We can't get there before midnight.'

'Yes, I think so.'

Ten minutes later after a VHF conversation with *Havella*, he corrected his statement: 'We are not going to Julianehåb.'

No one on board seemed to know during supper where we were going. 'I don't ask,' Gunnar said. 'That's better; it changes so much.'

Rikardur, visiting by gummiboat, was equally in the dark, and expressed surprise that we did not have detailed charts on board.

'We are now under tow, moving so gently that it does not feel as if we are moving at all, except for the quiet slooshing sound of the water under the keel,' I wrote. 'I suppose it does not matter where we are or where we are going – it's a perfect evening, showing these dramatic and unforgiving surroundings at their best.'

15   A Bit Hot in Greenland

It was not until late in the evening that we were given the first hint that we were after all going straight into Julianehåb, or Qaqortoq, to give it its Greenlandic name. A couple of kayaks shot round a corner towards us in the gloaming.

'Where the hell is Andrew?' Ragnar, who had just come back on board, shouted at David. 'Can't you see kayaks are coming out to meet us? Why aren't you filming? You come on this expedition and you don't want to film the capital of southern Greenland? It's unbelievable!'

We roused Andrew and Nigel, who after supper had given up trying to find out what was happening.

A third of the town's population of three and a half thousand turned out to provide an impressive welcome, with speeches by the mayor in both Greenlandic and Danish, and midnight hospitality in the tourist office showroom.

It had taken us more than two weeks to reach Julianehåb from Reykjavik. Without a support ship to tow them, the early Norse settlers, trading regularly between Greenland, Iceland and Norway, must often have taken even longer; but with a fair wind even a fully laden trading ship could have made the voyage in a week. As we had been under way for almost that long from Ammassalik, the hot showers and sofa beds of the Seamen's Home were welcome luxuries, although I never slept as well on shore as in my bunk.

Such are the miracles of modern communication that Jane was able to fax us an article printed in the *Guardian* from the copy I had faxed from Ammassalik. As usual, some editorial changes had been made. In particular, a general reference to Greenland's social problems had been deleted, although drunkenness, the most noticeable of these, was still mentioned in the last sentence: 'From a distance, the place will again look picturesque – we shall not be able to see the rubbish thrown from the multicoloured square houses set against the rock, and shall no

167

longer have to keep a watchful eye for drunken Greenlandic boarders, men and women.'

David and I walked to the tourist office to fax our next article. The first person we met there was Rikardur.

'Good morning. How are you?' David greeted him.

'Not good,' Rikardur answered unexpectedly. 'I'm very angry.' His voice, usually hesitant and gentle, was hard and tense, and his beard quivered with suppressed rage.

'What's the matter?'

A friend he had just spoken to in London had told him that I had written an article about alcoholism in Greenland. He was furious.

'I am very disappointed in you,' he said. 'You just repeat this old story, when in fact the stay in Ammassalik was the most peaceful of all. There was more drunkenness on Heimaey. Why didn't you write that Greenland is the most beautiful country in the world?'

His reaction was clearly a reflection of his loyalty to the country in which he had lived for four years, and which he therefore knew far better than I did. But I was not prepared to be judged by hearsay.

'Perhaps you should read what I wrote before criticizing it,' I said stiffly. I fetched my original copy, and the faxed article.

'I'm not going to apologize for sounding off,' Rikardur said, 'because I still don't like what you wrote. As a journalist, you must accept criticism of your work.'

'Maybe he was right, and that bit could have been better expressed,' I admitted to David later. There was however no chance to clear the air that day as Rikardur seemed to be avoiding me.

Our arrival in Julianehåb was celebrated with a communal lunch time barbecue, cooked and served outside in a small square round a fountain – the only fountain in Greenland and a source of considerable local pride. Several small children were playing with the water, putting their foreheads into the spray and splashing each other. Amplifiers and huge sound mixers were adjusted by a man wearing what looked like a floppy green bee-keeper's hat. Even the local people did not seem immune to mosquito attacks, and many adults, children and babies alike were wearing net bonnets. A local pop group struck up, and some of the adults started dancing in the street; but the dancers disbanded in disarray when two of the men fell out. It looked as if there was about to be a drunken brawl, but good humour prevailed, and the tension dissolved into laughter.

Bob and Beth Lux sailed in on *Rhodora* that evening while we were at an official mayoral dinner, at the end of which Ragnar informed David that he wanted to see the two of us on *Havella* the next morning. It was clearly not a social invitation.

Rhodora had left Reykjavik five days after *Gaia*, Bob and Beth told us over rum in their cabin. They had had a gentle crossing, and having listened to SSB radio knew more about our movements, which they had been able to plot on their charts, than we did.

When we reported next morning to *Havella* as instructed, Steinar ushered us down into the cabin, where Ragnar was sitting waiting for us with a pile of faxes on the table in front of him. He jabbed at a faxed copy of my Ammassalik article with his finger.

'You are here because of this,' he started. 'It is shit and because of it you, Judy are no longer on the boat.'

I reacted immediately and angrily to his choice of words and tone of voice. There was a brief and undignified exchange of insults before either of us had calmed down enough for rational discussion. I then apologized for the paragraph to which he objected: he was convinced that his reputation in Greenland would be ruined if any local journalist picked up what I had written, and felt that it reflected badly on the expedition.

'Kicking Judy off won't help,' David pointed out. 'As it's a hypothetical problem it might be wiser to wait to see if there is any complaint, and then dissociate yourself and the expedition from these sentiments.'

Ragnar and Steinar eventually went out on deck to consider what they should do. I was given a reprieve, accompanied by a warning that if I wrote 'any more shit' I would definitely be sacked, and that as a member of a project representing the governments of Norway and Iceland I was to write nothing critical or controversial.

The atmosphere was by then almost amicable. We were offered coffee, and the four of us had the sort of conversation we all agreed we should have had long before.

'This is the first time we've ever been invited on board here,' I commented.

'I was just saying to Ragnar on deck that this is the first time I've ever sat down and talked to you two,' Steinar said.

'Where do your loyalties lie?' Ragnar asked us. 'How do I know if I can trust you?'

'I suppose our loyalty is equally to the crew, to Knut, who made it all possible, and to professionalism,' David replied. 'And of course it should be largely with you as expedition leader.'

'Trust works both ways – we need to be able to trust you, too,' I added. 'I don't feel that you trust us, and that makes loyalty to you more difficult. With the rest of the crew, I feel that we all trust and respect each other, and so the question of loyalty doesn't arise. It's a natural part of the trust.'

The Norse all spoke such excellent English that we were perhaps too inclined to take it for granted that they understood everything we said; this, Steinar pointed out, was not always the case: 'I understand simple English, but you talk a different English I cannot always understand – it is . . .'

'Sophisticated,' Ragnar prompted. We all laughed.

'Please tell us when we don't make ourselves clear and you don't understand,' I said, apologizing for our lack of Norwegian. David and I left feeling that the air had been cleared, and agreeing that Steinar, who was amused when we told him that the Luxes knew more about our movements en route than we did, was a good go-between.

We were aware that faxes had gone backwards and forwards between Ragnar and Oslo. But the confrontation had been between me – or David and me – and Ragnar; and so we did not discuss it with anyone else. 'I understand it got a bit hot in Greenland,' Henrich Nissen-Lie said to us several months later.

As we walked away from *Havella*, we met a Danish policeman who had been seconded from Copenhagen for a three-month tour of duty. David asked him what were the biggest problems he had to face. Fraud, he said, was one – and 'there are a lot of drunk people here in Greenland'.

These people seemed from our observation to belong to all walks of life. Even if the Inuit as a race have a lower tolerance to alcohol than other races, as some people told us, this can only be part of the explanation. According to a recent survey, the average consumption of alcohol in Greenland is double that in Denmark, and four times that of Sweden. Greenlanders, in common with other northern peoples, often suffer from winter depression, linked with alcoholism and high suicide rates. They knew it as 'the burden' – *perlerorneq* – long before SAD (Seasonal Associated Disorder) was acknowledged medically elsewhere and attributed to the lack of sunlight, and therefore of vitamin D, during the long northern winters.

Alcoholism affects many other communities where the natural course of social evolution has been distorted, among the Australian aborigines, for instance. In Greenland, there has been a rapid transition from the traditional Inuit way of life, which was closely attuned to the environment, to the artificial complexities of modern Western society. The traditional kayak has, for instance, been replaced by fibreglass boats with outboard engines; although it has recently been reintroduced by a few sporting clubs, it is no longer used for hunting in southern Greenland. Numbers in Greenlandic stop at twelve – above that, there is a choice between *passuq*, 'many', or Danish; but it is now possible to fax Japan. At considerable expense, and with no obvious return, Denmark has provided education, medical care, housing and social welfare throughout the country; but there are still few indigenous Greenlanders with professional qualifications.

The gradual erosion of Inuit culture, which was unaffected by the Viking settlers, started when a Danish missionary, Hans Egede, set out in the seventeenth century to look for the Norse colonies. Nothing had been heard from them for several hundred years, and no one had realized that they had disappeared, probably at around the time Columbus 'discovered' the continent they had visited from Greenland five centuries earlier. Undeterred, Egede embarked instead on the conversion of the Inuit to evangelical Christianity from their animistic beliefs, in which hell was cold, and both living creatures and inanimate objects had souls.

Trade and religion went hand in hand, and the Danes assumed colonial rights, imposing a trade monopoly and closing Greenland to all but Danish shipping until 1950. Since the granting of Home Rule in 1979, a new sense of national identity has emerged. Most places now have two names, one Danish, one Greenlandic. More than four–fifths of the population of fifty–five thousand are still Inuit – which means 'people', and is preferred to Eskimo, 'eaters of raw flesh'. Most of the rest are Danes.

On the morning after our confrontation with Ragnar, *Gaia* and *Havella* set out for the Viking church ruins of Hvalsø, or Hvalsey – meaning Whale Island – with an assortment of guests, including a Greenlandic teacher Kaj, his Icelandic wife Edda and their small and energetic son, the Greenlandic mayor of Julianehåb and his half-Danish grandson, and the Danish tourist officer Hanna Lunde. Hanna and her husband had seen a post in Julianehåb advertised in a Danish newspaper, had decided they needed a new life, and had moved to Greenland twelve years ago.

Hanna told us that fish catches, the mainstay of the local economy, had been declining so steeply that the government was anxious to find a substitute. Tourism was a natural, she said, but there was a shortage of hotel capacity, boats and buses: 'We have suggested cooperating with some Canadian or American travel outfits and getting big numbers, but this has been frowned upon by many in the Home Rule government who want these things to be done in the Greenlandic way. Progress has been very slow.'

Many Greenlanders, as well as Danish and other immigrants, told us that they considered the government monopoly of trade through KNI – Kalaalliit Niuerfaat – to be unhealthy, preventing initiative and development. Edda, who had recently closed her gift shop because it could not compete, felt this strongly: 'As a form of socialism, it has been proved not to work everywhere it's been tried.'

She and Kaj were currently smarting about the expense of travel in Greenland. For what it had cost Kaj and his brother to buy their mother a helicopter ticket for an internal flight, they could have flown round the world. As an Icelandic, Edda felt able to view the Danish connection objectively. Contrary to what we had been told by several Danes, she was convinced that the Danish government must be making money from Greenland – for mineral rights, expeditions, NATO training exercises: 'They don't give something for nothing.'

Gaia was the first Viking ship in Hvalsey Fjord, or indeed anywhere in the old Eastern Settlement, for many centuries. From the fjord, the roofless stone church, once the focal point of thirty farms and a manor, looked insignificant against a steep rocky hillside. I was on the same dinghy to the shore as Rikardur, who pointedly ignored me until I caught him up on the stones above the water and apologized for giving a negative impression of Greenland.

'Accepted – ' he muttered. We walked together to the ruins through lush grass and a multitude of wild flowers: Hvalsey's Greenlandic name is 'Qaqorkulooq' – white daisy with a yellow centre. The only sign of current habitation was a solitary modern sheep farm farther up the fjord. For such a peaceful place, Hvalsey, haunted by the pagan ghost of Eirik the Red's cousin – it was part of his estate – has had its share of drama. It was at the church, built at the beginning of the fourteenth century, that a man accused of seduction by sorcery was tried, found guilty, and burnt at the stake in 1407. The woman concerned went mad and died. But it is for a wedding the following year that it is most famous, since it is the last Norse event in Greenland on record. The groom, Thorstein Olafsson, was an Icelander who later held high office in Iceland; of his bride, all that is known is her name, Sigrid Bjørnsdatter.

I wondered whether the wedding guests, who must have come as we did by boat, had been served some of the local delicacies Hanna had arranged for our neo-Viking picnic: seal meat and guillemot, minced reindeer patties, whale blubber and meat, and assorted dried fish. We ate in what had been a barn, between the great hall of the manor house and the church. Ragnar later pointed out, from a comparison with a photograph taken early this century, that more of the church had been destroyed in the last eighty years than in the preceding six centuries.

On the way back to Julianehåb, we stopped at a government-funded experimental and training farm, the only one in Greenland, at Upernaviarsuk. Erratics, boulders left by melting ice, balanced precariously on a ridge far above the makeshift greenhouses of an optimistic market garden. There were a few scrubby Icelandic horses and foals in a relatively rock-free paddock, but the sheep had been released from their winter barns to roam the hills until the autumn round-up in September. We were shown an assortment of vegetables, flowers and saplings, some under frames, some in the open ground, and tomatoes, cucumbers, peas, marigolds, lettuces and a special apple which looked more like a kiwi fruit in the greenhouses. The outdoor growing season is short, its start in May heralded every year by a blaze of dandelions.

The Upernaviarsuk women showed us their latest experimental knitting: scarves and sweaters knitted from a mixture of hard coarse Greenlandic sheep's wool, soft yellow-brown arctic fox and dog hair, and dark even softer musk ox.

As soon as we were all back on board, with some extra passengers, *Havella*, with Ragnar on board, took *Gaia* under tow.

I spent the fjord passage back to Julianehåb talking to two Inuit Greenlandic high school pupils, Karen and Lana.

'They don't sound very Greenlandic names,' I commented.

'People only started to give their children Greenlandic names after Home Rule,' they explained. 'Before that, they had Danish names, and older people were often given biblical names.'

'What do you think about Home Rule?'

'It's more Greenlandic than before, and that is good because it is our identity.'

At school, they had been taught in both Danish and Greenlandic, and had started to learn English at thirteen. Both were about to go to university abroad, there still being no university education in Greenland; Lana was going to a Danish university, in Århus, and Karen to Fairbanks in Alaska.

'When I go to Alaska, my boyfriend is going to study in Denmark,' Karen told me. 'We want to experience different things. Maybe he will get a new girlfriend, maybe I will get a new boyfriend, maybe we will wait. Girls in our villages get married and start having babies very young, too young – I don't want that.'

Among the many visitors to *Gaia* in Julianehåb was the bearded British leader of a multinational geological expedition. Although Greenland could no longer claim to have the world's oldest rock – its 3.8 billion years had been beaten in Australia – it was, he told us, a particularly good place to study, because of the lack of vegetation. He was about to take a group of students to the east coast, but hoped that they would not find any valuable minerals because that would inevitably damage the environment: 'A discovery near a centre like Julianehåb would at least contribute in some modest way to the local economy, but not on that unspoilt coast.'

When David asked him what he thought of an expedition calling itself 'Gaia', he said that he was in favour of anyone who could stimulate debate about environmental issues, no matter how. 'But the debate may well be thirty years too late. That's what many geologists think.'

Evidence about atmospheric and environmental changes over hundreds of thousands of years was gradually being collected through GRIP – the Greenland Ice Core Project, funded and undertaken by eight European countries, including Denmark, Britain and Iceland. From a field camp at the summit of the ice cap, 3240 metres above sea level, with maximum daytime temperatures of $-5°C$, cores of ice had already been extracted down to a depth of 770 metres, and back in time nearly four thousand years.

We heard about GRIP from Ivars Silis, a Latvian photo-journalist born in Riga, brought up in Denmark, and married to a Greenlandic artist, Aka Høegh. From a description of GRIP's investigations, he moved on to a defence of Greenlandic hunting. 'Hunting builds on an insight into and a respect of nature which has been transmitted from generation to generation for thousands of years,' he had written in 1987, which the Greenland Assembly had declared 'the year of the hunting trade'.

'I'd love to be able to take a sealskin jacket home,' I admitted.

'You are not brave enough?' Ivars asked. 'You should be.'

Ivars was one of the few people we had met since we had set sail on *Gaia* to comment on 'the red thread of the environmental strand' running through Vinland Revisited. It was a strand woven vividly into the paintings of his wife, whose murals at a new high school were based on Inuit mythology. Aka's version of the creation started from total darkness. Life came from the seas, where the water-born equivalent of Gaia combed whales and fish out of her hair as her gifts to man, the hunter, who had to prove himself worthy of them by living in harmony with nature. In the largest of several panels, painted in soft shades of blue and green, mottled seals like long-robed women rose from the depths of the ocean.

From what I had gleaned of ancient Inuit beliefs, they seemed more in tune with the environment than the more formal and less poetic dogmas of Christianity. Even so, it was a privilege to be present at a Greenlandic confirmation service for which the girls, and their mothers, were dressed in traditional costume: thigh-length white sealskin boots over dog-skin breeches, and capes covered with vivid multicoloured bead embroidery over bright red long-sleeved sweaters with decorated cummerbunds and wrist panels. The boys and men wore white.

'Go and see what I have made,' Ottar instructed me when we moved back on to *Gaia*. The hinged wooden seat above the plastic bucket in the heads seemed the height of luxury.

Ragnar, who had obviously seen the provisional plan we had presented as a basis for discussion about whether, or when, we should leave the boat, said tersely to David: 'You misunderstood me – I meant that you and Judy should get off the boat in l'Anse-aux-Meadows and not come back until Halifax.'

Western Greenland is not the easiest place from which to make complicated changes of plans for northern Newfoundland, which is only marginally more accessible.

'We didn't misunderstand,' I said to Ragnar at the first opportunity. 'But we'd like to talk about it.'

We left Julianehåb under tow. For the first hour, occasional icebergs loomed eerily from thick fog, from which we then emerged into brilliant sunshine under a clear blue sky. As there were still no Greenlandic charts on *Gaia*, even Gunnar had only the vaguest idea of where we were, although we had at least been told that we were going to Narsaq.

A mile short of our destination, sail was hoisted, although there was hardly any wind and icebergs and floes jostled on all sides. We were greeted in the fjord by three traditional kayaks with narrow paddles. The kayakers, encased in supple waterproof sealskin leather, demonstrated their skill with a series of rolls, some fast, some slow, all smooth and easy. Nigel, a keen canoeist, was particularly impressed.

On shore, wearing our Norwegian working sweaters, we were asked to line up, facing a group of local men and women in Greenlandic traditional costume. They sang us a haunting four-part choral welcome, against a backdrop of ice and rock and beneath a huge Greenlandic flag – symbolizing sun on ice, with half a red globe against a white background, the other half of the globe white on red. The ex-mayor and current local Landsting MP Agnete Nielsen, a tiny distinguished-looking woman whose national costume accentuated her high cheekbones, stepped forward from the choir to make a speech.

A full cultural programme had been arranged in Narsaq by Annemaria – Ria – Oldenburg, a Copenhagen historian, assisted by her husband Jens Hagemann, an ex-teacher who told us that he had 'dropped out' to concentrate on Norse studies in Greenland. Ria was responsible for a small but impressive museum on Narsaq's old quay. Among the displays was a collection of evil-looking east Greenlandic tupilaq, carved human- or animal-bone charms enlisted to bring misfortune or even death to an enemy – although there was a danger that the curse could turn the other way, depending on who had the stronger spirit. Frode had bought a replica two-jawed tupilaq in Ammassalik; I felt uneasy about it being on board.

From the museum, we were escorted to a paddock above Narsaq's small commercial wharf.

'Why are we being taken to look at two horses in a field?' Steinar asked.

Without Ria and Jens, we would not have realized that we were at Greenland's oldest Viking site, dating from Eirik the Red's reconnaissance in exile. The scattered stones round which a mare and foal were grazing were, Ria told us, the remains of an abattoir for Viking sheep. Jens was convinced that Eirik the Red had spent his first winter on an island facing Narsaq across the fjord, and the next at the site we were on.

'He must have been a very clever farmer,' Jens pronounced, 'since he knew the best places for keeping sheep.' A useful by-product of the sheep farming for which the grass along the fjords was primarily used by the Norse settlers was that it had the long term effect on the soil of repelling mosquitoes.

Jens had a theory that most of the original settlers had been slaves in Iceland who had bought their freedom by agreeing to sail to the west, and had practised a peasant subsistence economy. 'They must have been very hungry for new land to make that terrifying voyage in such hardship,' he commented. Only fourteen of the twenty-five ships which set out from Iceland with Eirik the Red reached their destination; how many of the others turned back, and how many foundered, does not appear to have been recorded.

The dirt road out of Narsaq to our next destination, Dyrnes, was built for a geological survey of uranium deposits, but after trial excavations the uranium project was abandoned as too expensive. Much of the road, one of the longest in Greenland, is regularly washed away by the ice and melting river water which are swept across it after every winter, but it is still possible to drive along the foreshore of a shallow bay littered with grounded icebergs and across a two-mile-wide stony river bed towards a summer ski run. A youth training camp on its coarse snow had just finished.

A minibus took us out of Narsaq past the town rubbish dump, a quartz quarry from which Rikardur told us that gravel was exported to Iceland, and a fox-fur farm abandoned because of the difficulty of feeding the foxes in the long sub-zero winter. We stopped beside a stream at the bottom of a grassy slope littered with jumbled boulders. Jens and Ria showed us how experts could tell from the way the stones had fallen that some of these were the ruins of a turf-roofed church.

According to a sign below the stones, this was probably the site of Dyrnes, claimed by Ivar Bårdsøn in the mid-thirteenth century to be 'the largest parish in Greenland'. As administrator of the cathedral at Gardar, Bårdsøn made an ecclesiastical survey of the Eastern Settlement.

We talked to Ria and Jens about Greenland's Vikings while we were drinking beer cooled in the stream, in which they told us there were sometimes trout. Even in winter, it was always a few degrees above freezing, no doubt a major reason for the Vikings' choice of the site. The church and farm buildings faced east across the wide sweep of the valley. The south-facing bay below provided shelter for boats which could easily be pulled up the gently shelving beach for winter repairs and storage.

As I lay on the lush grass, with its profusion of wild flowers, I tried to imagine everyday life in a Viking household. Women played a specific and important role in the Norse subsistence economy, Jens pointed out. 'They were responsible for skyr [the Nordic equivalent of yoghurt, a staple part of the Viking diet], for planning for the long winters, especially for making sure there were enough food stores, for day to day supplies and probably also for some trade, as well as for weaving.'

'Why do you think the Norse colonies disappeared?' we asked.

'There must have been a number of factors,' Ria said. The chief one, according to Jens, was the loss of contact with the motherlands of Iceland and Norway. 'They relied on supplies and contact – and they were forgotten.' He pointed out that the discovery of a Burgundy hat of a style not in fashion until long after the 1408 wedding in Hvalsey proved that contact with Europe must have been maintained for at least another half a century, possibly longer.

It would have been pleasant to loll around on the grass all afternoon, drinking beer in the sun and talking about life a thousand years ago; but we had another appointment, at Eskimo Pels in Narsaq. David was the last neo-Viking to board the minibus.

'Come on, Slowmax Lomax,' Øyvard chivvied him.

We were welcomed to the showroom of Eskimo Pels, Greenland's oldest sealskin factory and the only one in private ownership, by two Danish women with pictures of seals and the slogan 'I love Greenland' on their T-shirts. The older of the two, Hanne Hartvig, who had trained in Denmark, had moved to Narsaq as designer and consultant after four years in Julianehåb at the invitation of the government. Eskimo Pels was owned by a Dane, and managed by his daughter, Gitte.

It was Hanne who introduced the subject of Greenpeace, at the beginning of our tour of the factory: 'Greenpeace forgets to tell the world that baby seals are not born here but only in Canada,' she told us in Danish; Gitte translated into English. 'Greenpeace did such bad things, especially against the Greenlandic people because to live, they have to catch seals. The Greenlanders catch the seals for meat, and then the skin is the by-product – so we are using the by-product.'

Later in the tour, David asked what effect the Greenpeace anti-sealing campaign had had on Eskimo Pels' business.

'Stupid question,' Frode muttered irritably behind me, I assumed because he was pro-sealing and anti-Greenpeace. Later, when I knew him better, I was not so sure.

'In 1989 the firm was almost closed,' Hanne answered, 'but last winter it was on its feet again with twenty-two employees. And this summer we have made some sales to London for the first time since the Greenpeace campaign started.'

Although I could not bring myself to buy a sealskin coat – both on grounds of cost and because I knew that I would never wear it in England – I bought David a huge light-coloured hat of arctic fox and sealskin. This made him outright winner of the ship's hat competition, beating even Odd's Ammassalik dog and seal creation.

Halfway up the fjord next morning, under tow, Odd gave Jon an acupuncture session for headaches. After the treatment, Jon sat stoically with his head on the table while Odd chatted to us about acupuncture techniques: 'The Germans only put the needles in a millimetre or two, but I like to put them in deep.' When he was allowed to raise his head, Jon announced that he felt much better, except for the pains in his neck, which I suspected were caused by sleeping without a pillow and with his head hanging over the hard wooden edge of a bunk which was considerably shorter than he was.

By midday, we were anchored alongside *Havella* off a landing stage on to which a coastal boat was unloading crates of beer. There were no houses in sight. We scrambled ashore on to a beach of rounded pink pebbles and steep crumbling pink shale, and stood around wondering what we were supposed to do next. As Ragnar and Odd had set out ahead along a rough uphill track, we straggled along behind them. From the top of the track, we looked down over the modern sheep farming village of Igaliko, on the site of the Viking cathedral and farm of Gardar.

Much of the rock above the grassy plain on which the Vikings had built was pink *tugtupit*. Legend has it that Tugtup was a beautiful girl who went up into the mountains alone to give birth – a perfectly normal procedure in ancient Inuit times. The rock on which the afterbirth lay was stained red from the blood, and so has been called after the girl ever since.

For a village with a population of well under a hundred, Igaliko did us proud. We were welcomed with a speech in Greenlandic, translated line by line into Danish, and with superb choral singing by a small and elderly choir, followed by a feast in the community centre. Ragnar was presented with a commemorative plate for each member of *Gaia*'s crew, and made up for having brought nothing to give in return by introducing each crew member individually.

There is little to see in Igaliko of the Norse cathedral and farm of Gardar. Many of the stones from the ruins have over the ages been incorporated in later buildings, and hay is draped to dry every summer over the rest. In its heyday, Gardar was the centre of a large and well-developed Norse community, encompassing land twenty-five kilometres to the south and about as far to the north, and at least ten farms, as well as collecting tithes from a far wider area.

Several students, some from Denmark, one from France, were working on an archaeological dig at Gardar under the supervision of the Danish archaeologist Knud Krogh, who treated us to an exhaustive conducted tour of the site. The warmth of the sun encouraged a number of neo-Vikings to snooze at his feet on the grass while he expounded his theories.

His interest had, he explained, initially been in the system of agriculture in Norse Greenland: 'In spite of their seafaring reputation, the Norse settlers were first of all farmers. Everywhere they are known to have been there are stables, stalls, fencing, grazing stations in the hills. Life here in the early Middle Ages was not particularly tough. The people did not depend on contact with Iceland and Norway, they were self-sufficient. Conditions were very good for keeping cows and sheep. It was quite reasonable to have called the country Greenland – this part really was green. And today, too, the Greenlandic people want to use the vegetation. There are several sheep stations, for instance four here at Igaliko.'

One after another, he dismissed the theories about what happened to the Norse settlements. Deformities in skeletons from the Viking port of Herjolfnes had been thought to indicate disease, but had been caused while they were being shipped to Denmark. The more northerly Western Settlement, which according to Ivar Bårdsøn had by the mid-fourteenth century been abandoned to the 'Skraelings' – 'natives', or Inuit – had, Krogh claimed, been gradually depopulated: 'Summer in the Eastern Settlement starts a month before it does in the Western Settlement, and lasts a month longer; it was also two degrees warmer on average here. So whenever they could, people moved from the Western to the Eastern Settlement.'

He thought it unlikely that the 'Skraelings' had mounted a coordinated attack: 'The Eskimos were not a big group, and could only attack in small nomadic groups. Unlike the Norse, who met every Sunday at church, Eskimos did not meet each other much apart from within their own small nomadic hunting groups.' Emigration to the west he considered equally improbable: 'If they had gone from here to Vinland we'd find the traces and we do not see them. One Indian arrowhead has been found in the Western Settlement; this alone is no proof – it could have been brought by a goose.'

Most people wanted some kind of catastrophic solution to the problem of what happened to the Norse Greenlanders in the years after 1408, he admitted; but he thought that the explanation was 'a gradual undramatic depopulation', which was not widely reported since the saga age was over: 'The colony quite simply died out slowly. The young people gradually left, perhaps going to Iceland, leaving the farms in the Greenland fjords to be run by the old. The old died, and there was no one left to carry on.'

Ragnar and Odd walked back to the boats ahead of us, and went swimming in the nude – for about thirty seconds. The plan was to spend the night at anchor and proceed next morning to Narsarsuaq and Brattahlið. Odd disappeared on a long solitary walk.

Ragnar then became nervous about the weather – a gale was forecast, and it was already starting to blow up – and decided that *Gaia* should proceed instantly to shelter in Narsarsuaq. He, Steinar and Audun would wait on *Havella* for Odd. The atmosphere under way on *Gaia* was excellent, with an almost childish excitement about being allowed out without a chaperone, and a great sense of togetherness. After we had tied up at the Narsarsuaq jetty, we celebrated our brief independence with beer while we waited until well after midnight for the others to appear. Frode did his best to teach me how to open a beer bottle without an opener, a skill I have, however, yet to acquire.

'I would like a chat with you and David about life on board,' Odd told me next morning. We arranged to meet at the hotel near the international airport, a mile from the harbour, before a formal dinner which had been arranged there in our honour. I was quite unprepared for what Odd wanted to say to us, or rather, to me.

He had, he told us, gone for his long solitary walk the day before to think about what was wrong with the atmosphere on board.

'I have come to the conclusion that the bad atmosphere is caused because of you,' he told me, very quietly and politely. 'You talk a lot, and the others do not like this.' He suggested that I should stop talking.

I was also to stop doing anything traditionally undertaken by men: 'I understand that you want to help with work on the boat, but the others do not like this. So I want to ask you not to do any boat jobs. Leave these to the others.' I refrained from pointing out that the rope ends had still not been whipped, or enquiring whether I might still breathe.

'It is all right if you sit in the cabin writing, people are used to this and they don't mind,' I was told. 'And if you like you can do some extra cooking.'

Although this was not Odd's intention, the whole conversation – in which for once I did little of the talking – was both hurtful and insulting.

I accepted the criticisms, and agreed to do as Odd asked, in the interests of 'keeping the crew happy'.

Having relegated me to the position of a silent galley slave, Odd told us that he and Steinar were to act as go-betweens to sort out our difficulties with Ragnar.

At dinner that evening, I sat next to the mayor of Narsaq, an erudite and witty man with Danish, German and Russian as well as Inuit Greenlandic ancestry, and a hundred and forty-four cousins. He taught me the Greenlandic for skol: *kasuutta*, pronounced almost like *Gesundheit*. We practised it with some very good wine and cognac several times during the course of the evening, at the end of which he told us that we must not say 'Farewell', but *Inuulluarit*: 'Farewell means you won't come again; inuulluarit means "You must have your life a long time and come to this place again."'

In the opinion of a guest at the hotel, Narsarsuaq was 'where God forgot about creation'. It was, however, less God's fault that it seemed such a bleak place, than that of the modern developers – starting with the Americans during the war – who had taken advantage of the flat area between the ice cap and the fjord to build an airport, a hotel and a few hideous apartment blocks. But it was a good safe place to be while an unexpectedly warm forty-knot wind blew off the ice cap and down the valley, delaying our visit to Eirik the Red's place, Brattahlið, which we could see across Tunugdliarfik Fjord.

Qagssiarsuk, as it is now called, is again used for sheep farming, although its population is probably lower than it was in Norse times. With its relatively broad band of grassland between the water and steep bare rock, and the gently shelving beach essential for Viking boats, the attractions of the site are still obvious. It was from there that Eirik ruled his subjects, and from there that one after another his sons, starting with Leif, and followed by his illegitimate daughter, set sail for Vinland – although none of them stayed long.

It was a strange day. The impact of what Odd had said had hit me, and I was the one who kept wandering off alone, trying but often failing to keep back tears of self-pity. On the long motor and finally tow down the fjord back to Narsaq, I spent most of the afternoon in the dark refuge of my bunk.

An amicable compromise about our movements after l'Anse-aux-Meadows was, however, reached in Narsaq, with Odd and Steinar. Sitting in the sun on *Gaia*'s foredeck, it did not take long for everyone to agree that David and I would stay on board until St John's, where we would as usual move ashore, and that when *Gaia* left we would hire a car and drive down to Halifax, to film the relaunching of *Saga Siglar* and *Oseberg* after their transatlantic crossing on the deck of a freighter. Rather than being banished for a month, we would be having a ten-day working holiday.

'It will be good for everyone to have a break,' Odd pointed out. 'The crew feel very hemmed in at such close quarters with so many people on the boat. Frode for instance is used to a lot of space and just has to get away in the gummiboat to be on his own.'

'So that's why he zooms about so much,' I said, then added, 'Sorry, I forgot I'm not meant to talk.' If I could make a joke of it, perhaps I could jolt myself out of feeling so sorry for myself.

Steinar looked enquiringly at Odd, who explained: 'I told her.' We all laughed.

'I hope you didn't mind my straight talking the other day,' Odd said. 'Steinar and I agree that everyone feels much better about things now.'

20 July, Saturday, 17.00
We are under sail, somewhere in a fjord. I have kept well out of the way. While the sail was hoisted this was easiest in the cabin, but Odd was kind enough to tell me after hoisting that it was very beautiful outside, sailing in ice, and I must come and see. He was right.

It is so warm that many arms and even a few torsos and Nigel's legs have been seen. Before we left, he went off by gummiboat to record the sound of air bubbles escaping from ice floes, and then played it back over the loudspeakers. It sounded as if water was rushing into the boat – most alarming.

People have been falling asleep in various stages of nudity all over the foredeck. I snoozed for a while in the bows, but was woken when Ottar leapt on me with the boat hook to fend off a chunk of ice.

'Were you asleep?' Rikardur asked me a few minutes later. 'Yes – the sun was so hot.' That has been my sole exchange of words all afternoon.

As we motored into a tiny unnamed harbour on the north shore of Bredafjord in the early evening, several hundred reindeer appeared high above us on a cliff, then charged down a steep rock-face and out of sight. They were part of a huge privately owned herd which Rikardur told us were shot from time to time, but were not hunted because fear would spoil the taste of the meat.

For our last night in Greenland, Ragnar, with the benefit of Rikardur's local knowledge, selected an isolated but sheltered anchorage which we shared only with mosquitoes. There was enough driftwood for a fire, on which Steinar supervised barbecue cooking. Several bottles of chianti, whisky and brandy, and two crates of beer, were taken ashore and consumed. David and Øyvard led us in bawdy songs remembered from their misspent youths. Before we left the beach to the mosquitoes for the night, Rikardur threw the leftover food on the ground 'for the foxes'. The party continued on board *Gaia*. Ragnar, relieved of any public duties by the isolation of our anchorage, was in a particularly jovial mood.

We were woken at nine o'clock by Steinar, with an alarm clock which gave a horribly realistic and raucous imitation of a cock crowing. He then made us coffee with salt water – perhaps accidentally; *Gaia* had a salt water pump beside the sink, as well as a fresh water tap. Ragnar, who seemed highly amused by David's fragile morning-after appearance, sang the chorus of 'Oh what a horrible song'.

Apart from a number of well-deserved hangovers, conditions could not have been better for a departure for Labrador. Visibility was fifty miles, the sky clear, the temperature as tropical as it can ever be in Greenland. There was still ice to be negotiated, but nothing alarming.

I spent most of the day asleep in my bunk. 'I could pretend I'm ill, but it's usually called over-indulgence,' I admitted when David enquired solicitously after my health.

Others were feeling much the same. *Gaia* was, as Odd put it, 'a very quiet boat' as she left Greenland to cross the Labrador Sea.

16   Wild Ride to Labrador

As we were towed into a technicolour sunset, the icebergs and distant purple headlands beneath the vast solitude of the ice cap faded into the distance. All seemed well with the world, especially when we sighted several large whales.

Our book supply had been replenished by a swop with a British helicopter pilot in Narsarsuaq, and I immersed myself in one paperback after another. This had the effect of keeping me as quiet and inactive as anyone could have wished. The simplicity of shipboard routine, into which we fell back easily, dissipated the tensions felt on land. But we all knew that however calm it was to start with, the Labrador Sea was notoriously unpredictable, and the coast ahead as unforgiving as that behind us.

22 July, 22.30; on passage from Greenland to Labrador, 57 26 North, 51 27 West, heading 205

Two hundred and eighty-two miles to go (to Labrador), which the log read-out tells us will take thirty-three hours fifteen minutes. But we are unlikely to maintain this amazing speed – 9.1 knots. *Gaia* has been horsing along since the start of this wild watch at anything from 8 to 9.5 knots, with full sail plus jib. Nigel admitted that he was sick on his watch, but everyone on ours seems in fine form.

Ragnar on the helm keeps rocking the boat, although after tipping over the flowers I had picked in Narsaq he promised to keep her stable. At last I feel at ease with him as I did the first time we met. As soon as I finished my Jackie Collins novel, he grabbed it and whenever he is in the cabin is absorbed in its steamy rubbish.

23 July, 13.00

Two reefs were put in after *Gaia* reached 10.3 knots and began to feel as uncontrollable as a runaway horse. It has rained all morning, with some occasional big seas although the motion could be worse.

185

According to Ottar, it is not cold outside, but this all depends on the definition of cold. He says that he keeps thinking how nice it would be at home, and has made an important discovery: 'I am not a seaman.' No one would have known. The reason he so often makes cakes is apparently to avoid being on the helm.

Ragnar, after lunch: 'Where's my Jackie? I want my Jackie.' Having found her: 'I'm off to bed with my Jackie.'

16.30

Still wet and wild, now with three reefs and only a narrow strip of sail, low over the coach roof. David is roasting fatty lamb, a gift from Greenland, for supper.

There are big following seas roaring up behind us. Only one has actually splashed right over the boat, from the bows, a few seconds before I reached the heads, but things have bounced around a bit in the cabin.

After cooking supper, David did not feel like eating it – most unusual for him. The seas were mounting up behind us in an alarming way. Even Gunnar kept looking anxiously over his shoulder, and we resorted to trailing a canvas bag of oil to smooth the waves before they could break over the stern. Pouring oil on troubled waters proved effective, although we all hoped that it would not be tested in *really* rough weather – gale force wind and thirty-five foot waves were quite enough.

Gaia twisted and turned and leapt, groaning and creaking but at least not rolling convulsively like her chaperone. The two boats were often hidden from each other in the troughs, and for safety's sake had to keep their distance. In a twenty-four hour period, we clocked up a remarkable two hundred and four nautical miles under sail.

Then, to our dismay, we encountered ice: thick mush, with treacherous transparent glass-like pieces hiding in the spume, and occasional big scattered floes. It was a particularly dark evening watch. Ottar stood at the bows with a boathook trying to fend off on the starboard side, to prevent damage to the steering oar, while David shone a searchlight to show Odd on the helm when to take evasive action. I kept a look-out to port. We were going too fast, but slowing *Gaia* down was difficult; and we needed to maintain speed to avoid being pooped.

In a lull between patches of ice, Odd told me that he thought the atmosphere on board was 'much better'. 'It was all very amicable, but distinctly alarming and bloody cold,' I noted afterwards.

At some point, Ragnar said optimistically that the worst was over; he was wrong.

'Why do you think people want to go to sea in small boats?' Odd asked me as we stood side by side in the stern.

'Just at the moment I haven't the faintest idea, unless it's because it's so nice when it stops,' I said.

'That's the way I feel too,' he admitted, then added: 'For me, it is mainly because of the personal challenge.'

Eventually Ragnar decreed that there was no option to altering course so that we were no longer closing the coast. After two hours we seemed to have lost the ice, and crept below. The rice left over from supper had leapt from the galley on to the floor. I scooped it into the middle of the rug, which I rolled up and passed to Ottar to shake overboard. He missed, creating a minor rice storm on deck.

It was one of those nights when I had to get into my sleeping bag with care, planning each move and breathing deeply with my eyes shut. But in spite of the relentless crashes of water under the forefoot and against the bows, the creaking of the mast and the constant grinding of wood on wood as the hull flexed and the cabin resisted, insomnia lasted only a few seconds.

There was more ice evasion during the night watch, and the waypoint was changed, adding another hundred miles to our ordeal. This was then compounded by fog. At midday, Øyvard radioed to pass on a report of six-tenths ice at Hamilton Inlet. Ice conditions were unusually severe for late July, with many more southerly harbours still blocked, and scattered ice all along the coast. It was not a comfortable day, and I wondered how Bjarni Herjolfsson could have resisted three opportunities to go ashore when he was blown off course on his way to Greenland, and found Vinland by mistake.

The Vikings had had no choice but to go where the wind took them, or drift with the currents. We gratefully accepted an overnight tow from *Havella*. *Gaia* complained loudly – as well she might. The wind had by then gone round to the west, creating a vicious cross-sea but easing slightly.

'Who were these Vikings, coming to a place like this?' Gunnar asked as we approached a headland under which several large icebergs were grounded on the rocks.

'This is where they used to come for their summer holidays,' Nigel told him.

No wonder Leif Eiriksson had felt no more inclined to linger in

Labrador – Markland – than on Baffin Island, 'a worthless country' which he called Helluland, land of stone slabs.

'I wonder where the hell we are,' Ragnar said cheerfully. The GPS and a passage chart for the Labrador Sea had narrowed down the choices, assisted by harbour-entry details in a book of sailing notes. At last a sheltered bay opened up ahead of us as we rounded a large red buoy – leaving it to starboard, as the American buoyage system works the other way round from the rest of the world. 'They should be on the same side,' Gunnar said. 'It's very dummy.'

We tied up alongside a sheltered jetty at St Lewis, Fox Bay. It looked bleak and deserted at 7.30 am. Our unexpectedly fast passage – three and a half days – had caused more wear and tear on *Gaia* than the whole of the previous two and a half months together. It had also given us a week in hand before our official arrival in 'Vinland'. During the three days we spent in Fox Bay, there was time for Norse boat maintenance: tarring the shrouds, removing and refitting the gooseneck and yard, oiling the hull again. Nigel was invited to start whipping ropes. First, though, we all wandered ashore in dribs and drabs to explore.

Behind the scattered white-painted wooden houses above St Lewis Point, David and I found a swampy wilderness of miniature flowers and stunted trees. A wide track along the foreshore linked one end of the settlement to the other, with houses and a few shops loosely clustered round the bay. Angelica, thick-stemmed with large deeply divided leaves, grew as profusely as the giant British cow parsley it resembled, and can apparently be found wherever the Vikings settled. I wondered whether this meant that they had visited Fox Bay, either as Nigel put it for their summer holidays, or in search of wood, in which case they would probably have set up lumber stations, and have stayed for a few weeks or months at a time.

A fisherman, young but missing most of his front teeth, told us that he had recently been on a shrimping boat to the capital of Greenland, Nuuk – 'an arsehole'. We found him and his companion, wrinkled from years at sea, difficult to understand, and hoped that we were nodding in the right places. They told us that fishing so far that year had been poor, a complaint repeated by an equally wrinkled fisherman who came aboard *Gaia*. Although his baseball hat proclaimed that he was a 'grumpy old fart', he was, we learnt from the nurses at the Grenfell Clinic, the father of year-old twins. One had been delivered at the clinic, the other in the plane on the way to hospital. A new runway had recently been carved out of the trees above the clinic. Like most communities in Labrador, St Lewis had no road leading to anywhere else. Although for months at a time the sea would be frozen, making it inaccessible by water, this did not affect local mobility: skidoos just replaced boats.

The hospital, at St Anthony, eighty miles away round the north-eastern tip of Newfoundland, was, like the coastal clinics it administered, founded by Sir Wilfred Grenfell. At the girls' school I went to in England, we had a house called after Grenfell, along with Livingstone, Mallory and Scott; and he deserves to be remembered beside Britain's adventurers. But he was more: he was a reformer who left his mark all along the Labrador and Newfoundland coasts. From his first visit to their isolated coastal communities, as a young doctor in 1892, he was determined to alleviate the suffering he discovered. Labrador's 'liveyeres', originally settlers from Britain, lived off the land and the sea, as trappers and fishermen; but they were at the mercy both of the climate and of unscrupulous fish merchants. Many families lived in poverty, and no one seemed to care.

When Grenfell's employers at the Royal National Mission to Deep Sea Fishermen decided that the scale of the medical, educational and social care he advocated was beyond their scope, he carried on alone, enlisting support and raising money by lecturing in the UK and the USA. The hospitals and clinics he established have now been taken over by the government.

At the St Lewis clinic, we were made welcome and offered baths and showers – 'providing you take your shoes off outside and leave the bathroom as clean as you find it' – by its two resident nurses, Frances from England and Anne from Nova Scotia. They gave us tea, and bread and cakes baked by the clinic's housekeeper, Olive Rumbold. The majority of the Labradorians we met in St Lewis and its neighbouring communities were called Rumbold, Rumbolt, or Pye. The names featured in crew lists of fishermen who signed on in England in the 1780s for 'two summers and a winter' in Labrador: as it was put in a recent history of the province, 'some never returned to England but settled in small coves and harbours to fish on their own account'.

The arrival in Labrador of 'a replica of Leif Eiriksson's ship' was mentioned on Canadian Broadcasting's local morning news, which started: 'There could be good news today for fishworkers in St John's.' Good news about fishing was in short supply. The complaint of 'grumpy old fart' was echoed by Lucy, a teaching aide at a smart new school catering for a hundred children up to the age of twelve – a quarter of the community's population – who would then go on to secondary school as boarders, mostly in St John's, Newfoundland.

When she was a child, Lucy told us, by the second half of July boxes of fish were piled high on the wharf: 'This year, there's nothing.' She explained the local economy: the men had to catch as many salmon as they could in the season, which was short, and sell them to the local fish factory so that they could buy their unemployment stamps. Ten weeks work qualified them for the benefit on which they and their families would live for the rest of the year; a maximum, according to Lucy, of one hundred and thirty-nine Canadian dollars a week. There was, she said, no other work; but there was a great sense of everyone belonging together: 'We doesn't invite to dinner – we has no need to. If we comes when it's mealtime, another place is laid. It's just natural. Everyone is welcome.'

The Grenfell nurses felt themselves to be outside this magic local circle, although they were liked, respected and made welcome by everyone: 'Everyone knows everyone else's business, except us, and that is right.' The nearest policeman was at Mary's Harbour, six miles away; but in such closely knit communities crime was not a problem. Flies and mosquitoes were, as soon as the wind dropped. They kept us awake at night, and nothing we tried seemed to put them off our blood. They found Gunnar's and Ottar's particularly sweet.

'Everyone here should keep a sheep, as a mosquito repellent,' I suggested.

'No grass,' David pointed out.

There were, however, trees, stunted and shrivelled along the shore, but anyone could trek for a couple of hours inland and cut as many full-sized conifers as they wanted. Logging, using skidoos with trailers to bring back the wood, was a major winter occupation. The long weeks of unemployment were by no means inactive, and gave the men time for their homes and families. Many people did not want work, we were told; it would tie them down too much, isolate them from their children.

David and I were given the task of disposing of the ships' garbage. The foreman of the under-occupied fish factory came to our assistance with his truck. Just below the top of the hill, he reversed to the edge of a cliff and held the brake on while we tipped the rubbish into the void below. 'The council lights it once a year,' he told us. In the meantime, the dump was frequently visited by bears.

Within twenty-four hours, we had somehow accumulated another truckload of garbage. As we again tipped it over the cliff, it seemed a sad comment on modern society's waste and misuse of the environment. Our driver on our second garbage disposal trip was a young St John's engineering student who had been born and bred in St Lewis. 'I've lived here all me life, I'm related to most everyone here,' he told us proudly.

But he saw little future for St Lewis, and blamed the Greenpeace anti-sealing campaign for the decline of local fortunes: 'Folks here used to spend most of their time sealing. Seal meat was part of their normal diet then, and they could get an income from the skins. Now maybe a few folks catch seals now and then but sealing has basically been stopped completely. It was a major way of earning. Now there's only fishing. There are still millions of seals around, but fewer fish.'

For a short time, twenty years or so ago, he told us, the Americans had employed local people to build a radar station at the top of the hill above the tip. They used it for a year, and then they took it down again. The wreckage on the site still dominated an immense panoramic view of ice-scattered ocean and vast undeveloped land which made man's effect on Gaia seem puny and irrelevant.

'What potential is there here which could be developed?' we asked the student truck driver. 'Tourism?'

'Could be; but folks daresn't try starting anything and anyway they hasn't the money for it.' If they had, or if the place was more easily accessible, glossy travel brochures could describe the delights of fishing through the ice, cross-country skiing, winter cookouts, log cabins on skidoo trails leading inland through the forests or along the coast. In summer, the mosquitoes and general lack of tourist amenities might present more of a challenge to an advertising copy writer.

Although *Gaia* attracted a number of visitors, we were – to our relief – left to our own devices. As 'a real wife of the day' I invited the crew of *Havella* to join us on *Gaia* for lasagne, for which I managed to track down the main ingredients, as a change from our normal healthy but monotonous shipboard diet. The Norse had been working hard all day, in spite of Ottar's jocular reaction to Gunnar's mention of the word at breakfast time: 'First I have a smoke. Then I have a rest. Then I have a shower. That is my work for today.' Of the original smokers, only Ragnar and Gunnar were still not smoking.

Ottar informed us over beer on deck after supper that he and Frode had discovered why the Brits were not fluent in Norwegian: 'We must make you smoke, then you can speak Norwegian well.'

'In that case, why doesn't Andrew speak fluent Norwegian?'

'He does, but he hides it. He is one of us.'

A confusion in English between beer, beards and bears led to an excited exchange between Ottar and Frode about whether wolves should be hunted in Norway. To my surprise, Frode came out strongly against hunting in general, and of Norwegian wolves in particular, while Ottar took the farmer's view that livestock should be protected. The discussion started in English but became increasingly heated and carried on in Norwegian until long after everyone else had turned in. In the morning, I asked Ottar whether he and Frode had settled their differences. 'We discovered at the end that we think the same,' he told me.

The day we left St Lewis was Øyvard's birthday. He and Audun were leaving us in l'Anse-aux-Meadows, and we all wanted to show him that he was, as Frode put it, 'very special'. Steinar spent the day baking, and invited the crew of *Gaia* to a birthday tea on board *Havella*. After racking our brains for something to give Øyvard, we wrapped up a whale poster David and I had bought in Greenland, and all signed our names on one of the belts of our Viking tunics.

As official presenter of the gifts from *Gaia*, I gave Øyvard a reciprocal hug and kiss, to general applause. We all sang 'Happy birthday', 'For he's a jolly good fellow', and 'Why was he born so beautiful?'; and then we sang 'For he's a jolly good fellow' again in honour of Steinar, whose labours in the galley had produced waffles, chocolate, lemon and orange cakes decorated with fresh fruit, chocolate sauce and whipped cream. 'It was a feast fit for a king,' I noted afterwards, 'and Øyvard was the king. What a pity he goes back to Bergen and IBM in just over a week's time.'

Someone suggested that Odd should put his finger on each whale on the poster in turn while Øyvard, who was not allowed to see, said the name of a crew member. Ragnar was a long-finned pilot whale, Gunnar an ordinary pilot whale, and David a narwhale – 'I don't know what that long thing sticking out at the front is for,' Odd said; I was a minute harbour porpoise.

Gunnar was in a merry mood as we motored the few miles to Mary's Harbour. First he sang 'For he's a jolly good fellow'; 'Dat war I,' he told us, jabbing his chest with his thumb, 'me'. Then he asked, 'Shall I sing for you?' and broke into a lively falsetto.

We were greeted as we tied up by a dozen men who had just knocked off work at the Mary's Harbour fish factory, where there was some fish but less than usual, and by Sue, a British Grenfell nurse, who noticed with amusement that I was told not to tie off one of the mooring lines, but to pass it to Andrew. 'I don't know how to do this,' he muttered to me. 'I do, but I'm not supposed to,' I muttered back. So he handed the rope back to me, and I made it fast in the approved manner, to which I had been accustomed years before he had ever set foot on a boat.

'I have a warm and friendly feeling from and for these people,' I wrote that evening, about both the Labrador communities we had visited, 'and a sadness for them too, for their apparent lack of future which is dictated in part by the environment, in part by politics – the politics of the environment, of their distance from Ottawa, of the well-meaning but not necessarily clear-thinking anti-sealing campaign.'

David and I had walked only a few yards on shore that evening when we were offered a lift. We squeezed into the front seat of a pick-up truck driven by Tony Rumbolt, a young man with strange green eyes, alongside his plump young wife and their jam-faced year-old baby, Cody. Tony drove past the clinic, the mounted police centre, the local bank and shops, over a plank bridge, past the simple hotel (the only one in the area) and along a dirt road to Lodge Bay, eight miles away. The two communities were unusual in being linked by road, and Tony wanted to show us the bridge under construction across the Charles River. The road was eventually to be continued all the way to Red Bay, sixty miles away and already linked by road to Quebec.

He was a mine of local information, imparted with a strong Labrador accent, a mixture of rural Devonian with an Irish lilt and an American twang. Over a large area of rolling pinkish rock the conifers looked even more stunted than elsewhere; the result of a fire, Tony explained. 'How long ago?' I asked, expecting the answer a couple of years, or maybe four or five. 'Oh, I guess maybe forty year.'

Everywhere else, there was a fresh light green at the tips of all the branches and alongside creeks and lakes, giving the landscape a misleadingly lush look. 'It has all turned green just in the last couple of days, after the rain,' Tony told us. 'Summer should be well on here by now, but it hasn't hardly started.'

At the turning point of the road, men were still working on the bridge, although it was Saturday evening: 'They works all daylight hours.' The one-and-a-half-million-dollar operation, which had started only a week earlier, had to be finished by the beginning of December, before the winter snows. The road would, we learnt, 'in a few years' (fifteen, at four miles a year) make it possible to drive from Mary's Harbour and Lodge Bay to anywhere in Canada. Lodge Bay in the meantime was still a small sheltered winter community of twenty or so families, built compactly and even picturesquely at the navigational head of the river, nine miles from the sea. Traditionally, its inhabitants have always moved down-river to Cape Charles for the summer fishing. Upriver, there was fast-running, tumbling, salmon-fishing water.

After supper – fresh prawns in sauce with de-frosted flounders, cooked by Nigel – visitors came and went throughout the evening. They were polite and appreciative, asked intelligent questions about the boat, and never outstayed their welcome.

A couple of local men expressed surprise that *Gaia* did not have a deep keel to balance the weight of the yard. A large lady on holiday from Toronto asked me if I did all the cooking. A young man, another Rumbolt, who had his own small white fibreglass boat and had spent several years fishing in the Faroes, Svalbard, Iceland and Greenland, brought us a salmon. 'Whatever you're growed up to be, that's your culture and that's it,' he philosophized.

Next morning, twelve tons of snow crabs, late in the year for the first of the season, were unloaded from a smartly painted green and white boat. They were to be processed at the fish plant on the quay, for the American market. We were given a bagful to cook on board *Gaia*, and shown how to pull the legs and chest off together before putting them for twelve minutes into boiling salted water. In theory, it was Gunnar's turn to be 'wife of the day', but he allowed David and me to cook the crabs for lunch.

'I may have enjoyed crab more than this sometime,' Nigel commented, 'but I don't know when.'

When eventually the crab-eating finished, there was inevitably a mess, including the washing-up from several large late breakfast sittings. Since no one else seemed inclined to do so, I set about clearing up.

'If anyone else cooks anything else and makes more washing-up, I might scream,' I said.

'Why don't you just leave it?' Nigel suggested.

'Because I can't stand the mess,' I answered irritably, 'especially when people want to come on board – it's embarrassing.'

I was particularly irritated by a great heap of ground coffee which had been spilt on the side deck some hours earlier: 'Who spilt that coffee?' I asked fiercely. Gunnar was seen to clear it up with the dustpan and brush.

David and I were invited by the two Grenfell nurses, Helen and Sue, to stay the night in their flat at the clinic, with apologies that they could not offer beds to any of 'the boys': a married couple was one thing, unmarried or unaccompanied men another. Sue entertained us with stories about her time among the Indians at Davies Inlet, funny sad tales about how they made her laugh and she loved working with them, but how intensely frustrated she felt with and for them: the caribou stuck into a deep freeze which would not shut, so there it was in a living room, head and feet sticking out stiffly; the grandmother, a patient, hidden under all the other people on top of her in bed; garbage thrown out of the door; husky dogs in the house, and caribou bones all over the floor; and, most poignant of all, the fourteen-year-old-girl with sad eyes who missed school because she had to take care of a trail of younger children, while her mother was in the woods getting drunk, and who a couple of years later had two children of her own.

Although we laughed at her stories, we shared Sue's sense of the hopelessness caused by the transition from one culture to another, a transition which she felt to be at an earlier stage in Labrador than elsewhere, both for the Indians and the Inuit. 'Grenfell' often took the brunt of the bitterness and frustration, as the only identifiable symbol of the white man and authority. Dr Peter Roberts, whom we had met at St Anthony on our first visit there, showed endless patience, Sue told us.

'People think that there are thousands of Indians living in Labrador, but there are only seven hundred altogether, all living north of Goose Bay,' she pointed out. Benefit and special allowance money provided just about everything anyone needed, except pride and a sense of direction. The lack of initiative this engendered also affected the exclusively white population south of Goose Bay: 'There is always a reason why not, rather than why.' I read all I could find out about the tough old days, before Grenfell or welfare: collections of reminiscences in a series of publications called *Them Days*, biographies of Grenfell nurses and doctors, books by and about Grenfell himself. Time after time, the older generation underlined two great losses: the close understanding of the environment which had been essential for survival, and the proud independence of people who helped themselves and each other, but would, and often did, starve rather than ask for outside help.

Although Odd had given both Ottar and Ragnar acupuncture, as well as Jon, he could do nothing for a raging toothache which was making Jon's life increasingly miserable, and took him to the clinic.

Within a few hours, the patient had been flown to St Anthony, with a monstrously swollen face. The rest of us proceeded to Lodge Bay, Odd and Ragnar on foot, everyone else by boat under motor. We had our closest encounter with a whale in the Charles River, when a humpback leapt from the water only fifty feet away, then retreated slowly down our wake waving its great white flippers as if applauding our passage.

It was a perfect, clear, blue day, but with a breeze which made sweaters necessary, as we wound our way up the inlet leading to Lodge Bay. Occasional salmon nets set along the shore, beneath humps of rock with a thin covering of straggly stunted trees, were the only hint of human habitation. After dark, a small skein of Northern Lights played above our mid-river anchorage. We used Odd's borrowed military night-sight binoculars to examine it, and looked in vain for black bears wandering along the shore.

It had been wrongly assumed that there would be a shop near our anchorage, and both ships were short of basic supplies such as 'twenty breads'. David and I volunteered to go back by road to Mary's Harbour, first making our way by dinghy two miles upstream to Lodge Bay. Abandoned skidoos littered the grass between huge piles of logs.

The first person we met was a construction worker at the bridge site, Ward Pye, who immediately offered us the use of his pick-up, provided we had it back in time for his wife, Verna, to drive to work at the Mary's Harbour hotel at lunch time. 'Remember to pump the brakes a bit because they're leaky,' he warned. After buying all the bread, a dozen sliced loaves, at a store owned by a Rumbolt, we called at the clinic to enquire about Jon. He had been hospitalized, but was resting and comfortable.

Back at Lodge Bay, Verna Pye invited us into her house, which she told us was twenty-seven years old, the same age as her marriage. Built of wood by Ward, it was comfortable and well equipped, with electricity, plumbing, a CB radio and a plaque on the wall proclaiming that 'a wise monkey doesn't monkey with another monkey's monkey'. She plied us with tea, walnut cake and hunks of salmon freshly smoked with blackberry bush wood on their own smoker by the back door. Wild raspberries and blackberries grew freely outside many of the houses, alongside cultivated potatoes, cabbages, rhubarb and a few flowers. We asked her if bears were often seen near the houses. 'Just small ones,' she told us. 'How big is a small bear?' Her hand gestures did not make it seem small at all.

We were all woken unusually early next morning by the mosquitoes.

From dawn onwards, there was a variety of sounds from the shore and the water; birds, I assumed, although some could have been made by animals. Had I been a trapper, an old-fashioned Labradorian, even a generation ago, I would have known immediately what was making what noise, and why, and how to trap or shoot it if its skin or flesh could be put to use – and more or less everything could, from porcupines and red squirrels to bears, seals and whales.

There were still a few chunks of ice about, and one or two glisteningly photogenic full-sized bergs, as we motored out to Cape Charles, a collection of summer shacks surrounding a harbour about a mile across between granite islands. The two parts of the settlement, Tickle, where there was a shop, and the Cove, where we came alongside a jetty, were two miles apart by land, linked by a path across rock and past little highland ponds.

In a few hours, Cape Charles demonstrated some of the rapid weather changes with which coastal Labrador can catch out the unwary: sun, no sun; strong wind, no wind; clear visibility and fog. As the fog started to roll in, a foghorn three miles offshore gave its eery warning. The reopening of the fish harbour with a new summer coat of paint was being celebrated ashore, but there was no fish. Several small boats spent the early part of the evening zooming about at high speed, using large quantities of diesel bought with unemployment benefit. That the rest of Canada was supporting the province's unemployed was, we had been told, a source of considerable irritation outside Newfoundland–Labrador.

The white-painted board houses, set on pink rock amidst wild flowers and coloured mosses, looked picturesque from a distance; closer inspection revealed various stages of dilapidation. The largest and oldest house, two storeys, white with green shutters, belonged to 'Uncle Frank', we were told by a group of children: 'But he couldn't come this year 'cos he's not well and he can't get about in boats and things.' Their voices rose as if they were asking for verification at the end of each sentence. They pointed out the school, which had not been used since Cape Charles ceased to have any year-round residents, and was falling into disrepair: 'They keeps it locked now 'cos someone broke in and played schools.' The church, a tiny white building, was open, however; its plain interior was lined with remarkably light wood and equipped with five hymn books, two Bibles and a vase of plastic flowers.

Angelica grew along the track between the houses, although there was none at Lodge Bay. Perhaps the Vikings lingered at the Cove end of

Cape Charles, using it in much the same way as it was still used, as a summer fishing centre; it was too far from Labrador's forests to be much use as a lumber centre.

We left for 'Vinland', under tow with a light south-westerly breeze and a calm sea, on the morning of August 1st. It was time to start one of our minor ecological tasks, sampling sea water to assist a Rhode Island university marine biology laboratory with research into plankton levels. David had volunteered to do this twice a day, and took his first samples off the island of Belle Isle. Half a dozen large icebergs were lurking in the lee.

L'Anse-aux-Meadows lay shrouded in fog as we approached northern Newfoundland. *Gaia* was not to make herself seen, and so we anchored until evening out of sight of any habitation in eighteen metres of water, and not much farther from a headland. As *Gaia* had been thoroughly spring cleaned and oiled in Labrador, there was little to do except keep a wary eye on some large bergs which seemed to be standing guard over us. A pod of half a dozen dolphins, one a baby half the size of the others, greeted us, first humping their black backs out of the water, then trying little flat-bellied jumps out of the water.

In the evening, we moved closer inshore, to share an anchor with *Havella* in Quirpon Harbour.

'Look!' Gunnar exclaimed as we saw the first lights glittering, still in the distance, on shore. 'Lights!'

'Yes, Gunnar,' we all agreed.

'Where there are lights, there is electricity.'

'Yes, Gunnar.'

'And where there is electricity – there are GIRLS!'

Girls were of course from then on referred to as 'electricity' on *Gaia*.

Jon rejoined us in Quirpon, looking and feeling good, but minus one front tooth.

David and I were offered showers on *Havella* that evening; it was a small thing, but it seemed at last a symbol of acceptance.

We were almost at the climax of our Viking voyage, for although none of us knew for certain whether this was Leif Eiriksson's Vinland, l'Anse-aux-Meadows was our mecca, and *Gaia* had to play her part in a living pageant for dignitaries from Norway, Iceland and mainland Canada.

17 Revisiting Vinland

The Great Day – our arrival in Vinland, and Frode's twenty-first birthday – started as a photo call for *Gaia* under sail in front of an iceberg. A Canadian television crew filmed sail hoisting and manoeuvring – we managed several successful tacks – and an interview with Ragnar. David, Andrew, Nigel and I hitched a lift on a fishing boat so that we could cover the ceremonies on shore. As the New York public relations company had arranged for *Gaia* to sail in at the end, the crew would miss the speeches and presentations. It was the first time I had seen *Gaia* under sail: she looked good.

The world, it seemed, had come to l'Anse-aux-Meadows, an unlikely place for an international gathering, or even a rally of motor caravans, which was what it looked like from the sea. Many, we discovered later, had driven farther than we had sailed, just to see *Gaia* coming into the only known Viking site in North America. A family from an Alberta Sons of Norway Lodge, for instance, told us that they had driven four thousand miles. Above the sod houses of the reconstructed Viking settlement, next to the original site, visitors and journalists jostled for space inside the museum, part of which had been turned into a press room. Nicole Gorden, whom we had last seen in Iceland and who was in charge of PR, seemed disappointed that we could not provide any film of sinking or drownings for TV news bulletins.

Part of the museum carpark had been roped off as an official arena. I sat on the ground with Erik Bye, whose ambitious plans for a major multi-media happening at l'Anse-aux-Meadows had not yet crystallized, waiting for something to happen. We were entertained by a Newfoundland comedian, Ben Ploughman from Port-aux-Choix, with local patter jokes: 'Newfie goes to Toronto to get a job. Sees a sign on the road: "Toronto Left", turns round and goes back home again;' 'did you hear the one about the three Newfies who were drowned burying their friend at sea?'

It was not, however, all light-hearted. Ben Ploughman pointed out that the last international gathering in northern Newfoundland had been the 'great anti-sealing campaign', and recited his own song of mourning for 'the complete loss of the Newfoundland off-shore sealing industry':

> This is the last sealer's song,
> The end of the fishery gone wrong.
> Four hundred years of sealing we've done,
> Now the last of the sealer's dying young . . .

At last – it was a cold grey draughty day – the local Leif Ericson Canadian Sea Scouts marched from the museum at the head of an assortment of dignitaries, including the Newfoundland premier, the Canadian minister for the environment, the president of Iceland, Knut Kloster and the Norwegian minister of education, research and ecclesiastical affairs. Two Canadian Mounties, one magnificent in shiny brown leather boots and a big hat, added a touch of local colour.

The guests of honour were Dr Helge Ingstad and his wife Anne Stine, whose work at l'Anse-aux-Meadows was belatedly acknowledged with the unveiling of a commemorative plaque. Ninety-two-year-old Dr Ingstad looked and sounded frail as he gave a speech in English. There were tears in his wife's eyes.

Each of a long series of speeches rightly paid tribute to the Norwegian couple whose tenacity had proved that the Vikings really did reach the New World five centuries before Columbus. In keeping with the intended spirit of Vinland Revisited, emphasis was also laid by one speaker after another on the needs of the environment.

'The Vikings were looking outward while the rest of Europe was looking inward,' the Canadian minister of the environment stated. An Icelandic minister told us that we were 'indeed in the eleventh hour': 'Man has behaved as if he is the master of nature, he is not: he is but a part of it.'

Gaia made a stately appearance. A Norwegian folk singer in traditional costume stood at the head of the fish dock (which had been repaired for the occasion at the expense of the Norwegian government) and sang a haunting welcoming song. There was spontaneous applause from the crowds on shore – an estimated eight thousand people, more than had ever before gathered in l'Anse-aux-Meadows. For the Ingstads, it was clearly an emotional occasion: thirty years after they had first suspected that this might be Vinland, they were for the first time seeing a Viking ship sailing towards it. The mist added to the eery impression that this was how it must have been a thousand years ago.

As the sail was dropped, the crew hoisted a spar carrying a blue banner which *Gaia* was from then on to display in harbour:

> A thousand years ago . . .
> Europe and America were brought together by
> the Vikings.
> Since then . . .
> our knowledge of the world has grown faster
> than our sense to take care of it.
> Now . . .
> We must set the right course ahead
> and open up a new era.

Three huge cakes had been baked locally for the occasion, each decorated with a Viking ship. President Vigdis Finnbogadottir and Ragnar were given the first slices. David stood on a bench and announced to the crowd that it was Frode's twenty-first birthday; we all sang 'Happy birthday', and David and I gave him a two-dimensional model Viking ship we had bought from a stall on the quay. 'You'll have to make a slight alteration to it,' we apologized: not being a sailor, its maker had set its steering oar to port.

Finding out about plans for our time in Newfoundland had not been easy, and there was some confusion about who was meant to be where when. Ragnar, along with the dignitaries, had to make a hasty departure by coach to the airport at St Anthony; he was to attend meetings in New York at which it was to be decided whether *Gaia* would continue round the world after Washington, or proceed instead to the World Environmental Conference to be held the following June in Rio. The Brits had been booked into the nearest hotel, thirty miles away in St Anthony; fortunately David had arranged to hire a car. A bus appeared to take the rest of the crew to the town, for a Viking party, a splendid romp at which we were all the hotel's guests of honour.

Makeshift curtains were drawn aside to reveal two hotel staff, dressed as Newfie fishermen, talking about the need to build a bomb shelter because as everyone knew the Vikings were 'big, bad and ugly'. Two 'Vikings' staggered on to the stage wearing wigs with blonde plaits, long tunics and huge horned helmets which, as David commented, would have made Knut Kloster 'go bananas'.

Disco music went on afterwards until all hours, long after most of the crew had been returned to l'Anse-aux-Meadows. Frode, to whom we all sang 'Happy birthday' again during dinner, spent what was left of the night in Andrew's and Nigel's room – for which he was reprimanded by Odd when we returned him by car next day.

Our second evening's entertainment, also at St Anthony, was again riotously enjoyable. After a dinner given by the mayor and council, we were 'screeched in' as honorary Newfies; screech, the local rum, has a kick which rivals even Norwegian aquavit. The ceremony, of which we were told that the premier disapproves, usually involves kissing a cod before drinking a dram. It was a reflection of the state of Newfoundland's cod fisheries that we had to make do with a frozen salmon, proffered by a girl in oilskins and boots. Gunnar and Steinar braved the ceremony first, for which they were given a double dram.

Jon and I were next. 'What's your role on the ship?' I was asked. I turned to the others: 'What's my role?' Some replied, 'She's a Viking,' and others, 'She's a wife.'

Odd insisted on kissing the girl instead of the fish.

Compared with the settlements we had visited in Labrador, St Anthony was a real town. It had a main road, a village-sized population, and a shopping centre, the Viking Mall, to which we took the car and a long shopping list from Steinar. The new Curtis Memorial Hospital – Dr Curtis was Grenfell's successor – is both the biggest building and the largest employer in the area. On our first visit to Newfoundland, we had been given memorable hospitality by a British 'Grenfell doctor', Jez Hilyard, and his wife Jill. They lent David their elderly station wagon to drive to the airport with Andrew, Nigel, Øyvard and Audun.

We had all known from the start that Øyvard would be leaving, but Audun's decision had been made during the voyage. Both would, we knew, be a great loss; Øyvard for his unfailing good humour and radio skills, and Audun for his quiet professionalism and reliability. Steinar and Rikardur were the only two crew left on *Havella*. *Gaia* was temporarily three short – Ragnar, Nigel and Andrew – but was joined by a Canadian archaeologist, Bob McGhee.

The hope that once we had reached our primary nautical goal it would all be plain sailing was soon dashed. Frode was the first casualty. He was whittling away at a walking stick on the first afternoon at sea when his knife slipped. Odd stitched the gash in his hand, and I did his washing-up duty.

Early next morning, both boats stopped for adjustments to the tow rope which had become entangled round *Havella's* propeller. Gunnar was summoned with his diving gear. Odd too went across to help. Accompanied in heavy rain by a group of hopeful seabirds, *Gaia* lolled in the swell. After a couple of hours, we started moving slowly, still under tow.

'It's much better when Ragnar is on board,' Ottar commented, 'because he makes the decisions. Now there are three people to decide, Odd, Steinar and Gunnar. They are all talking on *Havella* about what we must do and where we must go.'

Forty-five miles off a place called Stinking, *Havella* stopped again, with transmission problems. The rolling became so unpleasant that David felt queasy, and I turned in without any supper. Temporary repairs eventually enabled *Havella* to move forwards, although her engine could not be put into neutral. A coastguard ship came out to investigate our plight, and a fishing boat from the island of Fogo led us into Seldom Come By, a harbour which in the old days the schooners never passed without calling in. We tied up alongside a new government wharf, and gathered at four o'clock in the morning for 'special coffee' in *Havella's* wheelhouse. New parts for the clutch had, we were told, been ordered, and would be waiting for us in St John's.

In spite of complaints about no fish, one boat was unloading cod when David and I explored later on, but they were so small that they hardly seemed worth the effort of gutting. Local children were cutting out the tongues, a local delicacy which David successfully tried on us next time he was wife of the day.

At midday, the Viking mechanics decided that *Havella* was movable, and we set out. A mile offshore, the trouble recurred. We returned to the harbour, where I whiled away the afternoon with sail repairs until our second, and successful, departure. *Gaia* proceeded under sail. Fifteen miles out, the gear box on *Havella* started its tricks again. In spite of a northerly sailing wind, it seemed only fair to stand by; but eventually the decision was made that *Gaia* must proceed alone so that she would make St John's on time, leaving Steinar and Rikardur on *Havella* to wait for a tow.

Big yawing seas made life uncomfortable, even with three reefs, two of which were shaken out just before the end of the night watch by Jon and Frode, neither wearing a harness or line. Jon so nearly fell overboard that for several seconds it seemed impossible for him to swing himself back. There was only a glimmer of light, and it would have been virtually impossible to retrieve him.

Odd was sleeping on the bench in the main cabin, looking drawn and white and at least ten years older. The more exhausted he became, the more he worried and the less he trusted anyone else's competence, double-checking everything, including a waypoint which he was afraid Gunnar had been too tired to enter correctly.

Havella meanwhile had been given a tow; but after twenty-four hours at sea, Steinar was told by Ragnar over the VHF to continue under sail to St John's, which they eventually reached more than twenty-four hours after us. It was by then, however, the sort of weather when being at sea for ever did not seem too much of a hardship – sun, blue sky, a glittering blue-green sea, a light following wind, and occasional entertainment by dolphins. Steinar and Rikardur confessed later that they celebrated whenever their speed under sail exceeded two knots.

While we drifted next day in perfect gentle weather under the cliffs a mile or so outside St John's, we discovered how difficult it was to hide a Viking ship. Our first visitor was a fishing boat, at breakfast time; others sought us out throughout the morning, their crew and passengers expressing interest, admiration, even incredulity: 'T'underin' Lord Jesus in the garden, did you come across the Atlantic on dat ting?'

Gunnar was on the helm as we eventually approached the steep-sided narrow entrance to St John's. 'Please go away!' he said under his breath when we had to tack in front of a huge orange coastguard ship just outside the narrows. Both to port and starboard, the cliffs were lined with people, many of whom ran to keep up with us. The cannon on Signal Hill fired a three-gun salute. Yacht crews came alongside, waving and cheering. Hooters, including those of some Russian trawlers, were blasted on all sides. Thousands had gathered behind a triumphal fir tree arch on the town quay.

Wearing our Viking tunics, we were ushered up a red carpet from the quayside to seats behind the governor general and his wife, the mayor, the premier, and Icelandic and Norwegian ambassadors. Children who had won an environmental Gaia poster competition were awarded certificates and prizes. Numerous speeches were made, all, including Ragnar's, emphasizing the environmental theme and its link with the Viking spirit of adventure. Groans from the crowd greeted the enthusiastic doggerel of the town crier. Fifes and drums played 'The British Grenadiers', and the signal that the welcoming ceremony was over was given by a lone piper.

Ragnar had negotiated a temporary cabin for David and me on a handsome orange factory-freezer ship, *Concordia*, with a crew from Molde in west Norway. Originally Norwegian, she had recently been re-registered in Halifax; her skipper, bronzed and wearing only Bermuda shorts and flip-flops, told us that he had waited four months for a licence from the Canadian registration authority, and was still waiting for official permission to start clam fishing for a Japanese company.

Our cabin was small, but warm and comfortable. The use of the ship's washing machine and tumble dryer was another luxury and we volunteered to act as 'Lomax Laundry Services' for the rest of the Vikings. The quay against which *Gaia*, *Havella* and *Concordia* were berthed ran along the bottom of the old town, which had retained the historic charm of its painted clapboard terraces in spite of several major fires during the nineteenth century.

The local tourist officer, Kay Coxworthy, whose powerful and warm personality was irresistible, told us that *Gaia* had attracted a far larger crowd than the British royal yacht *Britannia*. Kay had been brought up in one of the homes set up by Grenfell; her mother had died in childbirth at the age of thirty-two, leaving eleven orphans. Kay's husband, Ed, equally large and warm-hearted, became an honorary member of *Gaia*'s crew in St John's.

'I'll be in terrible trouble if some of you Vikings don't come with me,' Kay announced on the quay on our first morning. 'There's a bus trip, and you have to come.'

Ragnar had to stay to meet *Havella*. Frode was on boat guard duty, and Odd had important things to do on shore. Gunnar, Jon, Ottar, David and I went with Kay.

We were driven for an hour and a half through forests and farmland, past ponds and lakes – seventy-five per cent of Newfoundland is water – to a small museum commemorating a defunct whaling station, set up by Norwegians towards the end of the nineteenth century. The last whaling station to operate in Canada, it had also been a centre for the export of seal pelts to Norway.

Kay soon hustled us back on to the bus, which carried us on towards a village at the head of Trinity Bay. Almost enclosed by islands and the curve of the land, it looked well kept but not wealthy, with well-spaced neat clapboard houses. For two miles, the road round the bay was lined with cars and trucks. As we emerged from the bus, we were greeted enthusiastically: 'Welcome to Dildo!'

Twenty or more assorted local boats, many dressed overall with flags and balloons, were bouncing in a stiff breeze on the water behind a welcoming committee. A dory had been disguised as a mini *Gaia*. David was thrust in front of a battery of community TV cameras, and told to make a speech.

'We hoped you'd be wearing your Viking tunics,' Maude Williams, a leading Dildoer, told us. If only we had known: Maude and many others had been planning this for months, and we had come ill-prepared. We hoped that our genuine and obvious pleasure made up for any disappointment.

Lloyd George, Dildo's senior citizen and historian, an ex-civil servant and teacher, sat with us on the top deck of the largest boat of the colourful flotilla which escorted us to a tiny island, inhabited only by summer sheep. He pointed out his house, the second oldest in Dildo, and talked about the differences between his life and ours. 'We haven't got much pollution in the air out here yet,' he told us proudly.

There were apologies as we arrived at Dildo Island that the local people had not had time to build a landing stage; what with having to get their boats ready, and everything else they had had to do to prepare for our visit, they had not got round to it yet. We were all nevertheless safely carried ashore in various dinghies, with shrieks and squeaks from some of the local ladies, who claimed that they were not used to boats.

Lloyd George made a speech, standing on sheep-cropped grass beside a home-made stainless steel plaque commemorating 'the world's largest codfish hatchery'.

'This is a great day in the history of Dildo,' he started.

A couple of rusted and battered boilers on the beach were all that was left of the cod hatchery, set up by Norwegians.

Back on land, luncheon was ready at Dildo's community centre, the hall of the Society of United Fishermen. We did our best to do justice to the buffet of local fare: pea soup; buffalo cooked with and without honey; battered cods' tongues; cod 'n brewis – smoked dried cod, soaked, mixed with hardtack bread, also soaked, and served with pork scratchings; bakeapple pie, and many other sweets and cakes.

'Now it's your turn,' Maude told me. I was to introduce the crew for community television.

'Gunnar is skipper when the "admiral" is not on board. We have trusted our lives to him, and shall continue to do so. Ottar is also entrusted with our lives, as he built the boat. Jon is today's "wife", but he's getting off lightly as he doesn't have to cook after this wonderful meal.'

'What about David?'

'When I was asked in an interview before setting out what I thought the problems would be on this voyage, I was expecting a question about being the only woman with a boatload of men. Instead, I was asked: "Aren't you worried about being cooped up with your husband for such a long time?" So far, it hasn't been a problem.'

After various speeches, all filmed, the foreman of the fish plant entertained us with two songs he had written and composed, accompanied by his sons on electric guitar. The themes of his songs were of great local significance: the community's successful resistance to a government attempt to change the name of Dildo; and the serious decline in fish stocks, exacerbated by the permission granted to Russian trawlers to fish near Canadian limits.

> The way the fish is being taken from
> offshore,
> I don't know how long it's going to last.
> What will we do when our fish is all gone?
> Come all you Newfies, let's take a stand
> To save all our fish'ries here in
> Newfoundland,
> For the day here is coming, as I'm sure
> you'll agree
> When there won't be a codfish here left in
> the sea.

Gunner stood up before we left: 'I did not know that all this was going to happen,' he said. 'I do not know how to say what I feel, but I want to thank you. It comes from my heart.'

The day's surprises were not over. Our next stop was six miles away, between Hopeall and Backside Pond, at Green's Harbour, where we were to open a folk festival. I was thrust on to a stage, again in front of TV cameras.

Although nothing else could quite equal the warmth of our reception in Dildo, St John's continued to provide us with a wide variety of hospitality and entertainment. There was an informal evening with the Scandinavian Society, a formal fund-raising dinner, a guided tour to the tiny harbour of Quidi Vidi and Signal Hill, where Guglielmo Marconi received his first Morse code transmission, the letter 'S', from Poldhu in Cornwall, and where I discovered that shrapnel was invented by Henry Shrapnell.

Gaia attracted so much attention that we soon felt as if most of the city's population of one hundred and seventy thousand, and many from the rest of the province of Avalon, must have been on board or on the quay asking questions. More people were interested in what it was like to live and sail on a Viking ship than in the significance of her name; but occasionally the environment got a look-in, particularly from a group of teenage boys who wanted to talk about the Gaia hypothesis and its implications. One guest must have taken such a liking to our wooden sea god, Njord, that he or she returned during the night and removed him from his place in the stern. Although Njord was no beauty, he had been a comforting presence. We missed him, and hoped that his theft would not bring the wrath of the Norse gods upon us.

Several of our visitors had also been at l'Anse-aux-Meadows, where they felt that our welcome had been neither as warm, nor as well organized, as in St John's. But this too had its critics, among them Avalon Goodridge, commonly known as Ted. Avalon, meaning Divine Providence, is Newfoundland's most easterly province, a large and irregularly shaped peninsula to which the first English and Irish settlers came in the seventeenth century. Ted Goodridge was incensed that *Concordia* had not moved away from the quay for our arrival, as her bulk had blocked the view of *Gaia* from the shore.

Concordia, as we gradually became aware, was the cause of considerable controversy. 'Cape Breton shuckers angered by licensing of Halifax firm,' stated a headline in the Toronto *Globe and Mail* when permission was eventually granted for her to catch 17,500 tonnes of clams a year off Nova Scotia and Newfoundland. Part of the processing would be done on board. The angry Cape Breton shuckers were clam processors who had either just been laid off, or feared that the factory-freezer ship was a threat to their jobs.

While we were at St John's, *Oseberg* and *Saga Siglar* arrived in Halifax on the deck of a freighter. It seemed ironic that whereas *Gaia* had managed to cross the North Atlantic unscathed, *Oseberg* was discovered to have a large crack in her hull. There were long discussions about what should be done, and how serious it was, after which it was decided that Ottar and Gunnar should fly ahead to Halifax to assess and repair the damage. David and I were to go with them, as unskilled assistants – chauffeurs and gofers, as we put it.

We were met in Halifax by Martin Karlsen, one of many Norwegians involved in shipping and fishing in Nova Scotia. His dynamic energy inspired a wide network of volunteers, many of Scandinavian origin, to offer us assistance. 'I don't know how many people round the world are doing things free for Ragnar,' he commented. He had arranged accommodation for the four of us on board *Acadia*, an ex-survey ship. As she was one of the floating exhibits of the Maritime Museum, we had to vacate the cabins during museum opening hours.

Oseberg and *Saga Siglar* were sitting disconsolately on shore, caged in on three sides by containers and visible only from the water and then only to anyone actively looking for them in the docks. A door into the container cage was opened with a dockyard forklift truck, for which we were given the key so that we could come and go when we pleased. David and I busied ourselves removing the covers from the boats while Ottar and Gunnar examined the damage. It did not look spectacular – no great gaping hole – but was obviously serious: a long split in a plank, which, with those above it, had been pushed up and away from the lower planking.

'What do you think it needs?' I asked.

'A genius,' Gunnar replied gloomily.

'We must tell Ragnar that *Oseberg* can't be ready this year,' Ottar said even more gloomily.

We had flown from pleasant summer weather in St John's to the humidity of a Halifax heat wave, and had been up at five. The creaks of *Acadia*'s gangplanks against the hull did not keep me awake for long that night, although I was aware of a strange combination of smells, exacerbated no doubt by the heat: damp household cleanser from a quick scrub before we came aboard, even damper old dirt which the cleansing had not reached, and a strong whiff of sewage from the harbour water below my open porthole – through which I had been warned that Bert might jump on me during the night. Bert was boss of the wharf. He stalked along it, and on and off *Acadia*, with his fluffy black tail and his nose in the air, and had no idea that cats were meant to run away from dogs. The reverse was rather the case when he was about: rottweilers ran whimpering from his claws.

Two, or even three or four genii are better than one. Eggert, who had been on *Oseberg* in Norway, arrived next day from Iceland, and Bjarne, skipper of *Saga Siglar*, from Norway, not primarily to help with the repairs but to prepare their respective craft for the water. The masts and cabin boxes were craned off, and the experts set to work. We relinquished our cabins on *Acadia* (there were not enough for six of us) and moved into a hotel, idiosyncratically called after Lord Nelson. With such a wealth of maritime history in the area, it seemed strange to commemorate an admiral who had no local connections.

David and I hired a car, with which we made regular deliveries to the yard of cold drinks and ice – the heat remained excessive – and discovered where to buy screws, nails, caulking guns, sacrificial anodes, keel bolts, an axe, nuts and washers. While Gunnar, Ottar, Eggert and Bjarne performed complicated technical miracles, we demonstrated our willingness to be unskilled slave labour by scraping, sanding and antifouling the hulls of both boats below the waterline in preparation for relaunching. Then there was the oiling – masts, yards, hulls inside and out, deck, rigging.

Between chauffeuring, gofering and manual labour, we were drawn into the final Vinland Revisited preparations being made by Martin Karlsen and the staff of the Maritime Museum. A reception at the museum was threatening to get out of hand. From a provisional estimate of no more than two hundred people, the numbers had more than doubled, and they all had somehow to be fitted in round immovable and irreplaceable nautical exhibits.

We all took Sunday off. Ottar and Bjarne wanted to escape from the hot urban environment, and took the hire car out into the country. David and I were invited sailing by a couple whose yacht was moored free of charge in the river below their house, and who had a vast and uncrowded weekend cruising ground at their disposal – the three towns of Halifax, Dartmouth and Bedford merge into each other round one of the largest and most beautiful natural harbours in the world. The old warehouses and wharves of Halifax had recently been restored. Enclosed walkways and bridges link the waterfront tourist development to a compact city centre bounded on one side by an historic citadel and on another by a park.

The heat wave was swept away in torrential tropical-style rain, with alarming reports of an approaching hurricane. Fortunately it blew itself out by the time it reached Halifax. A week after our arrival, *Oseberg* had been expertly repaired, and both boats were ready for launching. There were a few anxious moments, then a burst of spontaneous applause from the crane driver and a handful of dock workers who had gathered to watch. By the time the rest of the crews of *Oseberg* and *Saga Siglar* arrived, the boats were in place outside the museum, their hulls gleaming and their rigging supple with fresh oil.

'How has the atmosphere been?' Herdis asked me a few hours after she arrived from Iceland. 'Has Ragnar been good?'

'Everyone wants to be positive and make things work,' I hedged.

Gaia and *Havella* meanwhile had managed to take shelter during the storm, and had then put into St Pierre, a French island off southern Newfoundland. I envied them that; we had heard nothing but good reports of the 'Frenchness' of the island's duty-free wine, food and general Gallic atmosphere.

I went with Herdis and Eggert on *Oseberg* to the rendezvous with *Gaia* ready for the fleet's grand entrance. Knut Rostad, to whom I had faxed a 'Letter from *Gaia*' from each port of call for the Vinland Revisited newsletter he was editing, was a passenger. He spent some time talking to me about how he wanted to warn the crew about what to expect and how to behave in America. 'Don't you think there's a danger of seeming patronizing?' I asked him.

It was so misty that morning that finding *Gaia* was not easy, but eventually, in company with *Bluenose*, a famous and majestic Halifax schooner which dwarfed the Viking ships, we all made our way back up river and into the museum's small harbour. The only interruption to a well-organized welcoming ceremony on shore, with speeches and music and marching, came from a heckler who kept shouting: 'What about the Micmacs?'

Although the Scandinavian immigrants to Nova Scotia were well represented, there were none of the descendants of the Indians who had been there long before either Leif Eiriksson or Columbus 'discovered' America; nor were they mentioned in the speeches. We discovered later that the Micmacs were at the time in mourning for the death of a chief.

Several crew changes were made in Halifax. Frode, at his request, was moved to *Oseberg*, where with only four people on board he felt less crowded. Rosa's place on *Saga Siglar* had been given to Jostein Tøvik, who had been replaced in the original crew because of an injury before we joined *Gaia*. Ragnar was joined by the rest of his family. He and Kari spent most of their time on *Havella*, with their older son Eirik theoretically replacing Audun as skipper. Njål Thorseth was on *Gaia*, instead of Odd who had officially moved up to the comfort of the support ship where he had his own space, the cabin which had previously been Øyvard's. Like Frode, he seemed more relaxed, even when I dyed all his socks and underpants – and mine – pink in the laundromat. I had wondered what the attitude of Kari and the boys would be to us, given the tensions there had been between us and Ragnar. Kari was as warm and friendly as she had always been, and although the boys were initially less so, I felt that this was only because they were not confident about their English and were naturally quiet and reserved. It was not long before they too relaxed.

According to a new shore regime, with a detailed table of instructions and times, one person was to be on duty on each boat from 8.00 am until 8.00 pm. Oversleeping was forbidden, as were late night parties on board. Attendance at official shore functions was compulsory, except for whoever had done the previous night stint: a twelve-hour two-person watch over all four boats, both people on duty to stay awake all night, and all pumps to be checked at hourly intervals.

The Brits had not been included in the shore rota, but we were asked if we would mind standing in on special occasions, starting with the formal Halifax dinner after the museum reception, and do Sunday nights between us, as well as being on question and answer duty from time to time. We probably found this less onerous than some of the others – in Canada and America we were after all usually questioned in our own language – but even I could get tired of talking.

The museum staff were delighted by the interest the Viking fleet aroused and reported a record number of visitors, particularly during a Scandinavian weekend featuring folk dancing in costume and saga-style story telling. But apart from well-deserved criticism by Ragnar of the water in Halifax harbour, and a gift of organically grown fruit by one of the few visitors who reacted to the environmental symbolism of the name *Gaia*, people in Halifax, as in St John's, seemed more interested in the practical aspects of sailing on a Viking ship. How the spirit this was supposed to demonstrate might set a caring course for the future of the planet was hardly mentioned.

Ragnar made a valiant attempt to recreate the atmosphere of our last evening in Greenland at a barbecue at Martin Karlsen's house. It was the first time that the four crews had been gathered together since the party at his house in Ulsteinvik. The only non-crew members were Martin and his wife, who catered nobly for us all in spite of being eight months pregnant, and Knut Rostad.

An atmosphere cannot however be deliberately resurrected, and the pep talks Ragnar and Knut Rostad felt it necessary to give – one in Norwegian, the other in English – prevented an enjoyable evening from developing into quite such a riotous one as the Greenland barbecue. This was probably just as well for Karlsen relationships with their neighbours.

We were beginning to be aware of an undercurrent of resentment about the authority exercised from *Havella*. I was no longer the scapegoat. An excellent rapport had been established between the six of us who had been in Halifax getting *Oseberg* and *Saga Siglar* ready, and had immediately been re-established with the rest of their crews, including Andrew and Nigel when they rejoined us. There was a sense of injustice, most strongly felt on *Oseberg*, when Pierre was expected to be on night watch within a few hours of his arrival from South Africa. Eggert, who was already nursing a grievance about not having been chosen on Håholmen for the crew of *Gaia*, insisted on doing the watch instead.

Ottar and Frode had been invited to go to an early evening concert, after which they planned to join the rest of us at a Scandinavian barbecue in Bedford – which Ottar in any case had assumed was voluntary, after doing the previous night watch. When it was decreed that they should not go to the concert, but must attend the barbecue from the start, they were both furious.

It was nevertheless a splendid evening, starting with a greeting at the water's edge by pantomime Vikings with flaming torches, and continuing with food outside and dancing and presentations in a marquee. David and I had been invited to stay the night by our hosts, Johann and Barbara Koppernæs. Johann was one of what we had started to refer to jokingly as the Norwegian Mafia, as there were so many west Norwegians involved in one way or another in Nova Scotian shipping and fishing. But we were the only crew members with a car, and David spent half the evening driving disgruntled Vikings back into town in relays before their rumblings of discontent erupted. Later, we were told that Ottar and Frode had been threatened with dismissal. Ottar started to count the days until he could return to Bjørkedal, 'the most beautiful place in the world', and Frode was emphatic that even if asked he would not continue on board to Rio de Janeiro, it having by then been decided that after Washington *Gaia* would carry her message to the environmental conference in Brazil.

An invitation to lunch on a Kloster cruise liner, the *Royal Viking Sun*, provided us with the greatest imaginable contrast to life on *Gaia*. For a minimum rate of six hundred dollars a day, seven hundred passengers at a time could be cocooned in a world of luxury complete with its own casino and electronic golf course. Our departures from Halifax were coordinated. It was a perfect evening for any photographers who might want to capture a replica Viking ship and its most luxurious modern counterpart against the sunset. Althought the forecast was for the wind to strengthen to gale force against us, Ragnar was hoping that we would have time first to reach Lunenburg, to meet yet more of the Norwegian 'Mafia'.

A few hours out in the dark, with *Gaia* and *Oseberg* under tow and *Saga Siglar* under her own inboard diesel engine, the welcome decision to turn back was announced. We had by then been ploughing for long enough into an increasingly lumpy sea against a freshening headwind – not the best way to test the repairs to *Oseberg*. Those asleep off-watch when we turned back were as dismayed as the museum staff to find us back in Halifax in the morning.

It was nearly two days before the weather moderated enough for a second departure, which gave us time to do some of the things we had not managed to fit in before, like go to an exhibition of paintings by the 'Group of Seven', Canada's leading landscape artists, some of whose work reminded me of Mikines, some of Van Gogh. We also visited the citadel, where I bought a book about 'the greatest man-made explosion before Hiroshima': in 1917, over a square mile of Halifax was destroyed, with thousands of deaths and injuries, when a Norwegian freighter collided with a French ship which was carrying explosives.

We started our downhill trip from Canada to America with a long dull tow in fog and mizzle, by-passing the coasts of Nova Scotia and Maine – to which, although there is no evidence to prove it, the Vikings must surely have sailed for cargoes of wood. Njål, who admitted that he had been miserably seasick on previous Thorseth voyages, accepted one of my earpatches, and was very smug when he discovered that his elder brother had been sick several times.

At last, for the final day of the passage, the sun came out, with a fresh north-westerly wind which gave us some excellent sailing with two reefs and a convivial atmosphere. We had done 'Vinland': now for the USA.

18 Downhill all the Way

As Ragnar had light-heartedly predicted, our progress down the American seaboard was 'downhill all the way' – and sometimes more literally than anyone had anticipated.

Our USA landfall was early on a Sunday morning at Gloucester, Massachusetts, a small town unaccustomed to providing customs' clearance for Viking fleets. It took most of the morning. When Herdis jumped ashore spontaneously to greet Knut Rostad and his wife and baby daughter, she was ordered back on to *Oseberg* by a customs' officer: 'That's the way it starts – you let one ashore, and ten more follow.'

At last we were allowed to proceed to what we hoped would be a quiet anchorage at Cocktail Cove, Misery Island. A well-kept uninhabited nature reserve, there was nothing except its name to betray that the island was once a leper colony. The cocktails came later, during prohibition, when it was the site of a hotel and golf course frequented by illicit drinkers.

Hiding a fleet of three Viking ships proved even more difficult than remaining incognito with one. A passing fisherman gave us half a dozen live lobsters. Two bronzed beauties toasted us with pewter goblets from a sleek power boat. Cans of beer, popcorn and a bottle of wine were thrown across by Sunday afternoon sailors.

'Say, does that thing float?' we were asked by the owner of a three-storey motor launch.

We prepared for our first night in the United States with a rousing neo-Viking singing competition which destroyed any remaining semblance of secrecy. A plaintive plea over the VHF from Eirik Thorseth for transport back to *Havella* from one of the Viking ships was answered only by the crowing of Steinar's electronic alarm clock.

To the floating questioner who enquired next day whether we were 'on a goodwill mission, or generating income', we explained that *Gaia*

215

was the flagship of an international environmental initiative. This seemed to make more sense in America, where we were told repeatedly that our message was 'so significant', than in the harsher environment of Labrador and Newfoundland.

What to do with our garbage presented us with a minor environmental problem, especially as shore visits were banned until we reached Boston. An exception was made for a rubbish run after two local police chiefs who paid *Gaia* an unofficial visit suggested that we could put our bulging black plastic sacks in the Manchester-on-Sea police station's bins, and offered to escort us upriver. We did not admit that one of the sacks contained the last stinking morsels of Faroese whale blubber, which we had had to retrieve after throwing it overboard – it refused to sink.

The fleet, under engine against a strong northerly wind, was greeted outside Boston by two fire tugs with full spray arching against the city skyline. 'Here come the shore captain and his wife,' Kari joked as she and Ragnar climbed aboard *Gaia* for the ceremonial entry, led by a schooner, the *Spirit of Massachusetts*. An armed officer waved from an environmental police launch as we came alongside in the Charlestown Navy Yard under the protective bows of the 204-foot USS *Constitution*, from which a cannon was fired in our honour. Built for the US Navy in the early nineteenth century, and the oldest fully commissioned warship in the world, she had been almost entirely rebuilt as a floating museum.

Njål nudged me as Ragnar was ushered in front of cameras and microphones. 'This is the bit he likes,' he whispered. I was not so sure. Being acclaimed as a heroic latter-day Viking, and acting as spokesman for Vinland Revisited, was part of Ragnar's job, and he did not shun the limelight, but nevertheless he often seemed ill at ease as he told yet another enthusiastic audience: 'I have been interested in Viking ships ever since I was a small boy.'

There were so many Icelandic and Norwegian flags, and so many colourful Nordic costumes, among the crowd waiting to greet us on shore that I wondered if there were any American Americans in Boston. Although the environment was mentioned in the welcoming speeches, the emphasis seemed rather more on the Viking past and American–Scandinavian present, especially during 'the Biggest Scandinavian Event Ever in Boston' at the weekend. Iceland was well represented: displays of Glima wrestling, a sport rarely seen outside Iceland, alternated with performances of *Light Nights*, a multi-media show based on the sagas. A group of visiting New York neo-Vikings in armour and chain mail were, they told us, members of the Historical Anachronism Society on the look-out for 'a bit of rape and pillage'.

Whether or not the Vikings ever reached Boston and the Charles River, as has been claimed but not proven, it is a matter of considerable local Scandinavian pride that the city boasts the first statue erected in Leif Eiriksson's memory in the New World. A Victorian bronze, it actually looks more like a Roman gladiator than a Viking adventurer. An open-sided tourist bus carried us to a wreath-laying ceremony at the statue, where there was so much Norwegian emphasis that Rikardur was moved to mutter between clenched teeth: 'Leif Eiriksson was *not* Norwegian'.

For Knut Kloster, Boston was part of the more recent and personal past, since he had studied at the Massachusetts Institute of Technology. As guest speaker at an MIT reception at the Navy Yard, he announced that for the next stage of her mission *Gaia* was to sail under a UNICEF banner with a cargo of children's messages to 'the so-called Earth Summit' in Brazil, and reiterated his personal and business commitment to finding 'ways of living within the means of the earth'. 'Since we all care for our children and their future,' he said, 'environment protection and sustainable development will become good business. There will be a growing demand for products and services that are in harmony with nature. And since environment and development go hand-in-hand, this is a process which will also be aimed at improving the human condition.'

A flamboyantly dressed man with long hair, a huge hat and a general appearance of energetic eccentricity leapt up and down pointing a video camera – sometimes at the speaker, sometimes at the listeners. Fox Tree, a Native American university professor in Native Nations People Studies, History, and Fine Arts, was obsessed by the atrocities he attributed to Columbus.

Over dinner with Knut and several others who had been at the lecture, Professor Fox Tree waxed eloquent about his 'Columbus War Crimes Tribunal', and about his conviction that Native Nations People – Indians of the Americas – had sailed round the world and had discovered Europe, China, Japan and other lands with their three masted sailing ships long before 1492. He was vague about quite how long before – maybe several thousand years, give or take the odd millennium.

'Will you come to Newport and stand beside me as my brother on the *Royal Viking Sun*?' Knut asked him.

'I'll come so long as I am not filmed or photographed. That gives me a pain here,' Fox Tree said, touching his chest.

'That's not fair. You filmed everyone else,' I pointed out.

Knut agreed. 'Good point. If you come, you must be photographed.'

'No photos,' the professor insisted.

'You say you want a platform, but then when you're offered one, you don't want it,' I objected.

'I have a five-hundred-year programme,' he told us. That, he explained, was how long it had taken for the 'crimes' of Columbus to be admitted.

History jumped a few hundred years when *Gaia* hosted a short, simple and dignified re-enlistment ceremony for a naval petty officer. By the time we left the protection of the *Constitution*, the next dockyard pageant was already under way: Vinland Revisited made way for American Rights Day.

Odd, Steinar and Ottar had been joined in Boston by their wives. As if to reassure Ingebjorg, Solveig and Marianne, who were sailing the rest of the way on *Havella* and *Gaia*, the passage from Boston to Cape Cod Canal was idyllic. When the wind dropped towards evening, so that we were drifting rather than sailing, Jon swam from *Gaia* to *Saga Siglar*, where he climbed the mast and jumped from the yard, egged on by the rest of us with cameras poised. 'On the way down I regretted it,' he admitted, 'but it was too late.'

Herdis had dived off *Oseberg* and was swimming across to visit us when David noticed that Gunnar had a bucket of water poised to throw over her, and signalled to the rest of us. As our guest grasped the gunwale, Gunnar bent to raise his bucket – and was unceremoniously thrown over the side. He climbed on to the gummiboat and sat there dripping, protesting with an expression of outraged dignity: 'But I am the shkipper!'

Coastguard and police boats escorted us under engine along the seventeen-mile Cape Cod Canal, excavated by US Army Engineers in 1928. Several thousand spectators, many waving Norwegian flags and including two entire primary schools, had gathered in small groups along the towpath to cheer us on our way.

At the Massachusetts Maritime Academy wharf, at the Buzzards Bay end of the canal, we were greeted by an admiral and a phalanx of senior cadets in dazzling well-pressed white uniforms with yellow neckerchiefs. In spite of their formal appearance, this was an informal stop, with an open invitation to avail ourselves of the academy's sport and canteen facilities; 'the chow' was indeed as we were told 'not bad'. Although it was a civilian establishment, the academy seemed to operate on military lines, with a style of education described as 'aggressive'. Frequent loudspeaker announcements in the barrack blocks all started with the words 'Now hear this', and a huge diagonal yellow notice on the door to the sports hall ordered: 'BE TOUGH'. Several hundred cadets in khaki uniforms, as well as their seniors in white, paraded in the morning for the raising of the US flag. The ensigns on *Gaia* went up two minutes later.

Admiral Cressey, who had been asked to take on the job while he was on Desert Storm duty in the Gulf War, outlined the college's new graduate courses in marine environmental protection, for which he was looking for industrial sponsorship. This seemed to us very much in keeping with Knut Kloster's thinking, and with our Gaian message. On the minus side environmentally, the cadets wasted huge quantities of food, to the disgust of the kitchen staff.

Once again, our departure was to coincide with the schedule of the *Royal Viking Sun*, which came through the canal in the dark on her way to Rhode Island. As she approached, a fast-moving floating city blazing with light, her inhabitants were unaware of the danger caused to the fragile Viking hulls by the great swirls of water she threw across the canal. *Havella* towed us behind her through a damp and windy night, greatly to Gunnar's frustration, and ours, as we could have been having an exhilarating nocturnal sail with a good beam wind.

I had been looking forward to our visit to Rhode Island, where Dolly Bjerke's brother-in-law John Macomber had promised us a rousing welcome long before we had thrown our lot in with the Norse, and I was not disappointed. It did us proud, avoiding the emphasis on ethnic flag waving from which we otherwise found it so difficult to escape, and using our visit as the focus for a series of lectures based on the various strands of Vinland Revisited – nautical, historical and environmental.

Heralded by cannon, we were escorted into Newport by a fire tug and two corvettes dressed overall, and processed round the harbour at the head of a fleet of local boats, most elegant among them Sir Thomas Lipton's J-class yacht *Shamrock*, which he could never have expected to fly the Stars and Stripes. The Newport Militia, which had been in commission for two hundred and fifty years and was the oldest military unit in the US, welcomed us in full historic costume. Knut Kloster reminded an audience of neo-Vikings and luxury cruise passengers over aquavit and snacks on the *Royal Viking Sun* that four thousand children round the world had died of starvation that morning.

Professor Fox Tree did not after all stand beside Kloster as his brother, although he put in an appearance later, to present 'A Native People greeting to all who love and protect the earth and water':

> Your sailing ships from far away
> Give courage as they point a way
> To save our mother planet's heart
> A last chance here before we part. . . .
> It's you and we against the sea
> For sharing our humanity
> To save a world's mortality . . .

The Native Nations People were well represented in Newport, where two historical camps had been erected side by side between Fort Adams and our berth. Sitting cross-legged on the grass in front of a wigwam, Native American Indians pow-wowed peacefully with neo-Vikings. A few yards away, men resplendent in scarlet and black colonial uniforms stood guard over a cannon, cooked in a billycan suspended over a camp fire, and slept in a small white marquee.

Enthusiasts who insist that the Vikings visited Rhode Island base their claim on a circular tower, rejecting the counter-claim that it is the ruin of a seventeenth-century windmill. Evan Smith, Newport's director of tourism, told us that a new form of carbon dating was to test whether the so-called Norse Tower really was the oldest building in America.

'What if the carbon dating proves that the tower is not Viking?' I asked him.

'In that case, it will remain a mystery.'

David, Emily (who joined us in Newport, and was to leave from New York) and I were staying with Evan and his wife in a single-storey wood-lined house overlooking the sea. Hurricane Bob had hurled huge chunks of granite across the sea wall into their garden, proof indeed of the power of Gaia.

This was the subject of a lecture at the University of Rhode Island by Dr Lynn Margulis, co-founder with Lovelock of the Gaia hypothesis, which, she claimed, 'happens to be true'. 'Gaia and Biospheres' was vividly illustrated with slides and video showing minute micro-organisms in full colour enlargement with Japanese subtitles.

'We are part of the biosphere,' Margulis told us, 'not above it, not superior to it . . . We are embedded in it.'

She was interrupted so that the blind behind the lectern could be raised to allow the audience to see *Gaia* sailing majestically across the bay. Those sitting near me found this, they said, a very moving experience. The lecture was then resumed.

'We cannot destroy the earth,' Margulis announced. That was the good news, the bad news was: 'But we can destroy ourselves.'

Ragnar had decreed that we should set out at midnight after a farewell dinner in our honour. 'Follow us and you will be all right,' Odd instructed over the VHF as we left under motor. It soon became difficult, however, to distinguish *Havella*'s lights from the many others in Long Island Sound, and *Gaia* was taken under tow through drizzle in a south-easterly force six and a nasty lollop. Frode read Jakob Sande over the VHF to us under way, including a poem specially adapted for David: 'Little David will go out into the world . . .' David retaliated with a variation on Hilaire Belloc: 'When Grandmama was told That Frode'd been as good as gold . . .'

Our first bite at New York's 'Big Apple' was an unofficial motor in perfect weather down the East River past Manhattan. There were two reasons for not sailing: there was no wind, and as we were a day early we were not to attract attention. We hid that evening and night at anchor off Coney Island. The order that no one was to go ashore did nothing for the general mood, especially of several crew members who had been threatened with dismissal during our progress down the American seaboard. 'I don't know how they dare talk about caring for the environment, when they can't even look after their own people properly,' one disgruntled crew member complained.

Pierre was deputed to negotiate on *Havella* for shore leave, with the result that we were after all allowed ashore, but were to keep together, not to go into any bars, and were to be back on board by eleven. The trolls – as the crew of *Saga Siglar* had been nicknamed, because of their beards – elected to stay afloat, wisely as it turned out. Leaving a watch on each boat, the rest of us from *Gaia* and *Oseberg* were ferried ashore, and spent a couple of surrealist hours in a Coney Island amusement arcade, then were soaked in a sudden downpour on our way back to the boats. At least we had all had a glimpse of aspects of American city life of which we were unlikely to be aware at our prestigious moorings in Manhattan and Washington.

A helicopter hovered and zoomed overhead as the Viking fleet passed under rain-darkened sail in front of the Statue of Liberty, and a paddle steamer carried press and VIPs out to take historic photographs. 'I hope there's no pollutant in that dye,' one of the crew commented as plumes of red, white and blue water from a fire tug mingled with the rain. There was plenty of ethnic flagwaving, mainly of Norwegian flags, from Scandinavians sheltering under umbrellas on the balconies of the South Street Seaport shopping arcade. The weather, and the feeling that we were being manipulated as part of a publicity stunt irrelevant to the intended spirit of Vinland Revisited, dampened our official arrival in New York.

It was considered quite a coup to have enticed the prime ministers of Iceland and Norway, and a representative of the mayor of New York, to participate in the official welcoming ceremony, for which Ragnar was to step ashore and move immediately up a ladder from the floating dock. The crews were however to stay on board, where we could neither hear nor see what was going on. The spectacular, expensive display of 'Vinland Revisited Fireworks' to Icelandic and Norwegian music over the East River that evening was however both audible and visible. If it had not been raining so hard, we might have been more appreciative of the pyrotechnic wizardry, instead of reflecting sourly on the gulf between such extravagance and caring for the environment.

We certainly earned our keep at the South Street Seaport, taking it in turns to stand at the top of the gang plank from the dock to answer questions. Only Ragnar, Kari and Gunnar were invited to the official functions, including a black tie benefit dinner. The exclusion of mere crew members was more than made up for by the hospitality we were given as luncheon guests on the Norwegian cruise ship *Nordic Prince*, humbler and homelier than the *Royal Viking Sun*, and by the Staten Island Lodge of Sons of Norway. I am told that there are more Norwegians in America than in Norway; many meet regularly as the sons and daughters of the homeland.

Knut Kloster and his New York World City colleague John Rogers were meanwhile planning the next stage of *Gaia*'s mission, as standard and message bearer for UNICEF and the children of the world. In preparation for this, David, Emily and I, with Rikardur and Njål Thorseth, were invited to join them and Staffan de Mistura of UNICEF at the United Nations International School (UNIS) to which we were driven in an immensely luxurious limousine. Njål experimented enthusiastically with its gadgetry.

The large international group of fourteen-year-olds we met first seemed more interested in whether the Vikings were violent than in the link with the environment, although this cause appealed to a smaller group of older pupils who had set up their own environmental group,

Save Today's Endangered Planet (STEP). They had already persuaded the school kitchens to use proper cutlery and crockery, and
reintroduce washing-up, rather than discard all the plastic and paper
which have become such a part of the fast food revolution – especially,
from our observations, in New York – and were raising money to buy a
few acres of rain forest. Their symbol was a whale, and they were, they
told us, hoping to adopt one. They had not thought about whaling from
the point of view of communities which traditionally depended on it,
they admitted.

During our Sunday night watch, after taking Emily to the airport at
the end of her two weeks, David and I spent some time talking to Frode.
I asked him why he had resented my presence so greatly to start with.

'Was it me personally you didn't like, or didn't you like having a
woman on board at all?' I asked.

'It wasn't personal. But if we had to have a woman on board, I
thought it shouldn't be an old one,' he answered. It was so obviously
not meant insultingly that I did not take offence.

The symbolic course for *Gaia*'s voyage from Washington to Rio as the
children's, and UNICEF's, ambassador was set at a waterborne PR
ceremony in front of the United Nations building. Ragnar was taken on
to a large motor cruiser, the *Spirit of New York*, on which Knut Kloster,
John Rogers, Staffan de Mistura, another group from UNIS, and
various publicity people and journalists had been gathered together.
Some of the UNIS STEP members, whom we had already met, were
brought aboard *Gaia*. While we waited for something to happen, they
wrote some additions to Ragnar's official 'cargo of messages from the
children of the world'.

'Let us respect our mother earth as she gives us life,' one of the girls
urged. 'Let us nourish her as she nourishes us. Let us not pollute her
water, air and soil, nor chop her down and cut her up. Most of all, let us
love her.'

'The bottom line is there is no excuse for going on like we've been
doing,' one of the boys wrote. Another suggested: 'Let's stop talking
and actually start to try to make a change.'

When Ragnar returned, the blue banner we had first flown at
l'Anse-aux-Meadows was replaced by one with the UNICEF logo and
the message: KEEP THE PROMISE . . . FOR A BETTER WORLD FOR OUR
CHILDREN. The official 'Children Who Care' message was propped up
in the bows, and read for the first time by the children on board. At a
captain's dinner (curry cooked by Andrew and Nigel) we had spent

some time a few nights previously discussing with Knut Kloster and Staffan de Mistura who should write the message, children, or adults on their behalf. In spite of its closing sentences – 'Please do not mistake this appeal as the naïve writing of children. It expresses our concern for the future, our future' – it read as if it had after all been written by an adult.

With the text, Ragnar had been given a young child's drawing: 'a picture of a Viking god named Odin and his wolf', although quite what this had to do with the environmental mission was not explained. I have a well-tested superstitious belief that mentioning Odin at sea is unlucky – and so it soon proved, on more than one occasion.

The first was on a hot soporific afternoon of lolling around in the sun, with occasional bursts of swimming between the boats, all three of which were under tow. While *Havella* was pulling us past a large buoy round which the current was sloshing strongly, *Saga Siglar* was swept close to a small boat anchored in the tide. To avoid damage, the men on board cut their anchor line, jumping up and down and shouting in Anglo Saxon. It was several hours before they could be pacified, and then only after visits from customs and police launches.

We rafted up that evening at anchor in pairs – *Havella* and *Gaia*, *Oseberg* and *Saga Siglar* – in a tide so strong that waves slopped over the foredeck. Ottar was soaked on his way to the sleeping cabin. In the darkest part of the night, we were woken by the sort of shout which makes sleeping sailors react before their brains are engaged.

'*Gaia! Gaia!* GAIA!'

Ottar landed on David, and I moved aside to let him and Gunnar through the door first. 'It's OK,' said Gunnar over his shoulder into the cabin. At least we were floating, although at a strange angle to *Havella* and with alarming noises of straining ropes and cracking wood.

It was difficult to see in the dark exactly what had happened, although it was immediately clear that the bow line to *Havella* had parted. David and I tried to untie the spring, which seemed a confused jumble of knots. A flashlight fetched by Ottar revealed that it had sliced horizontally through a foot of planking, like a wire through cheese. 'Oh my God,' Ottar exclaimed, drawing his knife and cutting the line.

It was worse aft. A two-foot long strip of planking had been torn out, leaving a jagged hole and a split across two further sections of planking. A cleat and line were missing.

The engine was started, and we belched in a cloud of diesel fumes into the darkness.

'Where are Andrew and Nigel?' I asked. Everyone else was accounted for, although Marianne and Njål were still asleep.

'On *Havella*, I think,' someone answered. To make sure, David called *Havella* on the radio.

'Yes, Andrew and Nigel are here,' Ragnar answered. 'What's the damage there?'

'We've lost a piece of planking.'

'We have it here, on the end of a rope.'

In the cabin, Ottar rubbed the back of his hand across his eyes. By the time Marianne emerged a few minutes later, his sense of humour had already reasserted itself.

'It's better on land,' he told her. 'There, no one wakes you in the night to say your house is moving and has a hole in it, and you have to try to tie it up or find out where it has gone.'

By midday, when a plank had been nailed over the hole and an excellent sail in convoy had banished the traumas of the night, we were again rafted up at anchor, in the muddy swirling water of a strong ebb tide off the historic little town of New Castle, Delaware. Our three-hour visit as the joint guests of the chemical company Du Pont and 'Delaware's Colonial Capitol' had attracted a sizeable crowd, including a gathering of neo-Vikings in costume. One group was trying to raise money to replace their small Viking ship *Raven*, which was, they told us sadly, no longer seaworthy: the headlines of the local newspaper had proclaimed 'Viking ship crashes into Buick' after its trailer broke loose in a busy street.

A more serious note was struck by the Du Pont band of young musicians, who played the Icelandic, Norwegian and American national anthems. I was sitting next to Pierre when the invitation to applaud 'the Norwegian and Icelandic crews of the Viking ships' was issued. We clapped heartily.

An exciting evening sail, with our engines running as we were in the canal, for a few moments became too exciting. Who had nearly rammed whom was a matter of some acrimony between skippers later on; it took several of us to hold *Gaia* and *Oseberg* apart until each answered to the helm and they separated, proceeding afterwards more sedately and with a greater distance between them.

Our final downhill run to Washington started soon after dawn, under tow in such heavy rain that for some hours no one not on steerboard duty took much notice of the rural scenery as the canal broadened into the cruising ground of Chesapeake Bay. By midday, we were at last sailing, with a fresh beam wind and warm October sun. The friendly rivalry between *Gaia* and *Oseberg* became increasingly competitive, with such light-hearted underhand tactics as visiting the rival ship so that an extra dinghy would add to the drag and slow her down. *Gaia* was in the lead when David and I retired for some sleep before our next watch.

I half woke some time later, aware that the speed had suddenly increased to a point where it felt dangerous, and thinking hazily that if *Oseberg* hit us, I was in a dangerous position on the outside bunk. Then the speed dropped just as suddenly, with a lot of shouting and stamping on deck. 'There are plenty of people doing whatever has to be done,' I thought lazily, and dozed off.

David scrambled out of the sleeping cabin to find Andrew sitting on the yard trying to tame the flogging end of the sail. It was dark, and the wind and sea had become wild. 'What's going on?' David asked. 'That's the first thing I've understood for ages,' Andrew answered. Gunnar and Pierre were shouting at each other in Norwegian over the radio. They had, we learnt later, continued racing under full sail while the wind rose, until a sudden gust which Gunnar later estimated at fifty knots flung *Oseberg* downwind out of control towards *Gaia*. He managed to take evasive action, but for a few moments it had seemed as if both boats might go over.

David woke me at 22.00 for our two-hour watch; two people on for two hours at a time had become the norm under Gunnar's regime down the coast. We were by then six miles from Lookout Point, round which we had to turn straight into the wind up the Potomac River towards Washington. The gale force wind was wild, but warm, as was the sea. With much flashing of lights, *Gaia* and *Oseberg* were both taken in tow; then we were abandoned to our watch in a swirling current which threw up phosphorescent spray.

'It was a horrible night,' Ottar said in the morning. 'I could not sleep, except the last hour, and then it was just like it used to be at the start. As soon as I was sleeping, I was being woken up for my watch.' He still insisted that he was not a seaman, and although Marianne never complained she did not become a sailing addict.

Apart from being reprimanded by a small patrol boat for having inadvertently wandered into an unmarked military area just before the start of a shooting exercise, the rest of our long tow up the Potomac River was uneventful. By evening, we were anchored in front of the George Washington Bridge waiting for it to open to admit us into the upper river at midnight. Early in the morning, we moored along the bank beside a flat open space so that the masts of the Viking ships could be craned off and laid across the decks. Then, leaving *Havella* behind, we proceeded under a series of bridges, past Washington's waterside parks and elegant buildings, and beneath what seemed an endless stream of jet aircraft, to Washington Harbour, where the masts were reinstated.

Two police boats escorted us upriver under a final but higher bridge to a tree-lined anchorage just out of sight of the harbour. A screech of brakes and a bang from an unseen road through the trees reminded us that we were still in the city centre. There was much amicable wandering between boats that evening, while Ragnar and Kari were at a black tie dinner at the Smithsonian.

America's Leif Erikson Day, the climax of Vinland Revisited, was blessed with perfect October weather: a blue sky, a light breeze and late summer warmth, a great improvement on the weather for our arrival in New York. Once again, the ceremonies had been master-minded by the PR company. Two separate groups of children were brought aboard *Gaia* at her early morning anchorage, one group from the Washington International School, WIS, and ten Native Americans, nearly all related in a complex extended family. Some of them were wearing Indian costume as instructed, although they were not sure why. The oldest, a girl, was dignified and elegant in a fringed bead-embroidered doeskin outfit, which it had taken her grandmother two years to make. None of them seemed to know what was supposed to be happening, except that they were to sing 'Kids Have Rights' as we came alongside. We tried to explain the link between the Viking ships, the environment and children.

As usual, Ragnar came on board for the final approach. Banners were raised. The children on *Gaia* sang. A band on shore played. Throughout, a harbour police launch held an anti-whaling protest boat far enough at bay for its chanting and slogans not to be an embarrassment.

When David, Andrew and Nigel, dressed in their Viking tunics, attempted to leap ashore with their camera gear before the formal welcome by Queen Sonja of Norway and President Vigdis Finnbogadottir of Iceland, they were pushed aside by a security guard.

'We've sailed five thousand miles to film this,' David pointed out.

'And I've come two blocks to stop you.'

At least from the coachroof, we could hear what was happening on shore, where Walter Mondale, the USA's most famous Norwegian–American, was M.C., and could see the backs of the dignitaries.

There was as usual much waving of Nordic flags in the crowd, especially from the many in Norse costume. Knut Kloster, whose speech again rejected ethnic flag waving, mentioned the three billion people in the world living in conditions of unacceptable poverty, and the forty thousand children dying daily of starvation. When twelve hundred local children had sung the 'Children in Need' song ('We are the world') on the quay, we were ushered ashore to a sumptuous buffet luncheon.

Queen Sonja, looking like a fairytale princess in a bright red suit, came on board with President Finnbogadottir before the luncheon. They were filmed at some length by a Norwegian Broadcasting crew. When David then asked for a brief interview for our film, his request was refused so brusquely by the Queen's security man that the Icelandic President seemed embarrassed, and asked if she would do instead. 'I had actually hoped for both of you,' David replied. That evening, when we were each presented in turn to the Queen at a reception at the Norwegian Embassy, David could not resist saying: 'Perhaps I can interview you next time I cross the Atlantic on a Viking ship.'

It proved easier to talk to the President of the United States, who made a surprise visit to the Viking fleet with his grandchildren during the afternoon, and whose security men kept discreetly in the background. President Bush was friendly, relaxed and informal, chatting about the technicalities of building and sailing a Viking ship. 'Pleased to meet you, ma'am,' he said as if he meant it as he shook my hand. 'You'd look down on my boat,' he told David. 'It's just a speed boat, but it serves my purpose.'

We had been looking forward to a stimulating and thought-provoking end to the day at a symposium at the Smithsonian's National Air and Space Museum: 'From Vinland to Mars – One Thousand Years of Exploration'. The Norwegian anthropologist and explorer Thor Heyerdahl, and the American astronaut Michael Collins, were among the five panellists. But after an hour of intense boredom we escaped, along with several other Vikings who were seated near enough to the exit to make a surreptitious getaway. Knut Kloster, who had been asleep in the row in front of us, admitted that he too was disappointed.

The next morning, David and I were on question-duty for a group organized by the Smithsonian. 'It was very comforting to have the boatbuilder on board,' David told them. 'There was a boatbuilder on the *Titanic*,' one of them reminded him. He refrained from mentioning how near the *Titanic*'s fate *Gaia* had twice come in American inland waters.

David had been appointed master of ceremonies for the Vinland Revisited farewell party, for the combined crews plus wives and four World City Discovery representatives; even such faithful supporters as the New York journalist Jennifer, who had followed us down the coast, were excluded. Knut Kloster was presented with the *Gaia* pennant, which we had all signed. The 'Speaking Hat', the sealskin and arctic fox creation I had bought David in Greenland, was passed from head to head, as jokes, speeches, toasts and entertainment by each ship's crew followed rapidly one after another. The crews of *Saga Siglar* and *Oseberg* revealed unexpected poetic and dramatic talents. Ragnar laughed as heartily as anyone at Pierre's line about his first solo nautical exploit – 'and even then he had trouble with the crew'. Our offering was a selection of 'Viking songs which should never be published – and probably never sung'. With the rest of the crew of *Gaia*, we sang a few of the less bawdy verses, such as one about 'a hotelier called Steinar, who pulled us along with his liner'.

The next morning, I hugged more men in one day than ever before. Some – Ragnar, Gunnar, Rikardur and Jon – would soon be setting out on *Gaia*'s next nautical mission. For the rest of us, it was the end of a strange way of life, alternating between red-carpet treatment on shore and shipboard routine at sea, to which we had all become accustomed. The general consensus was that it was for the friendships formed between us that we would most cherish the memories.

We had been away for nearly six months; it took six hours to fly home.

'Gaialogue'

Vinland had been successfully revisited, and although we all wished we had been towed less and had sailed more we had done enough Viking-style sailing to appreciate the stamina and skill of the Norse explorers who preceded Columbus to the New World – and to understand why winches, self steering and sea toilets were invented.

What it had all had to do with caring for the environment, and with setting a new course for mankind, it had sometimes been difficult to see, although our environment, the sea, had certainly put us in our place on a number of occasions. Give or take the nautical excitement, Vinland Revisited had often seemed primarily a complex and expensive publicity exercise; although quite what it was publicizing was another matter. In spite of Knut Kloster's emphatic rejection of ethnic flag waving, Norse – by which I mean Norwegian and Icelandic in particular, and Scandinavian in general – solidarity was the most prominent element on shore. We had been given memorable hospitality and red-carpet treatment, and could only hope that in return we and *Gaia* had contributed something 'meaningful'.

For those of us who were on board *Gaia* and *Havella* all the way, the months we spent together were an extraordinary kaleidoscope of experiences at sea and on land, of tensions and friendships, of self-discovery and of insights into the North Atlantic communities we had been privileged to visit. We were supposed to be demonstrating a spirit of adventure. That we resorted to modern navigational methods, not to mention tow-ropes, was the nature of the exercise; because it was 'official', we were subjected to a tight and detailed timetable which no Viking a thousand years ago would ever have considered.

From Washington, *Saga Siglar* and *Oseberg* were towed to Baltimore, ready to be freighted to Spain for Expo, while *Gaia* set out for Rio on her second 'Voyage of Exploration and Discovery – In Pursuit of a New Era'. She was again accompanied, and often towed, by *Havella*.

Although there was no historic Norse link, the Viking element continued to attract attention. In Cuba, for instance, Fidel Castro spent some time on board talking about Viking ships. We were kept in touch with *Gaia's* progress – the enthusiastic crowds of children, the official welcoming ceremonies, the support for her mission – through a 'Gaialogue' newsletter, in which Knut wrote: '*Gaia* sails to Rio as an advocate of the idea that planetary health and a sustainable, equitable future for mankind can be achieved only if *free enterprise* and *solidarity* become integral parts of the forces of change.'

Time had to be made en route for hull repairs: towing against adverse winds and seas had loosened her fastenings, and there was some doubt whether she would actually make it to Brazil. As the January 'Gaialogue' from Jamaica put it, 'she is a ship meant for sailing, not for keeping schedules, and after doing their share of "listening to Gaia", the crew decided that the sailing plan should be modified. "The Vikings were more sensible than we are," said Captain Thorseth. "They let wind and weather decide and never tried to defy the forces of nature."'

Of the four signatories to the Vinland Revisited 'Declaration of Purpose', representatives of all except NRK (the Norwegian Broadcasting Corporation having been primarily a sleeping partner) each contributed to the grand finale edition of the expedition's newsletter. From Norway, there was 'a special word of thanks ... to Ragnar Thorseth, a true present-day Norwegian Viking with an outstanding ability to represent his country abroad and with an intelligent and reflective attitude towards our common future on planet Earth', and satisfaction that the voyage had clearly shown 'the immense courage of our Viking ancestors and their remarkable skills in sailing such graceful and seaworthy ships'. For Iceland, Thordur Einarsson, in keeping with the presidential suggestion of the symbolic name *Gaia*, expressed confidence that the environmental message would be carried onward: 'Pollution has no borders and the state of the environment concerns all the Earth's inhabitants. We have an obligation to future generations not to leave the Earth to them in a worse state than we received it from our forefathers.' On behalf of both countries, satisfaction was expressed at the restatement and strengthening of historic, cultural and economic links with Canada and the United States: '... the people of North America, Norway, and Iceland, far from being separated by the Atlantic Ocean, are in fact united by it and because of it.'

Only Knut Kloster's question 'Did We Make It?' expressed any doubt: 'It is all in the eyes of the beholder. Each of the partners naturally had different visions and priorities. In the planning process with so much excitement surrounding the ships themselves and the adventure of it all there was sometimes a tendency to lose sight of the mission as reflected in our "Declaration of Purpose".'

'From the point of view of commemorating Leif Eiriksson and the voyages of a thousand years ago, Vinland Revisited was undoubtedly a great success,' Kloster acknowledged, with thanks to all those involved. 'However, taking our declared purpose seriously – as we should – we must ask ourselves: To what extent did we accomplish the task of actually showing how important it is that the spirit of discovery in our modern times be aimed at shaping our common future?'

'This, of course, is a question to which there cannot be given a clear cut answer. But I think it is fair to say that in their special way GAIA, SAGA SIGLAR, OSEBERG and HAVELLA, have touched the minds and hearts of thousands of people. If all of us use the memory of Vinland Revisited to re-shape our values and behaviour, then we will have made it, too.'

As for Gaia – Mother Earth Gaia: my respect for, indeed awe of, her power has grown immensely. I have no doubt that if mankind behaves in such a way that Gaia feels endangered by our species, she will be ruthless enough to get rid of us – so without any sentimentality about a loving caring mother, it is in our own self-interest to look after the environment, and to avoid upsetting its balances. Perhaps one thing I learnt on the way is that modern society has already lost the instinctive understanding of those balances which was previously an un-questioned part of survival – and which we can see at work if we look at the traditional life styles of some of the places we visited, where the environment imposed its own laws, and its own beliefs.

After our absence from England, it was encouraging to discover signs of increased environmental awareness close to our home: special garbage receptacles for tins and paper, as well as glass; an increase in organically-grown, chemical-free fruit and vegetables on sale; more use of recycled paper; and cleansing materials which vied with each other for environmental friendliness.

These are all small things; but although they have nothing to do with Vinland Revisited, or *Gaia*, they have plenty to do with Gaia. There is however one area of environmental concern about which I am still confused: whaling, which is indeed an emotional subject. Within a few weeks of our return from Washington, Norway's intention of hunting minke whales for scientific purposes was announced, and Iceland withdrew from the International Whaling Commission.

Post Script, May 1992
Oseberg and *Saga Siglar* were freighted to Valencia in Spain. On Sunday 5 May, they were on passage to Expo 92 in Seville when they were caught in a sudden and violent storm. First *Oseberg*, and then a few hours later *Saga Siglar*, capsized and sank. It was several hours before their combined crew of eleven Norwegians, including Frode Sætre and Bjarne Krekvik, were picked up. Miraculously, the most serious injuries were one broken leg and a few cracked ribs. Although the ships floated back to the surface, both were damaged beyond repair, and only the wreckage of *Saga Siglar* could be displayed to remind visitors to Seville that the Vikings crossed the Atlantic five hundred years before Columbus.

Gaia meanwhile had reached Brazil safely. At the World City Corporation in New York, Knut Kloster's colleagues were working on a 'Gaiaday calendar' for distribution at the Earth Summit. All nations and tongues were invited to abolish Tuesday, not to mention mardi, martes and martedi, since both Tiw and Mars were gods of war. Instead, there would be a weekly 'Gaiaday', 'an earth sabbath, the "green" day of the week for tending to Mother Nature – with the added advantage that the change would be a blow for women's lib and a move towards sexual equality, since Frigga (wife of Odin and mother of the gods) is currently the only female deity to have given her name to a way of the week.

After disgorging her cargo of childrens' messages at the environmental conference, which was to open in Rio on the last Tuesday, *Gaia* was to be freighted back to Norway. If Knut Kloster's big ship plans eventually come to fruition, the first of his mega-ships, *Phoenix World City*, may be ready to host environmental conferences at sea by the end of the millenium.

Acknowledgements

There are so many people to thank, of so many nationalities, in so many places and for such a variety of support, that a future of international cooperation seems entirely possible.

Living and sailing together forms a special bond, whatever occasional frictions may (inevitably) occur, and David and I shall always remember our fellow neo-Vikings with affection and gratitude:

Crews of *Gaia* and *Havella*, in alphabetical order, under the leadership of Ragnar Thorseth: Ottar Bjørkedal, Nigel Chatters, Andrew Dearden, Gunnar Marel Eggertsson, Jon Folde, Audun Gården, Øyvard Karlsbakk, Steinar Kulen, Odd Kvamme, Rikarður Már Pétursson, Frode Sætre

Crews of *Saga Siglar* and *Oseberg*, with a particular poignancy as it seems unlikely that either ship will sail again: Bjørnar Rangøynes Dahl, Pierre de Billot, Bjarne Krekvik, Ellen Rosa Gunnarsdóttir, Herdis Ellen Gunnarsdóttir, Jan Nessa, Knut Rangøy, Eggert Sigður Sigurdsson, Jostein Tøvik; Svein Flem, Kari, Eirik and Njål Thorseth and the wives of several of the crew, who joined the fleet at various stages in North America.

I have no idea quite how many people were involved in Vinland Revisited, and with our own Viking expeditionary plans, directly or indirectly, on both sides of the Atlantic and at all the many stops in between; but I am grateful to all those I know personally, and who fall more or less into geographical and chronological groups:

Pre-WCD: the Marquess of Aberdeen; Dr Alan Binns; Alf Bjercke; Harald, Rikki and Dolly Bjerke; Sheila Browne; Erlend Clouston; Peter Davies; Susan Davis; Henry Farrar; Clare Francis; Sir Richard Francis; Scott and Svea Fraser; Malcolm Fuller; John and Susan Gau;

Sir John Harvey Jones; Hans Kraft Johanssen; Ludovic Kennedy; Vivian Lomax; Magnus Magnusson; Robert Morfee; Hilary Nesbit; Peter Pagnamenta; Slade Penoyre; Jim Reeves; John Speirs; Flemming Rieck; Anthony Smith; Max Vinner; Charles Harrison Wallace; Clodagh Wallace; Brian Wenham; Piers Wilson

England: AFS: Ailsa Eckel, Elaine Maberly, Lisa Tylee; H.E. Helgi Agústsson, Icelandic Ambassador; Paul Bebbington; David and Pam Bowerman; Hugh Cannell; John Coleman; Martin Dale; Carol Daughtrey; Roger Eldridge; H.E. Kjell Eliassen, Norwegian Ambassador, and Mrs Eliassen; David Fairhall; Alan Goodenough; John Gore-Grimes; Willy Ker; Barry Kernon; Jane Lighting; Henri-Lloyd Ltd; Jane, Alistair, Megan and Emily Lomax; Professor James and Sandy Lovelock; Tim Luton; Michael Massey and the BBC TV 'Clothes Show' team; Pål Moe; Michael Narduzzo; Lee Needham; Robert Olive; Helen Price; Father Wilfrid (Paul) Sollom (G3 BGL); Sandra Rubery; Niven Sinclair; Steve Whettam; Anthony Whittome; Ian Wright

Norway:

Oslo: Harald and Dolly Bjerke; Erik Bye; Merete Fonstad-Smith; Svein Erik Furulund; Odd Grann; Helge and Anne Stine Ingstad; Knut Utstein Kloster Sr; Jens and Ann Karina Lassen; Anne Marie Mathiesen; Elin Gullhav Moltubakk; Henrich Nissen-Lie; Per Paust; Jørgen Randers

Trondheim to Bergen: Ragnhild Øverland Arnesen; Einar Belboe; Trygve Berg; Magne Bjørno; Jan Bredeveien; Torbjørn Fjesme; Tom Fossingen; Prof. Rolf Grankvist; Torbjørn Halvorsen; Kjell Moltu Jacobsen; Hans Kjærem; Elin Moltubakk; Dag Nordtømme; Sigbjørn Notøy; Bengt Martin Olsen; Nils Standal; Ivar Ytreland; Bengt Audun Øiestad

Scotland:

Orkney: J. William (Bill) Spence; Robin Cheer; Matthew Gloag Ltd; Bergljot Gundersen; Orkney Islands Council; Orkney Sailing Club

Shetland: Maurice S. Mullay; the Jarl Squad; Shetland Islands Council; Lerwick Boating Club; Christopher and Valentine Thornhill

Fair Isle: John and Betty Best; Ian and Lisa Best; Dr Peter Evans; staff and guests of the bird watching hostel, and islanders

Faroes: Harbour Master, Mayor and Commune of Tvøroyri; Captain and crew of Russian tug; Sigmund Groven; Edvard Heen; Jan Kløvstad; Sissel Kyrkjebø; Ingigerd a Trødni; Påll and Sólva Patursson; Trondur, Borgny and Diana Patursson; staff of Seamen's Mission; ring dancers and rowers of Torshavn

Iceland: President Vigdis Finnbogadottir; H.E. Sir Richard Best, British Ambassador, and Mrs Best; Estrid Brekkan; Tordur Einarsson; Eggert Feldskeri; Valgeir Gudjonsson; Ingjaldur Hannibalsson; Jormundur Ingi; Thorstein and Katie Jonsson; Prof. Jónas Kristjánsson; Hermann Ottðsson; Birgir Thorgilsson; staff of Hotel Leifúr Eiriksson; Mayor of Heimaey, and Gunnar Eggertsson's mother and daughter

Greenland: Mayor and Commune of Angmassalik, Qaqortaq (Julianehåb), Narsaq; staff of Julianehåb Seamen's Mission, Arctic Hotel in Narsarsuaq, and Hotel Perlen in Narsaq; Sven Erik Danielsen; Kai Egede; Chris Farmer; Jens Hagemann; Hanne Hartvig; Aka Hoegh; Gitte Jensen-Jakobshavn; Knud Krogh; Poul and Hanna Lunde; Bob and Beth Lux; Kaj and Edda Lyberth; Annemaria Oldenburg; Ivars Silis; Poul Henning Thureby; Lars A. Wensell

Canada:

Labrador: Frances Federowicz; Helen Macklin; Anne MacLean; Ward and Verna Pye; Tony Rumbolt; Sue Sellars

L'Anse–aux–Meadows and St Anthony, Newfoundland: Bruce Bradbury; Bernard Bromley; Nonnie Crawford; Kaye Fulton; Dr Jez and Jill Hilyard and hospital staff; John Moyes; Tony Stephenson and staff of Vinland Motel; Christine Taberner; staff of Parks Canada Visitors' Centre, l'Anse–aux–Meadows

St John's, Newfoundland: Robert Collingwood; Kay and Ed Coxworthy; Dr Anthony Dickinson; Avalon Goodridge; Shelagh Guy; Pamela Karasek; Peg Magnone; Ronald Rompkey; Clyde Rose; Robert M. Sinclair; Captain and crew of *Concordia*; Lloyd George, Maude Williams and the Dildo Local Development Committee

Halifax, Nova Scotia: Ann Acland, Maurice and Kathy Brown, David Fleming and crew of *Acadia*, Museum of the Atlantic; Marilyn A. Belec; Larry Cooke; Robert B. Dauphinée; Steinar and Debbie Engeset; Gordon Flemming; Helen Wickwire Foster and Tony Foster;

Kenneth Jacques; Andrea Johansen; Melanie Jollymore; Martin Karlsen; Johan and Barbara Koppernaes; Fred Macdonald; Captain Per Moen; Andrew Sinclair; Christine Taberner

USA:

Boston: staff of Charlestown Navy Yard; Pat Barki; Scott and Svea Fraser; David and J.B. Greenway; Terje Korsnes; Myron D.A. Olson; Mitchell T. Rabkin; Chris Viegaard

Buzzards Bay: Staff and cadets of Massachusetts Maritime Academy

Newport: John Macomber; Jim and Lega Medcalf; Evan and Amy Smith; Harbour Master; staff of Museum of Yachting; Sara Hickox; Dr Lynn Margulis; Thomas A. Wuchler; Captain and crew of *Royal Viking Sun*

New York and Washington: the many members of Sons of Norway and other Scandinavian groups who gave us hospitality; Nicole Gorden; Kitty Jones, Stephanie and Chick Gallagher, John S. Rogers, Knut Rostad at World City Corporation; M. Le Henaff and pupils of UNIS; Jennifer Merin; Peter Neill, South Street Seaport, NY; Angel Perez and staff of Seaport Suites, N.Y.; pupils of WIS and Native American children who came on board *Gaia* in Washington; staff of the Channel Inn Hotel, Washington DC.

To all these, and to many others whose names are not mentioned, but who supported Vinland Revisited in any way – by assisting with shore plans, or welcoming us at one of our ports of call (to which many people drove far farther than we had sailed): Thank you.

Bibliography

Here are some of the most relevant, useful and interesting books we acquired during, before and after the Viking voyage, divided into categories.

The Vikings and Norway
Barrett, Clive: *The Viking Gods: Pagan Myths of Nordic Peoples*, Aquarian Press 1989
Bertil, Algren, and others: *The Viking*, Nordbok, Sweden, 1975
Blindheim, Joan Tindale, trans: *Vinland the Good: the Saga of Leif Eiriksson and the Viking Discovery of America*, Tano, Norway 1986
Brønsted, Johannes: *The Vikings, the background to a fierce and fascinating civilization*, Pelican Books 1965
Crossley-Holland, Kevin: *The Norse Myths: Gods of the Vikings*, Penguin Books 1982, Folio Society 1989
Donovan, Frank R.: *The Vikings*, Cassell 1965
Farrell, R.T., ed.: *The Vikings*, Phillimore 1982
Francek, Thomas: *The Northmen*, Time-Life Books 1974
Grankvist, Rolf: *Leif Eiriksson and the Royal City of Trondheim*, Trondheim, Norway 1991
Hødnebø, Finn and Kristjánsson, Jónas, eds.: *The Viking Discovery of America*, J.M. Stenersens Forlag, Oslo 1991
Ingstad, A.S.: *The Discovery of a Norse settlement in America*, Oslo 1977
Ingstad, H.: *Westward to Vinland*, Jonathan Cape 1969
Jesch, Judith: *Women in the Viking Age*, Boydell Press 1991
Jones, Gwyn: *A History of the Vikings*, OUP 1984
The Norse Atlantic Saga, OUP 1986
Magnusson, Magnus: *Vikings!* Bodley Head/BBC 1980
Magnusson, Magnus and Pálsson, Herman, trans.: *The Vinland Sagas: the Norse Discovery of America*, Penguin 1965
Midgaard, John: *A Brief History of Norway*, Johan Grundt Tanum Forlag, Oslo 1964

239

Mowat, Farley: *West Viking*, McClelland and Stewart 1973
Prytz, Kåre, trans. Myhre, Liv and de Stefano, Charles: *Westward Before Columbus*, Norsk Maritimt Forlag 1990
Sannes, Tor Borch: *Christopher Columbus – en europeer fra Norge?* Norsk Maritimt Forlag 1991
Savage, Anne, trans.: *The Anglo-Saxon Chronicles*, Papermac 1982
Smiley, Jane: *The Greenlanders* (fiction based on Sagas)
Sturluson, Snorri, trans. Magnusson, Magnus and Pálsson, Hermann: *King Harald's Saga: Harald Hardradi of Norway*, Penguin 1966
trans. Monsen, Erling and Smith, Dr A.H.: *From the Sagas of the Norse Kings*, Dreyers Forlag, Oslo 1984
Wilson, David M.: *The Vikings and their origins*, Thames and Hudson 1980

Sailing, Viking ships, exploration
Andersen, Magnus: *Vikingfærden*, Oslo 1895
Anderson, J.R.L.: *Vinland Voyage*, Eyre & Spottiswoode 1967
Binns, Alan: *Viking Voyagers Then and Now*, Heinemann 1980
Bockstoce, John: *Arctic Passages: A Unique Small-Boat Voyage in the Great Northern Waterway*, Hearst Marine Books, N.Y. 1991
Crumlin-Pedersen, Ole, ed.: *Sailing into the Past*, Viking Ship Museum, Roskilde 1986
Cunliffe, Tom: *Topsail and Battleaxe, a voyage in the wake of the Vikings*, David & Charles 1988
Ingram, Michael: *The Voyage of Odin's Raven*, Clearwater, Isle of Man 1982
Jankuhn, Herbert: *Nydam und Thorsberg*, Karl Wachholtz Verlag, Germany 1987
Lopez, Barry: *Arctic Dreams*, Picador 1987
Millman, Lawrence: *Last Places: A Journey in the North*, Houghton Mifflin, Boston 1990
Nansen, Fridtjof: *Farthest North* (2 vols.) George Newnes 1898
Olsen, Olaf and Crumlin-Pedersen, Ole: *Five Viking Ships from Roskilde Fjord*, Danish National Museum, Copenhagen 1985
Pohl, Frederick J.: *Prince Henry Sinclair, His expedition to the New World in 1398*, David-Poynter Ltd 1974
Severin, Tim: *The Brendan Voyage*, Hutchinson
Stamp, Tom and Cordelia: *Greenland Voyager*, Caedmon of Whitby 1983
Swaney, Deanna: *Iceland, Greenland and the Faroe Islands*, Lonely Planet 1991

Thorseth, Ragnar, trans. Cowlishaw, J. Basil: *Alone Across the North Sea –
and Adventurous Voyages in the Arctic Ocean*, Nordvest Informasjon,
Ålesund, Norway, 1980
Saga Siglar: Århundrets seilas Jorda rundt, Nordvest Forlag, Ålesund,
1988
Willis, Thayer: *The Frozen World*, Reader's Digest 1979

Scotland, esp. Orkney and Shetland
Bridges, Antony: *Scapa Ferry*, Peter Davies 1957
Brown, George Mackay: *Portrait of Orkney*, Hogarth Press 1981
Crawford, Barbara: *Scandinavian Scotland*, Leicester University Press
1982
Donaldson, Gordon: *A Northern Commonwealth: Scotland and Norway*,
Saltire 1990
Irvine, James W.: *Up-Helly-Aa*, Shetland Publishing Co. 1982
Kjørsvik, Liv and Moberg, Gunnie: *The Orkney Story* and *The Shetland
Story*, John Murray
Linklater, Eric, revised Nicolson, James R.: *Orkney and Shetland: an
historical, geographical, social and scenic summary*, Robert Hale 1990
Mackie, J.D.: *A History of Scotland*, Penguin 1991
Maclean, Fitzroy: *A Concise History of Scotland*, Thames and Hudson
1973
Marwick, Ernest: *The Folklore of Orkney and Shetland*, Batsford 1986
Pálsson, Hermann and Edwards, Paul, trans.: *Orkneyinga Saga: the
History of the Earls of Orkney*, Penguin 1981
Smout, T.C.: *A History of the Scottish People*, Collins/Fontana 1967

The Faroes, Iceland and Greenland
Fisker, Jørgen: *Tassiilaq, Angmagssalik*, Norske Landes Bogforlag,
Greenland 1984
Herglund, Joel: *Hvalsø – the Church and the Magnate's farm*, Qaqortoq
Commune, Greenland 1982
Jackson, Anthony: *The Faroes*, Robert Hale 1991
Jákupsson, Bárdur: *Mikines*, Emil Thomsen, Torshavn, Faroes 1990
Kjørsvik, Liv and Moberg, Gunnie, ill. Patursson, Tróndur: *The Faroe
Islands*, John Murray 1991
Krogh. K.J.: *Viking Greenland*, Copenhagen 1967
Lauritzen, Philip: *Highlights of an arctic revolution: the first 120 months of
Greenlandic Home Rule*, Atuarkkiorfik, Greenland 1989
Magnusson, Magnus: *Iceland Saga*, Bodley Head 1987

Magnússon, Sigurdur A.: *Northern Sphinx: Iceland and the Icelanders from the Settlement to the Present*, Reykjavik 1984.

Rodahl, Kåre: The Ice-Capped Island: Greenland, Blackie & Son 1946

Young, G.V.C.: *From the Vikings to the reformation: A Chronicle of the Faroe Islands*, Shearwater Press, Isle of Man 1979

Young, G.V.C. and Clewer, Cynthia: *The Faroese Saga*, Føroya Skulabokgrunnur, Belfast 1973

North America (Labrador, Newfoundland, Nova Scotia; USA)

Bird, Michael: *The Town That Died: a chronicle of the Halifax disaster*, McGraw-Hill Ryerson, Canada 1967

Floyd, Candace: *The History of New England*, Portland House, USA 1990

Grenfell, Wilfred Thomason: prolific writings include eg *Adrift on an Ice-Pan; Labrador, The Country and the People; Forty Years for Labrador; A Labrador Doctor: the autobiopgraphy of Sir Wilfred Thomason Grenfell*, Hodder and Stoughton 1954; ed. Pope, William: *The Best of Wilfred Grenfell*, Lancelot Press 1990

Handcock, W. Gordon: *Soe longe as there comes noe women: Origins of English Settlement in Newfoundland*, Breakwater, St John's, Newfoundland 1989

Hansen, Ben, photographer: *One Hundred Outports*, Vinland Press, St John's, Newfoundland 1990

Horwood, Joan: *Viking Discovery: L'Anse aux Meadows*, Jesperson Press & Newfoundland Historic Parks Association 1985

Josephy, Alvin, M., Jr.: *The Indian Heritage of America*, Houghton Mifflin, Boston 1991

Loder, Millicent Blake: *Daughter of Labrador*, Harry Cuff Publications, St John's, Newfoundland 1989

McNaught, Kenneth: *The Penguin History of Canada*, Penguin 1988

Norman, Howard: *Northern Tales: Traditional Stories of Eskimo and Indian Peoples*, Pantheon Books, N.Y. 1990

Paddon, W.A.: *Labrador Doctor: My Life with the Grenfell Mission*, James Lorimer & Co. 1989

Pilgrim, Earl B.: *The Price Paid for Charley*, Tromso Enterprises Ltd, Newfoundland 1990

Powell, Ben: *Trapline*, Jesperson Press Ltd 1990

Rompkey, Ronald: *Grenfell of Labrador*, University of Toronto Press 1991

Rowe, Frederick W.: *A History of Newfoundland and Labrador*, McGraw-Hill Ryerson Ltd, Canada 1980

Them Days: Stories of early Labrador, Nos. 1, 2 & 3, Vol. 16, Happy
Valley-Goose Bay, Labrador 1991

The Gaia theory and the environment, including the 'very emotional question' of whaling, and sealing:

Brown, Lester R., Project Director: *State of the World 1991: A Worldwatch Institute Report on Progress Toward a Sustainable Society*, W.W. Norton & Co. 1991

Davies, Brian and Porter, Eliot: *Seal Song*, The Viking Press N.Y. 1978

Environmental Protection Agency: *The Global War Against Small Cetaceans: The IWC and the Politics of Extinction*, EIA 1990;
. . . : *A Second Report*, EIA 1991

Francis, Daniel: *Arctic Chase: A History of Whaling in Canada's North*, Breakwater, Newfoundland 1984

Henke, Janice Scott: *Seal Wars! An American Viewpoint*, Breakwater, Newfoundland 1985

Jenkins, J.T.: *A History of the Whale Fisheries*, Kennikat Press 1921

Joseph, Lawrence E.: *GAIA, the growth of an idea*, St Martin's Press, N.Y. 1990

Lovelock, James: *Gaia: a new look at life on earth*, OUP 1979
The Ages of Gaia: A Biography of Our Living Earth, W.W. Norton & Co. 1988
GAIA, the practical science of planetary medicine, Gaia Books Ltd 1991

Ottoway, Andy: *The Whale Killers*, Greenpeace 1991

Patey, Francis: *A Battle Lost: An Unsuccessful Attempt to Save the Seal Hunt*, St Anthony, Newfoundland 1990

Porritt, Jonathon: *Save the Earth*, Dorling Kindersley 1991

Raundalen, Magne and Tora Synøve, and others: *Now – or too late*, Research for Children, Norway 1991

Vestergaard, Elisabeth, ed.: *North Atlantic Studies: Whaling Communities*, Aarhus University Press, Denmark 1990

(All books published in the UK unless otherwise stated)

Index